Sarah Knowles Bolton

Famous Types of Womanhood

Sarah Knowles Bolton

Famous Types of Womanhood

ISBN/EAN: 9783742812582

Manufactured in Europe, USA, Canada, Australia, Japa

Cover: Foto ©ninafisch / pixelio.de

Manufactured and distributed by brebook publishing software (www.brebook.com)

Sarah Knowles Bolton

Famous Types of Womanhood

FAMOUS

TYPES OF WOMANHOOD

BY

SARAH KNOWLES BOLTON

AUTHOR OF "POOR BOYS WHO BECAME FAMOUS," "GIRLS WHO BECAME FAMOUS,"
"FAMOUS AMERICAN AUTHORS," "FAMOUS AMERICAN STATESMEN,"
"FAMOUS MEN OF SCIENCE," "FAMOUS EUROPEAN ARTISTS,"
"SOCIAL STUDIES IN ENGLAND," "STORIES FROM LIFE,"
"FROM HEART AND NATURE" (POEMS), "FAMOUS
ENGLISH AUTHORS," "FAMOUS ENGLISH
STATESMEN," ETC., ETC.

"My business on earth is to do what good I can."
JOHN WESLEY.

NEW YORK: 46 EAST 14TH STREET.
THOMAS Y. CROWELL & CO.
BOSTON: 100 PURCHASE STREET.

COPYRIGHT,

1892,

BY THOMAS Y. CROWELL & CO.

TO

FRANCES E. WILLARD,

A Noble Type of Womanhood.

PREFACE.

When Matthew Vassar gave a million dollars to found Vassar College, he said, "I considered that the mothers of a country mould its citizens, determine its institutions, and shape its destiny." Without doubt he was right. Though not all the women in this book were mothers, they helped to do that which Mr. Vassar considered directly traceable to woman's influence. Queen Louise was the inspirer of German unity; Madame Récamier will always be a social force from her charm of manner and loveliness of character; the results of Mrs. Wesley's life are incalculable; Harriet Martineau moulded public opinion as few have moulded it; Jenny Lind taught the world how to use a marvellous gift for good; Miss Dix will show to future generations what a retiring, devoted woman can do for humanity. The power of true womanhood, in all civilized lands, is increasing year by year, and with increase of power comes increase of responsibility.

S. K. B.

TABLE OF CONTENTS.

	PAGE
QUEEN LOUISE OF PRUSSIA	9
MADAME RÉCAMIER	62
SUSANNA WESLEY	105
HARRIET MARTINEAU	150
JENNY LIND	196
DOROTHEA LYNDE DIX	241
ANN, SARAH AND EMILY JUDSON	273
AMELIA BLANDFORD EDWARDS	327

QUEEN LOUISE OF PRUSSIA.

NO one can read the life of the grand old Emperor of Germany, William I., without seeing how his love for his beautiful young mother brightens every page. No one who has ever stood before his writing table in his Berlin palace can forget the lovely face that always hung before him, or, in summer, the blue corn-flowers at his side, dear to him because they were dear to her.

He said, when confirmed at the age of eighteen at Charlottenburg, where Louise is buried, "I will ever bear in mind the virtues of the late queen, my mother. As long as I live my mother shall live in my heart in sweet, affectionate, and grateful recollections." He kept his word, and for over half a century Louise has been also the ideal and the idol of the German nation.

Louise Augusta Wilhelmina Amelia was born at Hanover, March 10, 1776. Her father was Prince Charles, afterwards Grand Duke of Mecklenburg-Strelitz, the brother of Charlotte, wife of George III. of England. Her mother was Princess Frederica Caroline Louise of Hesse-Darmstadt.

When Louise was six months old the family removed from the unpretentious home in which she was born to the old castle of Herrenhausen, the father having been made Governor-General of Hanover. Here she passed her happy childhood in the midst of the fountains, trees, flowers, and statues of that famous garden of one hundred and twenty acres.

Princess Frederica, the mother, died in May, 1782, at the birth of her tenth child, leaving six children under twelve years of age. Louise was six. Two years later, feeling that the lonely children needed a mother, Prince Charles married Charlotte, his wife's sister, who died in fourteen months, leaving an infant son.

The duke, saddened by his double loss, resigned his governorship in 1786 and went to Darmstadt, where his children could have the care of their maternal grandmother, Princess George William of Hesse-Darmstadt. She was a noble woman, and with the governess, a Swiss lady, Mlle. de Gélieux, reared Germany's future queen with wisdom and in Christian principles.

The child was delighted to visit the poor and the sick in the neighborhood of the palace. Catherine E. Hurst, the wife of Bishop John F. Hurst, in her sympathetic life of Louise, relates many touching incidents.

The children of the servants of the royal household were allowed to play with the little princesses. One day a thunder storm came unexpectedly. The mothers ran for their children, all except one little girl named Hannah, who had no mother. When Louise saw that no one came for the child, she said, "Be quiet, dear Hannah; do not be afraid of the thunder and lightning and rain, for our dear Saviour sends it; and do not be sad, for you are not alone, I am with you, and your father will come soon and take you home."

"But," said the child, "who will take care of me when my father dies?"

"Who says that your father will die?" asked Louise.

"Oh, my aunt says that he suffers so much from pain in his breast when he must run so rapidly to keep pace with the horses, that he can live but a very short time."

"Be assured your father shall not die, for I will tell this to grandma, and she will give him another position," said Louise.

When evening came Louise told her grandmother, weeping, that she could never have any more pleasure in driving if the footmen who ran beside the carriage were to lose their health in consequence. The grandmother abandoned the barbarous custom.

A short time after this, scarlet fever appeared in its most malignant form in the town, and many of the children were laid in their graves. Hannah was taken ill. The grandmother gave orders that a physician should attend her, and report to the palace. Finally, when the fever had left her, and Princess George felt that it would be safe to visit the little girl, she did so. What was her astonishment to find Louise sitting at the foot of the bed, reading to Hannah, while the sick child amused herself with the princess's embroidered handkerchief. The grandmother left the place unobserved.

When Louise returned Princess George said, "Where have you been, my child?"

"O grandma," she said, "I have been with a sick child, who has no mother, and no grandmother like you, and who would have died long ago if I had not visited her. Will you not forgive me for not telling you of my visits to her before?"

"You know, my child, this disease could so easily have taken you from us, and then what should we have done? Oh, the grief we should have at your loss!"

"I knew well," replied Louise, "that I should not get

the disease, for der liebe Gott — the dear God — saw that I was doing good."

Louise was always giving to those in need. When she was thirteen she met a poor widow in the village, who was begging for her hungry children. She gave the widow all she had, and then borrowed from an old servant to make other gifts.

Her grandmother reproved her for making debts, and told the servant that he ought not to have loaned to the child, but she granted Louise an increase of spending money, stipulating that the princess should pay the debt herself. This habit of giving continued through life, and Louise always spent for others in preference to herself.

E. H. Hudson, in her life of Louise, tells this incident. Monsieur Mideaelis, the editor of a periodical, gave lessons to Louise and her sister. He was not prosperous, and the children saw that he was troubled. One day Louise offered him a gold cross, saying, "We are afraid you want money, and we are so sorry that we have not any to give you; but we have talked it over and have agreed to ask you if you will accept this gold ornament, which is the most valuable thing we have."

The gift was courteously declined. The teacher saw happier days, and died, in 1843, professor of French literature in the University of Tübingen.

Louise made two happy visits to Frankfort, — one when she was fourteen, to witness the coronation of Leopold II., the son of Maria Theresa, and the other when she was sixteen, to be present at the coronation of Francis I., the son of Leopold.

All Frankfort was in commotion over the crowning of Leopold II. The jewels, the sword of Charlemagne, and the Gospel printed in golden characters, on which the coronation oaths were taken, were brought from the towns of Aix-la-Chapelle and Nuremburg, the attendants bearing them in state carriages drawn by six horses. These precious jewels were placed in the chapel of the cathedral, where the Emperor was to put on his robes.

At ten o'clock, Leopold, forty-four years of age, mounted on his richly caparisoned horse, his robe of purple glistening with diamonds and pearls, and the crown of Austria on his brow, rode toward the cathedral under a crimson canopy carried over his head by twelve senators of Frankfort, who rode on each side of the Emperor.

Before him were borne the crown on a cushion of cloth of gold, the scepter, the orb, and the drawn sword of St. Maurice.

The long procession was most picturesque and gorgeous. The imperial body-guard, the pages in black and yellow velvet, the halberdiers in black velvet tunics laced with gold over a red bodice, long lines of princes and nobles, made an imposing sight.

Within the cathedral the king was anointed with consecrated oil, received the Holy Communion, and ascended to the imperial throne; without, bells were rung, cannon were fired, and thousands of people cried, "God save the Emperor."

After the coronation the Emperor was escorted to the Römer palace, over a bridge carpeted with red, black, and gold, which carpet the people immediately seized and divided into thousands of pieces.

Louise spent these days of the coronation at the home of Goethe's mother. Frau Goethe was delighted with the natural, merry princess, and her vivacious sister Frederica, and often told the story of a pump back of their house, which Louise, espying, said, "Oh, I wonder if we could make the water rush out. I should like to try."

She did try and succeeded, greatly shocking the lady attending her, but Frau Goethe was pleased, and said: —

"I would rather have brought any vexation on myself than permit them to be disturbed in the innocent pleasure that was permitted them nowhere else; but in my house the young people greatly enjoyed the liberty granted to them. When they left they said to me that they would never forget how happy they had been."

Leopold did not reign long. His sister, Marie Antoinette, was passing through the terrors of the French Revolution, and urging her brother to aid and save her family. He feared to make enemies of the successful revolutionists, lest harm should come to her. He therefore tried to conciliate the people. When matters became desperate, he and Frederick William II. signed a treaty which united Austria and Prussia against the French. Leopold addressed a letter to the French government, which only exasperated. They declared war against Austria and Prussia, April 20, 1792, and hostilities almost immediately followed.

Leopold died suddenly a month before the war broke out, and Francis II., his son, at the age of twenty-five, came to the throne. Louise saw Frankfort again in its gala dress at this coronation.

The war went on in earnest. The French captured Mayence and advanced towards Frankfort. Then Princess George with her granddaughters, Louise and Fredererica, retreated to Hildburghhausen in Thuringia, where Charlotte, the oldest sister of Louise, had married the Duke. The beautiful country was enjoyed by the princesses, but all were filled with anxiety about the war.

Prussia and Austria, urged on by the brave and energetic statesman, Stein, turned the tide of battle. They recovered Frankfort, Dec. 2; the King of Prussia made it his headquarters, and both armies went into camp for the winter.

Princess George ventured to return to Darmstadt, stopping at Frankfort to see the king, who was her nephew by marriage. She called with Louise and Frederica, and was invited to dine with the king and his sons, Frederick William and Louis.

Louise was seventeen, with an exquisite complexion, large, blue eyes, light hair, frank, natural manner, and was very graceful. Frederick William, the crown prince, was twenty-three, tall, and well-proportioned. He had a thoughtful face and somewhat grave manner. He was well-educated and of admirable character. He loved Louise from the first. He told Bishop Eylert, years after her death: —

"I felt when I first saw her,' 'T is she, or none on earth,' — that expression is somewhere in Schiller, I forget where, but I have it, and it exactly describes the emotions which sprang up in my heart at that moment."

Bishop Eylert found it afterwards in "The Bride of Messina."

That love never changed, but remains one of the beautiful things of history which keep bright our faith in human nature.

The brother Louis likewise became devoted to Frederica, and the double betrothal was celebrated a month later in Darmstadt, the king assisting, and distributing the rings with his own hands. Later, the brides-elect and their grandmother were invited to see the camp at Mayence.

Goethe, then forty-five, saw the king and the court

party. He wrote: " Toward evening there was prepared for us, but especially for me, a lovely sight. The Princesses of Mecklenburg had dined at the headquarters of his majesty the king, and after dinner visited the camp. I confined myself to my tent, and could thus most perfectly observe the high-born personages, who walked up and down before me quite at their ease. In this tumult of war, one might really consider the two princesses as heavenly visions. The impression which they made upon me will never be obliterated."

The war went on with varying success. Meantime the French Revolution was doing its work. Louis XVI. had perished on the scaffold, Jan. 21, 1793, the beating of drums drowning his last words, " I am innocent of all the crimes laid to my charge; I forgive those who have occasioned my death; I pray to God that the blood you are about to shed may never be visited on France; I heartily wish — "

Marie Antoinette was guillotined eight months afterwards, Oct. 16, 1793, at the age of thirty-nine.

Two years later, Frederick William II., worn with the war, his country drained of men and money, concluded the treaty of Basle with the French Republic, Jan. 22, 1795.

The marriage of the crown prince and Louise was set for Christmas Eve, 1793. The bridegrooms, Frederick William and Louis, waited at Potsdam the arrival of the princesses. Troops of horsemen rode out to meet them, while the town was thronged with various guilds in showy costumes.

The butchers wore brown coats with gold bands on their sleeves, red waistcoats embroidered in gold, and hats with red feathers. Many years afterwards Louise gave them a new standard in remembrance of this day, when the one which they then unfurled was worn out.

Two days later, the stately entrance was made into Berlin. Six royal secretaries at the head of forty postilions led the procession. Now followed guilds, corporations, merchants, citizens, — a great concourse of people. To the royal carriage eight horses were harnessed, while six drew the state carriage in which rode the princesses and the lady-in-waiting.

About noon, Dec. 23, the royal procession entered Berlin through the Potsdam gate. Opposite the Royal Palace a triumphal edifice had been erected, where the statue of Frederick the Great now stands, the pillars covered with evergreens, while chains of flowers were suspended from arch to arch.

Thirty boys in green and more than fifty girls in white and pink, with green wreaths in their hands, were stationed near the triumphal arch to await the coming of the princesses. When the state carriage arrived, a little boy came forward to recite a poem; then a little girl proffered flowers, and on the impulse of the moment, Louise bent over and kissed her.

"What has your Highness done?" said the lady-in-waiting.

Louise was startled and exclaimed: —

"What, is that wrong? May I never do that again?"

At three o'clock the princesses were received by the queen. The following day, at six o'clock on Christmas Eve, all the members of the royal family assembled in the queen's apartments, when the diamond crown of the Hohenzollerns was placed upon the head of Louise. After spending a little time with Elizabeth Christine, the aged widow of Frederick the Great, the company repaired to the white drawing-room which is decorated in white and silver; in the middle of the room, under a crimson canopy embroidered with gold crowns, Frederick William and Louise knelt on an elegant cushion, and were united in marriage.

After the wedding banquet, served in five state apartments, a ball followed. Everybody spoke of the beautiful bride. She was dressed in silver glacé, her corsage glittering with diamonds to correspond with her crown. She bowed and smiled with that artless grace which she possessed through life. Fouqué, the poet, said: —

"The arrival of the angelic princess spreads over these days a noble splendor. All hearts go out to meet her, and her grace and goodness leave no one unblessed."

The citizens of Berlin wished to celebrate the wedding with a great illumination, but at the request of the Crown Prince, the money, which would have been thus expended, was given to the widows and orphans of those who had fallen in the late war.

Prince Louis and Frederica were married three days later, Dec. 27.

Frederick William and Louise went at once to live in their own palace, at the head of Unter den Linden. Here Frederick lived and died, bequeathing it to his grandson, afterwards Emperor Frederick I., who married Victoria, Princess Royal of Great Britain.

At the palace a happy married life began. The crown prince was called the handsomest man in Prussia; tall, and with military bearing, and as good as he was handsome. His wife attracted everybody by her sweetness of manner, her musical voice, her joyous disposition, her brilliant conversation, and her generous heart.

King Frederick William II. was very fond of Louise,

whom he called the "princess of princesses," and on March 10, the first birthday after her marriage, when she was eighteen, he gave her the palace of Oranienburg (Orange-burg), about twenty miles north of Berlin. It was built for Louise of Orange, the lovely and cultivated mother of the Elector of Brandenburg, who became the first king of Prussia.

The king asked Louise what would most gratify her on her birthday. She replied, "A handful of gold, to distribute among the poor of Berlin."

"How large a handful would the birthday-child like to have?" asked the king.

She replied quickly, "As large as the heart of the best of kings."

She received a large sum, which was carefully distributed. She gave a feast to her servants on this birthday, each being allowed to invite several guests, and eighty came. She wished the number had been one hundred. Both Frederick and Louise disliked the ceremonial of court life. Once when they had returned from some court festival, the crown prince took hold of both her hands and said, "Thank God, you are my wife once more."

"Am I not always your wife, then?" she asked.

"Alas! no," he said; "you must too often be only the crown princess."

The prince would not use the customary six horses and pages, but sat beside his wife, in a carriage drawn by two horses, like any citizen. He was conscious of the financial condition of his country, and wished to practice a reasonable economy.

They read much together, Louise being especially fond of history and poetry. She took delight in the works of Goethe, Schiller, Richter, and others. Herder's poems she carried with her in her journeys. She read Shakespeare in English, and the Greek tragedies in translation, making long extracts which pleased her, and adding her own pertinent remarks on the margin. Schiller's "History of the Netherlands," and "History of the Thirty Years' War," and also Gibbon's "Decline and Fall of the Roman Empire," with the "History of England," she read carefully. Several years later, when Richter dedicated his " 'Titan' to the four beautiful and noble sisters on the throne," the Mecklenburg princesses, and sent Louise a copy, she wrote back: —

I have received your "Titan," and observed with pleasure from it that you continue to interest your contemporaries in truths which cannot fail to influence them, dressed as they are in the garb of romantic poetry. Your object, to free mankind from many a dark cloud, is too beautiful not to be realized, and it will therefore be a pleasure to me to see you during your stay here, and to show you how much I am,

Your kindly affectionate, LOUISE.

Once when talking with Frau Goethe about German literature, Louise unclasped a gold necklace, and gave it to her as a tribute to the genius of her son. The mother was very proud of it, and wore it only on rare occasions.

Both Frederick and Louise were musical, the former understanding the science of music so well that he often composed marches, which were played by the bands.

In the year 1794, Louise lost her first child, a daughter. The next year, Oct. 15, 1795, her first son, afterwards Frederick William IV., was born at Oranienburg. He had many sponsors: his two grandfathers, the Empress Catharine of Russia, Francis II., George III., Queen Charlotte, and others.

Oranienburg was too stately for two persons who desired a quiet home, so the estate of Paretz, the former home of one of the crown prince's tutors, was purchased, with its castle, for thirty thousand thalers.

Frederick said to the architect who rebuilt it, "Always bear in mind that you are building for a poor proprietor." The house was furnished simply, and the garden was a restful retreat. The tall poplars and other majestic trees were a great delight to the young wife, who loved nature intensely.

"Amid the quiet and beauty of nature," she said, "I can best rally and collect my mind, whose chords, like those of an instrument of music, need each day to be drawn up in order to get the right tone. If I neglect this, I feel out of harmony."

A rural village was on the estate of Paretz, and soon the people came to know her and to love her. Once she gave all the children of the village new clothes for the harvest festival.

Not far from Paretz, in the river Havel, is Pfaueninsel (Peacock Island), which Frederick converted into a park. Here, after they had become king and queen, they often dined with their children beneath the beech trees.

One summer evening, as they were sitting under some great oaks on the island, they requested Bishop Eylert to read a sermon which he had recently preached on Christian marriage from the words of Ruth to Naomi: "Entreat me not to leave thee, or to return from following after thee: for whither thou goest, I will go; and where thou lodgest, I will lodge: thy people shall be my people, and thy God my God: where thou diest, will I die, and there will I be buried."

They sat till the moon rose, and distant music floated

through the air. Frederick broke the silence, laying his hand on Louise's shoulder, saying with tenderness, "This is my intention, dear Louise: I and my house, we will serve the Lord."

He went down by the river alone to meditate, while Louise conversed with the bishop: "Only in faith can I find support," she said. "In the longing after happiness I become sensible of a deep emptiness in my heart which nothing earthly can satisfy. . . . What elevates me most and gives me the most happiness, is the thought that the king and I fully accord in our religious convictions. I believe he is the best man and Christian on earth. Did you hear, as you finished reading your sermon, how he said, with heartfelt emotion, 'This is my intention: I and my house, we will serve the Lord'?"

Two English travellers rowed over one day from Potsdam to Pfaueninsel, and were told by the court chamberlain that the grounds were not open to the public, as the king and queen were there. They communicated their disappointment to a gentleman and lady, simply dressed, whom they met.

"Ah!" said the gentleman, "that was Herr von Mossow. I know him well, and if you like to walk round the island I will excuse you to him."

"You had better come with us," said the lady, "for you are strangers here, and we can show you every thing worth looking at."

They talked of England, and the lady's sweet face seemed to them full of expression. As they approached the castle, breakfast was announced, and they perceived, to their astonishment, that they were in the presence of the king and queen, who had been their guides. They were cordially invited to the breakfast.

Death came once and again to disturb this happy life. Prince Louis, to whom his brother Frederick was devotedly attached, died Dec. 28, 1796, of typhus fever, leaving Frederica at eighteen with an infant son. The crown prince would not leave him, and took the disease, but recovered. The young widow was at once taken to the home of Louise.

Three weeks later the widow of Frederick the Great, Queen Elizabeth Christine, died at the age of eighty-one, and was buried in the royal vault back of Berlin cathedral.

She must have led a lonely life with Frederick, who, at the command of his father, married her rather than the Princess Amelia of England, of whom he was fond. He would never live with her. He had been reared by a most tyrannical father, who once condemned him to death for trying to escape to England, but he was saved by the generals of the army and the representatives of foreign powers, who assured the king that the heir to the throne belonged to the nation more than to him.

Frederick passed his life either on the battlefield or surrounded by men of letters at Sans-Souci, his pet greyhounds for his dumb companions. His sister Wilhelmina, the playmate of his childhood, whom he tenderly loved, died when he was in middle life.

Once a year, on her birthday, he went to call upon Elizabeth Christine at her secluded abode at Schönhausen. She gave herself to charities, and wrote several religious books, a copy of each of which she presented to Frederick, who had them handsomely bound, though whether he ever read them or not is doubtful. He sometimes made her valuable presents, but she was never permitted to come to Sans-Souci, though she adored him.

Elizabeth Christine grieved sadly on hearing of his

death at Sans-Souci, on the night of Aug. 16, 1786, when he expired in the arms of a servant at twenty minutes past two, his little Italian greyhound watching beside him. Observing the dog tremble, he directed that a covering be thrown over it. He would not allow his wife to be sent for.

She survived him eleven years, and had the small comfort of making a handsome cloth for the communion table, which stands before the chamber where he lies buried in the Garrison Church, at Potsdam.

After her death, Frederick William II. said, "It will be my turn next." He died the same year, Nov. 16, 1797, and was buried in the crypt of Berlin Cathedral. With all his failings, and his life had been far from moral, he had been a good father to Louise. He left, says E. H. Hudson, "a legacy of three very great evils, — a demoralized nation, his own cabinet ministers, and an exhausted treasury. . . . The most imminent, though the least important, of the dangers arising out of these evils, was the want of money. Frederick the Great had left the sum of ten million pounds in the treasury, — it was all gone, and instead of it there was a heavy debt which the new king felt bound to discharge as quickly as possible."

The crown prince now became King Frederick William III., and Louise was queen. They did not change their home, for Frederick said: —

"The king will have to live on the revenues of the crown prince."

A second son had been born to them, March 22, 1797, Frederick William Louis, afterwards Emperor William I. of Germany. The king and queen walked arm-in-arm as formerly in the Unter den Linden, and belonged to their people as their great son William did after them.

They visited the Christmas fair in Berlin. At one of the stalls, a woman about to make a purchase, recognizing them, stepped back. "Do not go away, my dear woman," said the queen. "What will the stall-keeper say, if we drive away his customers?"

She then inquired if the woman had come to buy toys for her children, and asked how many she had. On learning that there was a son about the age of her eldest, she said: —

"Take these toys and give them to your crown prince in the name of mine."

The queen seemed never to forget the small courtesies of life, showing how thoroughly kind she was at heart. When a count and the court-shoemaker were announced at the same time, she received the shoemaker first, saying: —

"The mechanic's time is far more valuable than the count's. The tradesman must be attended to first, and the count must wait."

At a military festival, the Garrison Church at Potsdam was so densely crowded that a woman by mistake sat in the royal pew. The lady-in-waiting reprimanded her after the service, as not showing proper respect to the queen. Louise heard of it, and sent for Bishop Eylert.

"Come and drive with us to-day on Pfaueninsel, and tell me that you have set the good woman's mind at rest. Bring her to me to-morrow, for I should like to know her personally, and to speak to her myself."

To a friendly note of invitation to Scheffner, the aged councillor of war, she added this postscript: "Pray wear your boots, and do not come in thin stockings; I am sure they cannot be good for you; and as you know, I am fond of old friends, so I like to take care of them."

The distinguished soldier said: —

"I have never seen in any woman's face eyes of a purer, freer expression, such gladsome ingenuousness, almost bordering upon childishness."

The queen often asked Bishop Eylert to inquire into the cases of various applicants, and wished him to be lenient. She said: —

"The lines which separate deserved from undeserved suffering are very seldom distinctly drawn; they run into each other, and we ought not to forget how unworthy we are to receive the rich blessings that God bestows on us."

She wrote in 1797, "To train my children to become benevolent lovers of mankind is my warmest and dearest wish. I even nourish the glad hope of fulfilling my aim." And she set them a wonderful example.

Six months after the death of Frederick William II., the king and queen made a tour of their Eastern provinces. At Stargard, in Pomerania, where a great crowd had assembled, nineteen little girls strewed flowers in their way. One of the children told Louise that one of their number had been sent home "because she was not pretty enough."

"The poor child," said the queen, "she has rejoiced over our coming, and now she must be weeping at home." The queen immediately sent for her, and showed her much kindness.

At Elbing, a man knelt before the king, presenting a petition. The king took it and bade the man rise, saying, "No man should kneel before any human being."

At Dantz'g, the amber-workers gave her a beautiful necklace, which she wore as long as she remained in the city, much to the joy of the artisans. At Königsberg, they stayed a week. The merchants collected a large sum of money amongst themselves, and made a dinner for the poor, giving each a useful present and a dollar in remembrance of the royal visit.

On their return, they repaired to one of their favorite homes, Charlottenburg, the former residence of Sophia Charlotte, the first queen of Prussia. She was a woman of unusual mind, and a friend of the great Leibnitz, with whom she corresponded for many years. When near her death, she said to her attendants: —

"Do not grieve for me; I am now going where my intense curiosity will be satisfied as to the primeval cause of those things which Leibnitz has never been able to explain to me, — time, space, and eternity."

On July 13, 1798, the fourth child of Queen Louise, a daughter, Frederica Louise Charlotte, was born at Charlottenburg. She married, at the age of nineteen, Nicholas, the Tsar of Russia, and died in 1860.

On Oct. 13, 1799, a fifth child, a daughter, was born in the royal family; she died in the following year, of whooping cough.

In August, 1800, Louise took another journey with the king. The coal mines at Waldenburg deeply interested her. Dressed in the garb of a miner — a suit had been especially prepared for her — she went into the cavern in the hillside in a boat, as a stream runs through it.

Twenty years afterward, Prince Radziwill asked the miners if they remembered the visit.

"Yes," said an old man; "about half of us are alive who had the honor of rowing the boat on that day: three of us are with you now. I sat at the rudder. I could see the queen's sweet face well by the light of the lamps. I had never seen such a sweet face before in all my life. She looked grand as a queen should look, but she

was as gentle as a child, and had the sweetest smile I
ever saw.

"We sang the ninety-sixth psalm: 'O sing unto the
Lord a new song: sing unto the Lord, all the earth.'
The queen took the king's hand, and said softly, 'My
favorite psalm; this is heavenly!' And then turning to
me, she said, 'More slowly, my good steersman.' The
king and queen made us all presents. She gave me with
her own hand two new Holland ducats. I gave them to
my wife, and she wears them as a necklace when she goes
to church, for what *she* touched is holy. Ah! that was a
woman indeed! Why did the good God take her from us
so soon? She did everything kindly, and loved us all.
She took away her mining dress to remind her of us, as
she told us."

Louise was now twenty-four years old.

"She reminds me," says Mrs. Richard Trench, in the
life of her written by her son, the Dean of Westminster,
"of Burke's star (Marie Antoinette), glittering with life,
splendor, and joy, and realized all the fanciful ideas one
forms in one's infancy of the young, gay, beautiful, and
magnificent queens in the Arabian Nights. She is an
angel of loveliness, mildness, and grace, tall and slender,
yet sufficiently *embonpoint;* her hair is light, her complexion fair and faultless; an inexpressible air of sweetness reigns in her countenance, and forms its predominant
character."

After the queen's early death, another lady wrote: —

"Why can I not hold fast such features of her noble
image as still float fresh in my mind? The nameless grace
of her greeting, the inimitable rhythm of her walk and
bow, or the childlike repose of her gentle and yet earnest
glance, or the gliding of her royal form into a splendid

assembly in which, however large it might be, she appeared always the fairest, the first, the only one. Of her was true in its full sense Ossian's praise, 'beautiful among thousands.' If one tried to compare others with her, and considered their forms more beautiful in single features, none stood the comparison. The character of her beauty lay in the harmony of her nature. Here prevailed tenderness, gentleness, and perfect naturalness."

In 1801, June 29, a third son, Frederick Charles Alexander, was born to them. In the summer of 1802, Frederick and Louise made another tour of their provinces, receiving an ovation from their people.

At Memel, Alexander I., Emperor of Russia, spent a week with the king and queen. The ship-owners and merchants gave a brilliant ball which was opened by the Emperor of Russia and the Queen of Prussia. The emperor was commanding in appearance as well as winning in face, with many admirable qualities.

The next year, Feb. 23, 1803, the seventh child, Frederica Wilhelmina Alexandra, was born. She afterwards became Grand Duchess of Mecklenburg-Schwerin.

The royal home continued happy and peaceful. The king visited the nursery every morning, and received the children from their mother, kissing and playing with each. Every night, before retiring, the king and queen visited their sleeping children and kissed them. The king was always quiet and somewhat grave; the queen, light-hearted and witty, the joy of every circle, and the idol of her children.

One day when she was standing before the window of the castle at Potsdam, holding one of her children, and allowing it to play with a gold piece, a poorly dressed old man approached, and asked charity.

The king responded pleasantly, "Ask this lady; you see she allows her child to play with gold pieces. I have not my purse with me."

The queen gave the little prince some money (between fourteen and fifteen dollars), and said: —

"Give them to the man."

The old man received them with tears in his eyes. As soon as he had gone, the queen called him back and asked his name.

"Berghof," he replied. "I was formerly a saddler in Brandenburg; for twenty-three years I served Frederick the Great, and was discharged as sergeant."

"Without a pension?" asked the queen.

"Yes, madam."

"This gentleman," said Louise, pointing to the king, "says he has not his purse with him; but he has pen, ink, and paper, and his hand-writing is as good as gold."

Whereupon the king wrote on a slip of paper and gave to the man: —

Old Berghof, of Brandenburg, is to receive a pension of twelve thalers monthly from the extraordinary treasury of war.

FREDERICK WILLIAM.

At another time she saw a sick man on a bench at Potsdam. Thinking him needy, she asked her servant to give the man ten dollars, while she walked on.

The man, who was a master-mason, refused it. Fearing that she had hurt his feelings, she returned and said: —

"I hope you will pardon me if I have given offence. I did not intend it."

She asked if he would not come to the palace and let her cook prepare his dinners till he was well, which kindness he gladly accepted.

The queen gave so much in charities that the treasurer felt that he must confer with the king about it, and she gave him leave. The next time she opened the drawer of her writing-desk, she found that it had been refilled with money.

"What angel has filled that box again?" she asked.

"The angels are legion," replied the kindly king.

While generous himself, he was prudent in expenditures. He said:—

"The secret of dollars lies in groschen; whoever would possess the one should be careful of the other."

When he was ten years old, being very fond of cherries, a basket was brought him from the hot-house, grown in winter. When he found that they cost five dollars, he refused to eat them. Yet, while averse to spending for himself, he sent at this time twenty dollars to a poor shoemaker to buy leather.

While there was peace in the royal home, and peace in Prussia, Europe was passing through troublous times. Frederick the Great had foreseen that Frederick William III., his nephew's son, would need a strong hand and earnest purpose. In their last talk together, he said:—

"Fritz, you should prepare yourself for the future which is preparing for you; my career has come to an end, my day's work is done. I am afraid that when I am gone there will be great confusion, things will go on *pêl-mêle*. The whole world is in a ferment, and the rulers, especially those in France, unfortunately foster the exciting elements instead of appeasing or neutralizing them. . . .

"Qualify yourself to pass through trials; prepare to meet them firmly. When that day comes, think of me; watch over the honor of our house; be guilty of no injustice, but, at the same time, tolerate none. . . . The supporting foundation is the people, the nation in its unity. Stand by it faithfully, that it may love and confide in you; through the people only can you be strong, prosperous, and happy. Do not forget this hour."

Since the treaty of Basle, in January, 1795, Prussia had remained neutral in the conflicts between Russia and Austria, England and France. Frederick William III. knew the financial weakness of Prussia, and though he had two hundred thousand soldiers, he dreaded war, both from its barbarities and its enormous expense. He refused to join the coalition of 1798, when Russia and Great Britain concluded a treaty of alliance against the encroachments of France.

About two months after the peace of Amiens, in 1802, Prussia made an alliance with France, by which the former gained considerable territory. In a little more than a year after the peace, Great Britain and France were again at war. Napoleon at once seized Hanover, disbanded its German army, levied over seventeen million francs, occupied Hamburg and Bremen, and closed the Elbe and Weser against British merchant ships. Hanover begged the king of Prussia to deliver her, but he still abstained from war.

The execution by Napoleon of the Duke d'Enghien, March 21, 1804, shocked all Europe. The courts of St. Petersburg and Stockholm went into deep mourning. Alexander of Russia and Frederick wrote letters of protest to Napoleon, but they were not heeded. The Duke had been arrested at Ettenheim in Baden, between the Black Forest and the Rhine, and that country being under the protection of Frederick, he was personally interested.

When Napoleon was proclaimed emperor, Dec. 2, 1804, Alexander refused to recognize the title. Foreseeing that war with Russia must soon occur, Napoleon made an

QUEEN LOUISE OF PRUSSIA. 33

agreement with Prussia, by which the latter promised to maintain a strict neutrality, and not permit Russia or any foreign troops to march across her territory.

A coalition was formed against Napoleon by Sweden, Russia, Austria, and Great Britain. Napoleon at once marched his troops through Anspach, which belonged to Prussia, thus violating his treaty, surrounded the Austrian army near Ulm on the Danube, and cut it to pieces. The Austrians felt that crossing a neutral country, and falling upon them almost before they were aware of it, was one of the principal causes of their defeat.

A strong war party had been growing in Prussia. Frederick was urged on every side to join the other powers. The queen believed that the time had come to check Napoleon, and rebuke some of his unjust acts.

On Oct. 25, 1805, Alexander came to Prussia to see the king and queen. No Russian emperor had visited Prussia since the time of Peter the Great. The streets were crowded with people to give him a hearty welcome. The Emperor Francis II. sent his brother, the Archduke of Austria, to confer with the two sovereigns. An agreement was finally made with Russia and Austria, that Prussia should send one hundred and eighty thousand men into the field if Napoleon did not yield to the conditions of the allies.

Alexander remained for ten days, and on the night of his departure, Nov. 4, dined with the royal family at Potsdam. He expressed regret that he had not seen the tomb of Frederick the Great. "There is yet time," said Frederick, and gave orders to have the church lighted.

At midnight the emperor, with the king and queen, stood beside the plain zinc coffin. Alexander bowed and kissed it, and reaching his hand across to Frederick, pledged eternal friendship to him and his house, and an alliance against Napoleon. Louise consecrated the scene with her tears; tears that were remembered by Germany long after she was in her grave. It is said that Louise planned the meeting at the tomb, and with her woman's tact and heart, it is not improbable. A knowledge of this midnight treaty came to Napoleon, and he said, "The King of Prussia shall pay for this."

The Prussian army was made ready, and a letter sent to Napoleon by the Prussian minister, Haugwitz, who, reaching Vienna, and finding Russia and Austria on the eve of a great battle, deferred giving the letter.

Napoleon, on Dec. 2, 1805, the first anniversary of his coronation, swept all before him in the terrible battle of Austerlitz. The Russians, according to Alison, in his "History of Europe," lost thirty thousand in killed and wounded, and the French twelve thousand. It was reported that Alexander was killed, and the Grand Duke Constantine barely escaped with his life.

Haugwitz, who had come with a threat of war, concluded to make a treaty of peace, whereby Hanover was given to Prussia, and Prussia ceded Cleves, Neufchâtel, and Anspach to Napoleon.

The Prussians were enraged at Haugwitz, and the king at first refused to sign the treaty, but finally did so, at the request of his ministers, saying, however, that he would keep Hanover only till a general peace could be arranged. He said to Count Hoym, "I have signed, but I tremble for the consequences."

Napoleon felt that Prussia was in his power. He demanded that the king should renounce his connection with Russia, and make a closer alliance with France.

Napoleon had consummated his long-cherished plan

of the "Confederation of the Rhine," whereby several states had separated themselves from the German empire, and put themselves under his protection. Sixteen million men transferred their allegiance to Napoleon with the promise that hostility committed against one should be considered as a declaration of war against the whole. Francis II. saw that the German empire was destroyed, and renounced the imperial crown.

England was angry concerning Hanover, and Napoleon made her a private proposal to restore it to her — he had just ceded it to Prussia — if she would make peace with him. Before Anspach knew that she was given over to France, forty thousand Frenchmen took possession. The heart-breaks of war had begun. When by Napoleon's order the ports of Hanover were closed to Great Britain, the latter at once declared war against Prussia, and Sweden was ready to join her. It was discovered also that Napoleon meditated the seizure of Westphalia.

Frederick William III. was worn and anxious over these dire events. Louise was in ill-health. Her eighth child, a son, Frederick Julius Ferdinand Leopold, born Dec. 13, 1804, had died April 6, 1806, at the age of sixteen months. Prostrated by a nervous fever, she was advised by her physician to go to the baths of Pyrmont. Here she staid six weeks with her father and brother George, but she was anxious to be at home and share in the joys and sorrows of her beloved Germany. She returned Aug. 3 to Charlottenburg, where the king had planted some poplars and beeches in honor of her coming. At Berlin she was received by the people with the greatest enthusiasm.

Frederick had at last determined to meet the demands of Napoleon by war. The army was made ready for marching. The patriotic queen, at the request of the king, rode beside him when he reviewed the troops. When the queen's regiment, the Anspach-Baireuth dragoons, came into Berlin before going to the field, the queen wore above her riding-skirt a spencer trimmed with the colors of the regiment. This was given to the regiment and is tenderly preserved.

Alexander offered at once to put himself at the head of a large army to help Prussia. Frederick and Louise went to Naumburg to meet the first body of Russian troops sent by Alexander. The Russians were charmed with the queen. She had lost something of her girlish light-heartedness, but none of her enthusiasm and spirit. She was thirty, still beautiful, brilliant, and thoroughly womanly.

The letter of Frederick to Napoleon, stating his grounds of complaint, was hastily read, and then Napoleon dictated his proclamation to his army: "Soldiers! the order for your return to France was issued. You were already within a few days' march of your homes, triumphal *fêtes* awaited you, and preparations for your reception had commenced in the capital; but while we too confidently resigned ourselves, feeling too secure, new plots were hatching under the mask of friendship and alliance. . . . We ought not to return except beneath triumphal arches. What! have we braved inclement seasons, the ocean, and the desert; have we subdued Europe, often united against us; have we extended our glory from the east to the west, only to return like deserters? and are we to be told that the French eagle has fled in dismay before the Prussian?"

Frederick told his soldiers, "On this war depends not only the honor of the Prussian arms, but the very existence of the monarchy."

The king chose Erfurt for his headquarters, and thither the troops marched, singing triumphant songs. A portion of the army was at Weimar. Louise was with her husband inspiring the troops. She had not instigated the war as Napoleon said, but he well knew that the love felt by the German nation for her was to be more dreaded by him than many armies. For her they would face death on any battlefield.

When moving with the army the king and queen travelled in a close carriage, followed by twenty other carriages, and surrounded by troops and artillery. One of the generals, Kalkreuth, said one day to Chevalier von Gentz, a diplomatist from the court of Vienna, "You are hoping to have the honor of being presented to the queen. If you should have an opportunity of saying a few words to her on the subject [her remaining with the troops], pray say all you can to induce her to remain. I know what I am asking. Her presence with us is quite necessary."

Gentz had an audience with the queen at nine o'clock on the morning of Oct. 9. She showed neither fear nor irresolution. She said, "I think we could not decide otherwise than on war; our position had become so equivocal that it was necessary to get out of it at any price. It is much less on calculation than on a sentiment of honor and under a sense of duty that we were obliged to take this course. . . . I was fully convinced that the great sources of true security were to be found only in the closest union of all who bear the name of Germans; as to Russia's assistance, I always regarded it only as a last resource."

The "union of all who bear the name of Germans" was always dear to the heart of Louise. Her son Frederick William IV. said, "*The unity of Germany concerns me deeply: it is an inheritance from my mother.*"

Gentz was delighted with the queen. He said, "You could not find another such woman in Germany. The intellectual and refined ideas she developed every moment during our three quarters of an hour's conversation were wonderful; she argued with independence and energy, yet with precision and self-control, evincing a prudence that would have been admirable in a man. At the same time, everything she said was so full of deep feeling as not to allow me for one moment to forget that it was a woman who claimed my attention. It was a combination of dignity, benevolence, and grace such as I never met with before. Not a word was out of place, not a sentiment, not a reflection which was not in exquisite harmony with the general character of her conversation." She spoke guardedly and gently of both Napoleon and Josephine.

On Oct. 10 the main army which had proceeded to Weimar was shocked by the news of the death of the brave Prince Louis Ferdinand, nephew of Frederick the Great, at the head of six thousand men, surrounded by thirty thousand of the enemy. The fight lasted for five hours. His horse got entangled in a hedge, and left his rider struggling in the bushes. The prince had extricated himself, when his surrender was demanded. He replied by a cut of his sabre, and the next instant fell by the sword of his antagonist. His conquerors took the body to Saalfeld and gave it military interment in the church, from which it was removed in 1811 to Berlin cathedral.

On the evening of Oct. 13 the king and the aged Duke of Brunswick reached the heights of Auerstädt. The king had made arrangements for the queen to remain at the ducal castle in Weimar; but anxious for the king and the army, the heroic and fearless queen left that afternoon, and was soon travelling with him, with the enemy in full view. The Duke of Brunswick insisted on the wisdom of her return, and she was finally persuaded to go back to Berlin, attended by a guard of fifty men. A circuitous route was marked out for her, as many Frenchmen were in the country.

The next day, Oct. 14, 1806, the dreadful battles of Jena and Auerstädt were fought. At Jena, Napoleon, Ney, and Murat led the French against Prince Hohenlohe; at Auerstädt, Davoust led the French against the king and the Duke of Brunswick. The king fought bravely and with great coolness, having two horses killed under him. The Duke had his left eye struck out by a bullet, and was carried senseless from the field in the early part of the day.

Alison says, "The astonishing battles of Jena and Auerstädt in a single day prostrated the strength of the Prussian monarchy, and did that in a few hours which all the might of Austria, Russia, and France in the Seven Years' War had been unable to effect. The subsequent disasters of the campaign were but the completion of this great calamity; the decisive strokes were given on the banks of the Saale. The loss of the Prussians was prodigious: on the two fields there fell nearly twenty thousand killed and wounded, besides nearly as many prisoners; and two hundred pieces of cannon, with twenty-five standards, were taken. Ten thousand of the killed and wounded fell at Auerstädt. . . . Nor was that victory bloodless to the conquerors: their total loss was fourteen thousand men, of whom seven thousand five hundred belonged to the corps of Davoust." When Napoleon entered Berlin, Davoust and his corps took the lead, in reward for their bravery. Napoleon followed the retreating Prussians into Weimar.

He took no rest on the night of the fourteenth. He was dictating orders to his various corps in their pursuit of the enemy. Towards evening on the following day he took possession of the palace of the Duke of Weimar.

The next morning, before the sun had risen, an officer entered the apartment of Napoleon. "Sire," said he, "I have a good report to give you, but we have failed in our attempt to take the Queen of Prussia."

"Ah! that would have been well done," said Napoleon, "for she has caused the war."

The queen pursued her sad journey towards Berlin. At Brandenburg a courier met her to tell her that all was lost, and that she must flee with her children. Her physician, Hufeland, accompanied her to the Schwedt on the Oder, where the children had been sent already. Her agitation frightened them as they had always seen her so happy.

She said to her two sons, Frederick and William, eleven and nine years of age: "You see me in tears; I lament the destruction of the army! . . . Destiny has destroyed in one day a structure in the erection of which the great men of two centuries have labored. There is no Prussian state, no Prussian army, no national glory longer; it has disappeared like that mist which on the fields of Jena and Auerstädt hid the danger and terrors of that ill-starred battle. . . .

"Call back to memory, in the future, when your mother and queen is no longer living, this unhappy hour; weep tears as you remember me, as I now at this sad moment lament the downfall of my fatherland. But let not tears alone content you; act, develop your powers. Perhaps

Prussia's tutelary genius will alight upon you; then deliver your people from the disgrace, from the reproach, of degradation in which she languishes. . . .

"Oh, my sons, do not allow yourselves to be swept along by the degeneracy of this age; become *men*, and covet the glory of great commanders and heroes. If you should lack in ambition, you would be unworthy of the name of princes and grandsons of the great Frederick. If with every exertion you cannot raise up again the prostate state, then seek death as Louis Ferdinand sought it."

They soon went to Stettin, and after a day hurried on to Cüstrin, where the king met her. He remained for some time, examining the defences, the noble queen in her long travelling cloak walking up and down the ramparts with him. Many men in high positions counselled surrender to Napoleon, but the queen urged continuance of the war rather than submit to the hard terms of the Emperor of France. Napoleon's victories seemed to have paralyzed the Prussian nation. Cüstrin was given up. Stettin surrendered without firing a shot. Lübeck surrendered after a heroic defence.

The court retreated to Marienwerder, where they staid ten days, and then to Ortelsburg. The royal family suffered every privation. They had but one scantily furnished room in a wretched house. They were ankle deep in mud whenever they stepped out of doors. Provisions were very scarce. "But," says Sir George Jackson, "we have some reason to be satisfied when we think of the privations which the poor queen is enduring, whose dignified resignation under these distressing circumstances renders her even more interesting than does her great beauty."

The queen felt all this keenly, for she quoted in her notebook, as expressive of her heart, this verse from Goethe's "Wilhelm Meister":—

> "Who never ate his bread in sorrow,
>   Who never-spent the darksome hours
> Weeping and watching for the morrow —
>   He knows ye not, ye gloomy powers.
> To earth — this weary earth — ye bring us,
>   To guilt ye let us heedless go;
> Then leave repentance fierce to wring us,
>   A moment's guilt, an age's woe."

The people sympathized deeply with their king and queen. The sect of Mennonites sent two hundred gold Fredericks which they had collected among their people, and begged the royal family to accept the money with their love and respect. They accepted it, and repaid it in better times.

A farmer's wife brought some butter for the "poor, dear king." "No, no," said the king, "not poor; I am a rich king, blessed with such subjects."

Magdeburg soon fell. Marshal Ney heated twenty-four-pound shot to red heat, and began to throw them into the town. The people begged their leaders to surrender. Sixteen thousand troops in arms, four thousand in the hospitals, six hundred pieces of cannon, eight hundred thousand pounds of powder, a pontoon train complete, and immense stores of all kinds fell into the hands of the enemy.

Late in 1806 the royal family went to Königsberg. The queen was prostrated by nervous fever, and her life and that of her child, Prince Charles, were in great danger. Before she had recovered they were obliged to flee to Memel, as the French were approaching. She begged to be removed, saying in the words of King David, "Let us fall now into the hand of the Lord; for his mercies are great: and let me not fall into the hand of man."

They were three days and nights on the journey. The first night the queen lay in a room whose windows were broken, and the snow blew on the bed. But she was full of trust and courage.

Meanwhile Napoleon had entered Berlin in triumph, amid the hatred and despair of the people. He visited Sans-Souci and looked upon the room where Frederick the Great died. He traced a large N in the dust on Frederick's coffin, saying, "If he were alive now, I should not stand here." He sent Frederick's sword, hat, and scarf to Paris; these were destroyed in 1814, just before the Allies entered.

At Charlottenburg he entered the queen's private rooms and read her letters, in some of which she showed her aversion to him. But he was much impressed with her picture, and wished to see her.

Early in 1807, the remnant of the Prussian army under Gen. Lestocq combined with the Russian troops and fought the desperate battle of Eylau, Feb. 8. The Russian and Prussian loss was said to have been twenty-five thousand in killed and wounded, and the French thirty thousand. Alison says of this battle, "Never was spectacle so dreadful as the field of battle on the following morning. Above fifty thousand men lay in a space of two leagues, weltering in blood. The wounds were for the most part of the severest kind, from the extraordinary quantity of cannon-balls which had been discharged during the action, and the close proximity of the contending masses to the deadly batteries which spread grape at half musket shot through the ranks.

"Though stretched on the cold snow, and exposed to the severity of an arctic winter, they were burning with thirst, and piteous cries were heard on all sides for water, or assistance to extricate the wounded men from beneath the heaps of slain, or loads of horses by which they were crushed. Six thousand of these noble animals encumbered the field, or, maddened with pain, were shrieking aloud amid the stifled groans of the wounded."

Napoleon suffered so severely that he proposed to make a favorable peace with Frederick if the latter would break with the Emperor Alexander, which Frederick refused to do. Napoleon also sent word to the queen that he would be happy to pay his court to her at Berlin. This was impossible after his unjust and sarcastic words about her in his bulletins. The Germans never forgave and never forgot them.

The queen still had hope. She wrote her father, "Only by patient perseverance can we succeed — sooner or later I am sure we shall do so." Brave Gen. Blücher told Bourrienne, whom he met at Hamburg, "I reckon much on the public spirit of Germany, on the enthusiasm which reigns in our universities. Success in war is ephemeral; but defeat itself contributes to nourish in a people the principles of honor and a passion for national glory. Be assured that when a whole people are resolved to emancipate themselves from foreign domination, they will never fail to succeed. I foresee that fortune will not always favor your emperor. The time may come when Europe in a body, humiliated by his exactions, exhausted by his depredations, will rise up in arms against him."

But hope was soon well-nigh quenched by the battle of Friedland, June 14, 1807. The Russians lost seventeen thousand in killed and wounded, and the French eight thousand. The queen wrote her father three days after the battle: —

"We are on the point of forsaking the kingdom. Consider how I feel in so doing, but I implore you do not misjudge your daughter. Do not believe that pusillanimity bows my heart. There are two principal reasons why I am lifted above everything. The first is the thought, we are no sport of blind chance, but we are in God's hand, and his providence guides us. The second is, we shall go down with honor. . . . To live and die in the way of right, and, if need be, eat bread and salt, will never make me wholly unhappy, but I can no longer hope. If good fortune comes, oh, no one will receive it more gratefully than I, but I no more expect it. If misfortune comes, it will stun me for a time. When not deserved it can never overwhelm me. Only wrong on our part would bring me to the grave."

The defeated Alexander, his people clamoring for peace, proposed an armistice, which Napoleon accepted. It was agreed that the terms of peace should be settled between Napoleon, Alexander, and Frederick, at Tilsit, on the Niemen.

Napoleon desired to have as much dramatic effect as possible. The bridge at Tilsit having been burned, a raft was placed in the river, with a gaily decorated pavilion upon it. At one o'clock, the short but alert conqueror, with his strong pale face, and keen, controlling glance, surrounded by his officers, stepped into the boat which was to bear him to the raft. At the same moment, in sight of the great crowds which had gathered, the tall, handsome Alexander started with his suite from the opposite bank. Napoleon arrived first, and opened the door for Alexander, whom he met cordially. They conversed for three hours.

The next day, June 26, 1807, the king of Prussia was called to the conference. Napoleon treated Frederick coldly from the first, but he treated Alexander pleasantly. The three dined together each day, but Alexander only was asked to spend the evening and talk till midnight.

It seemed impossible to gain much for Prussia, when it occurred to Alexander that the beautiful queen might win concessions where he failed to obtain them. The king, with an aching heart, sent for her.

When she received the message, she burst into tears and exclaimed: "This is the most painful sacrifice that I can make for my people."

She wrote in her diary: "God knows what a struggle it cost me! For although I do not hate the man, yet I look upon him as the author of the unhappiness of the king and his people. I admire his talents. I do not like his character, which is obviously treacherous and false. It will be hard for me to be polite and courteous to him; still the effort is demanded, and I must make the sacrifice."

Napoleon sent an escort of French dragoons and his state carriage drawn by eight horses for Louise. She reached Tilsit July 6, and Napoleon at once called upon her, Talleyrand accompanying him. She was dressed in white crape, richly embroidered in silk. The conversation lasted for half or three quarters of an hour. Napoleon said, with h's usual abruptness, "How could you ever begin war with me?"

"Sire," replied Louise, "even if we have been imposed upon in other respects, could the glory of Frederick deceive us in regard to our powers?" She begged that some of the fortresses be spared to Prussia, especially

Magdeburg. "You ask a great deal," said the emperor, "but I will think about it."

Later Napoleon remarked to Talleyrand, "I knew that I should see a beautiful woman, and a queen with dignified manners, but I found the most admirable queen, and at the same time the most interesting woman I had ever met with."

Talleyrand thought he might yield to her influence, and responded, "Sire, shall posterity say that you have not profited by your great conquests because of a beautiful woman?"

At the sumptuous banquet to which Napoleon invited her, she sat at his right hand, and the king on his left. The emperor talked freely, but the king was silent. The queen was quick-witted in her answers to Napoleon, brilliant, and with great tact, yet with one purpose ever in mind, — better terms for fallen Prussia.

Napoleon offered her a rare and beautiful rose. She hesitated about taking it, but did so, saying, with her sweet smile, "At least with Magdeburg!"

Napoleon replied, "I must observe to your Majesty that it is I who present, and you who are about to receive it."

Again, though much against her will, she dined with the emperor, after she had heard that he would yield nothing. "The conversation," writes the lady-in-waiting, "was constrained and monosyllabic. After dinner the queen talked once more with Napoleon; on going away she told him that she was about to depart, and felt deeply that she had been deceived."

Louise said herself, a year later, "What I suffered then I suffered more on account of others than on my own account. I wept; I implored in the name of love and of humanity, in the name of our misfortunes, and of the laws which govern the world."

Count de Las Cases, in his "Memoirs of the Life, Exile, and Conversations of the Emperor" at St. Helena, gives these words of Napoleon in those lonely days of remembrance: "The queen of Prussia was unquestionably gifted with many happy resources. She possessed a great deal of information, and had many excellent capabilities. It was she who really reigned for more than fifteen years. She also, in spite of my dexterity and all my exertions, took the lead in the conversation and constantly maintained the ascendancy. She touched, perhaps too often, upon her favorite topic, but she did so, however, with great plausibility and without giving the slightest cause of uneasiness. It must be confessed that she had an important object in view and that the time was short and precious. . . .

"I was determined not to yield. I found it necessary to keep a great command over myself, that I might continue exempt from all kind of engagement and every expression which might be taken in a doubtful sense."

By the treaty of Tilsit (signed July 7), the king of Prussia was obliged to give up half his dominions, to reduce his army to forty-two thousand men, and to pay a war indemnification of one hundred and fifty million thalers.

How little Napoleon dreamed that this would be paid back with interest in the war of 1870! The queen wrote her father, "I am convinced that the way in which this peace has been concluded will, at a future period, sooner or later, bring down a blessing on Prussia, although I may not live to see it."

The state was near bankruptcy, and the king was

advised to declare it, but he said, "I may be unfortunate, but God will preserve me from committing a base act."

The sovereigns and the people bent their energies to paying the war debt. The gold dinner service of Frederick the Great was sent to the mint to be coined into money. The queen parted with all her jewels save one ornament of pearls, which she said "betokens tears, and I have shed so many."

The royal table at Memel was furnished like that of an ordinary citizen. A Russian diplomatist who spent a night at the king's house said, "Not a thousand court feasts, with golden uniforms and stars, would I give in exchange for the memory of that night. A queen sits at a poorly furnished table, that, like herself, is divested of all external adornments; but her grace, beauty, and dignity shine all the brighter.

"By her side sits the eldest princess, Charlotte, as the bud by the unfolded rose. She shared with her mother the little household duties. Both delighted by their amiable attentions, and left behind in my soul a living picture which no after event can efface"

The queen walked every morning and evening with the king to cheer him. The Countess Voss, the lady in attendance, said the king was so sad, "it touched one's heart to the quick, and one could not listen to him without hot tears."

After the peace of Tilsit, Baron von Stein, who had differed from the king some months previously, was recalled, to the great delight of Louise. She wrote, "How happy I am that Stein is again here; yes, I feel, since I know that he is at the head of affairs, as if I could raise higher and carry more easily my head, burdened with a weight of care."

"I implore you," she wrote to Stein, soon after his coming, "have patience during the first months; the king will certainly keep his word. . . . I pray God that the good may not come to nought on account of the patience and delay of three months. I implore you for the sake of myself, my children, my country, the king, have patience."

In all the great projects for the reform of Prussia in education, in the army, in the emancipation of the peasants, Louise was Stein's helper and friend. She greatly influenced her husband, who was naturally more conservative than she.

She aided every good work. On her birthday in 1807 the Luisenstift, or Louise's Association, was organized for orphans, most of them the children of soldiers. She gave both money and time to it. She still made charming little *fêtes* for her own children, who loved to make wreaths of blue corn-flowers for her.

The cold air of Memel was affecting her health, and the royal family removed to Königsberg early in 1808. On the first of February, of this year, the queen's ninth child was born — a daughter — to whom was given the endeared name of Louise.

"You will be pleased to hear, dear father," she wrote a little later, "that the misfortune which has fallen upon us has not affected our domestic happiness; indeed, it seems to have drawn us nearer together, and strengthened our affections. The king, who is the best of men, is kinder than ever. Often I fancy that I see in him the lover and the bridegroom; more in actions than in words do I perceive his constant devotion to me.

"Only yesterday he said to me, looking at me with his guileless eyes and earnest expression of countenance, 'Dear Louise, thou hast become dearer and more precious than ever to me in misfortune. Now I know by experience what I possess in thee. Let the storm continue without, as it will; if only our happiness remain undisturbed, we are secure. Because I love thee so fondly, I have desired our youngest-born daughter to be called Louise. May she become a Louise!'

"This tenderness on his part affected me to tears. It is my pride, my joy, and my happiness to possess the love of the best of men, and because I love him in return with all my heart, and we are so united that the will of one is the will of the other, it is very easy for us to preserve this harmony day by day. In a word, he pleases me in all points, and I please him, and we are happiest when we are together. . . .

"Our children are our treasures, and our eyes rest upon them with satisfaction and hope. The crown prince is full of life and spirit. He has superior talents, which are happily developed and cultivated. . . . He is particularly attached to his mother, and could not be purer-minded than he is. I love him most tenderly, and often speak to him of the duties which will devolve upon him if he lives to become king.

"Our son William will, if I am not mistaken, take after his father, and be simple, upright, and wise. Also in outward appearance he bears the greatest resemblance to him, only he is, I think, not so good looking. You see, dear father, I am still in love with my husband."

After describing her other children to her father, she adds, "It may be well for our children that already in their youth they have learned to know the serious side of life. If they had grown up in the lap of plenty and ease then they would suppose everything must ever be thus. But they see by the grave countenance of their father, and the grief and frequent tears of their mother, that things can change."

The baby Louise, when grown to womanhood, married Frederic, the second son of William I., King of the Netherlands, and died in 1870. During the year 1808 the queen spent much time in reading history. "I read history diligently," she said, "and live in the past because there is no more future for me."

In the winter of this year, 1808, the king and queen visited St. Petersburg at the request of Alexander. Twelve elegant rooms were made ready for the queen, one with hangings of pink silk and a toilette of gold. Six superb Turkish shawls were presented to her, besides a sumptuous table service of crystal, vases, silks, and other costly things. She visited the benevolent institutions with great interest. On her return she said, "I have returned as I went. Nothing dazzles me any more. My kingdom is not of this world."

During the spring and summer of 1809, the queen was ill much of the time. France and Austria were at war, and Louise feared that Prussia would be drawn into the conflict. After the battle of Wagram, July 5, 6, 1809, she wrote her father: "With us it is all over for the present, even if not forever. I look for nothing more during my life. . . . It becomes more and more clear to me that everything had to come as it has. Divine Providence is unmistakably introducing a new order of things in the world; there will be a different arrangement, since the old order has outlived itself and is falling to pieces. *We have fallen asleep on the laurels of Frederick the Great*, who, as the master of his century, created a new epoch. We have not kept pace with the age, therefore it has left us behind. No one is better aware of this than the king.

I have just had a conversation with him, in which he repeatedly said, as if speaking to himself, 'This also must be changed among us.' . . . Better times will certainly come. Faith in the most perfect Being is a guaranty for this. But only through goodness can the world become better. Therefore, I do not believe that the Emperor Napoleon Bonaparte is firm and safe on his glittering throne. Only truth and justice are strong and secure. . . . He has no moderation, and he who cannot observe moderation loses his balance and falls. . . . What has taken place is unmistakably neither final nor abiding, nor for the best good of all, but only the opening of a path to a better end. This end appears to be at a great distance; we probably shall not see it, and shall die before it is reached. As God wills; all as He wills."

The French troops had left Berlin, and the royal family were to return Dec. 23. The queen had longed for the day. She said, "A homesickness that I cannot describe draws me thither [to Berlin] and to my Charlottenburg!"

On the anniversary of the day and hour on which Louise entered Berlin as a bride sixteen years before, she entered it again Dec. 23, 1809. She rode in a handsome carriage lined with lilac, her favorite color, the gift of the citizens. By her side were her two daughters and her son, Prince Charles. The king was on horseback with his generals, while Frederick and William, the two sons, were on foot as officers of guards in the queen's regiment. The citizens seemed wild with joy. The royal family went first to the cathedral to attend a national thanksgiving service, and then to the royal box at the opera house to please the people.

Fouqué said, "The queen sat beside her husband. As she conversed she often raised her eyes to the king with a very touching expression; had she, perhaps, already the presentiment that she would not long be the comforter, the consoling guide of the severely-tried monarch? I do not know; but when she bowed to the public, before leaving the house, as was at that time the custom, I could not help being struck by her expression, and I said to my friends as we were returning home, I had thought that Prussia could now give up all thoughts of war, and settle down to peaceful pursuits, as Frederick had done after the battle of Molwitz, which he lost; but now I feel quite differently.

"Our beloved queen has thanked us with tears. Bonaparte has dimmed those heavenly eyes, and I wish Prussia could gain a victory to brighten them. That may not be granted to us, but at all events we must do everything that can be done to make those eyes sparkle again."

Borowsky, the court preacher, said, "Our dear queen is far from joyful, but her seriousness has a quiet serenity, and the calmness and repose, which God gives her, sheds over her entire life a noble grace. Her eyes, it is true, have lost their former sparkle, and one sees that they have wept much, and still weep; but by this they have received an expression of gentle sorrow and quiet longing which is even more charming than that which mere enjoyment of life would give. The bloom on her countenance is indeed gone and a soft pallor overspreads it, yet her face is still beautiful, and now the white roses on her cheeks please me almost more than the red of other days. At times is seen a slight trembling of the mouth, around which formerly a sweet, happy smile hovered. Sorrow is implied by this, but it is not bitter. Her dress is ever exceedingly simple, and the choice of colors indicates her frame of mind."

The king, as was his usual custom, thought how he might benefit the poor. He gave five thousand dollars to them, remitted all punishments for light offences, and set at liberty all whose terms of imprisonment were less than a year.

To commemorate this return to Berlin, the people placed on an island in the Thiergarten a beautiful vase, by the sculptor Schadow, which each year is filled with flowers on Louise's birthday, the 10th of March.

The queen's tenth and last child, Prince Albert, had been born two months previously, Oct. 4, 1809. She was in failing health with lung trouble. On her last birthday, March 10, 1810, when she was thirty-four, she said, "I think this will be the last birthday I shall ever celebrate."

The country was unable to meet the money demands of Napoleon. The latter said, "If the king cannot pay, nothing remains to be done but to surrender Silesia." The queen wrote Napoleon, begging for a modification in the interests of Prussia, but it availed nothing. Napoleon's descendants were to learn later on that magnanimity to a fallen foe would have been the part of wisdom, at least.

On May 20, Louise wished to go to Paretz. She twined a wreath of oak leaves and flowers, still preserved, and was so loath to depart that she staid until the moon came up, and then walked arm-in-arm down the long avenue with her husband, and passed out of the gate near the summer-house. Not long after, the king locked the gate out of which she went for the last time, and it has never been reopened. In the grotto where she used to sit and teach her children is an iron table, with letters in gold: "Remember the absent."

On June 25, Louise started for Charlottenburg, to make a long desired visit to her father. On her arrival only one day was given to a public reception. On that evening she showed some of the ladies a locket which she wore containing her husband's picture, saying that it was her most precious treasure. On the following day the king arrived. Being in a room with her brother George, and in front of her father's writing-desk, she sat down and wrote the last words she was ever to put upon paper:

My dear father, — I am to-day very happy as your daughter, and as the wife of the best of men. LOUISE.

New Strelitz, 28 June, 1810."

These words were always carefully treasured by Emperor William, her son.

Louise went soon after with the family into the country to the castle of Hohenzieritz. The king was obliged to return to Berlin, but he wrote her affectionately. One day when a letter came she said, putting it next her heart, "Oh, what a letter! How happy the one who receives such a letter!"

Louise soon became ill, and was tenderly watched by her sister. "Oh," she moaned, "if only their anxiety for me were not so great! It will make them ill."

On Monday, July 16, she was attacked with spasms, which lasted five hours. The king had been sent for. "Will he come soon? How late is it?" she asked repeatedly. "Think of my dying and leaving the king and the children!" she said to her physician At four o'clock on the morning of July 19 the king arrived with the two elder sons. With eyes full of affection she looked on the two boys, saying, "My Fritz! my William!"

When the king was told that she could not recover he

said, sadly, "Oh, if she were not mine, she would live; but since she is my wife, she will surely die!"

He left the room to gain control over his feelings. "Tell him," said the queen, "not to be so agitated, or I shall die instantly." The king sat on the edge of the bed and tried to warm the cold hands of the queen. At ten minutes before nine o'clock, in the forenoon, Louise looked upon them all with her clear, open gaze, and then towards heaven, saying: "I am dying! O Jesus, make it easy!" She drew a long breath, and life was finished.

All Germany seemed in tears. Blücher said, "Our saint is in heaven." When four years later he led his victorious army to the heights of Montmartre, when the Allies entered Paris, he said, remembering those agonizing days, "*Louise is avenged!*"

The precious body of the queen was carried to Berlin, and lay in state until July 30. Six months later, on Dec. 23, the anniversary of her wedding day, the mausoleum at Charlottenburg having been made ready, she was carried thither.

The exterior of the temple is of red granite, four Doric columns supporting the entablature. The building is sheltered by trees — appropriate, since, with their shade and graceful motion, they seemed to her as friends. The exquisite recumbent statue of Louise in its soft blue light, from the blue glass above, as though the sky were reflected upon it, is by Rauch, who worked on it two years as a labor of love, for the queen had befriended him. He had been a footman in the royal household. Seeing his love for art Louise furnished the means for his study at Rome. Frederick thought of asking Canova to make the statue, but Rauch was so disappointed that the work was given to him; he died in 1857, honored by his nation.

The king founded several institutions and orders in memory of his beloved Louise. The Order of the Iron Cross was instituted on her birthday, 1814.

Napoleon, when he heard of the death of Louise, said, "The king has lost his best minister." He too was coming into sorrow. France and Russia were again at war.

The terrible march from the burning Moscow had been made, the battle of Leipsic fought, and Alexander and Frederick, — the crown prince and William riding behind him, — with their army, entered Paris, March 31, 1814. Napoleon abdicated at Fontainebleau, April 5, and soon after retired to Elba. When, Aug. 7, the troops returned to Berlin victorious, Charlotte now sixteen, in the place of her beloved mother, greeted them with much feeling and dignity. The king said, "If this high honor be given to those to whom it is due, to Gen. Blücher and the Prussian army, I will enter with them as the sovereign head of a grateful people."

After Napoleon's escape from Elba, and his crushing defeat at Waterloo, June 18, where Blücher had one hundred and sixteen thousand Prussian soldiers, he was sent to St. Helena, where he lived in isolation for six lonely years, dying May 5, 1821. What a contrast to Tilsit, when Louise was the beautiful suppliant and he had it in his power to be generous!

Fourteen years after the death of Louise, Frederick married the Countess von Harrach, a lovely woman, though as she was not of royal blood she could not become queen. He said to Bishop Eylert: "My last daughter, my darling Louise, so like her mother, is leaving me; I would not have it otherwise. . . . I cannot be so selfish as to wish to keep her with me through the remainder of my life, but what should I do without her?

Womanly companionship and sympathy have become necessary to me, therefore I must marry again."

He died sixteen years later, June 7, 1840, having reigned forty-three years. Under the decoration of the Black Eagle which he always wore was found the face of Louise.

Frederick William IV., his son, reigned twenty-one years, and died Jan. 2, 1861, without children. He directed by will that his body should be opened, and his heart taken out, and buried in a granite heart of proportionate size, at the feet of his mother at Charlottenburg.

King William came to the throne on the death of his brother. Early in 1870 trouble arose with France because Spain wished to make Prince Leopold of Hohenzollern her king. France wished King William to interfere to prevent it, which he declined to do.

A declaration of war was delivered at Berlin, July 19, 1870. King William said, "God knows I am not responsible for this war; the demands were such that I could do no other than reject them."

Sixty years before, on July 19, he had knelt beside his mother's death-bed. Before going to war he went to Charlottenburg, and stood with uncovered head beside her tomb.

The Prussian army numbered a half million well-drilled men, with a half million more ready for service. Moltke knew France almost as well as he knew Germany, and Bismarck was a born leader by the side of his brave king.

Battle after battle was gained by the Prussians, culminating in the surrender of Napoleon III., at Sedan, Sept. 2, 1870, with from eighty to ninety thousand French soldiers. He was sent a royal prisoner to Wilhelmshöhe. Metz surrendered Oct. 27, with one hundred and seventy-three thousand Frenchman. A little more than a month later, Jan. 18, 1871, King William, in the palace of Louis XIV., at Versailles, was crowned Emperor William I. of Germany. His ancestor, Frederick the Great, on that day one hundred and eighty years before, had been crowned king of Prussia.

The terms of peace, concluded between Bismarck, Jules Favre, and Thiers, included the ceding of nearly the whole of Alsace and Lorraine with other territory, about six thousand square miles in all, to Germany, and a war indemnity of one thousand million dollars.

As soon as the emperor returned to Berlin, he went alone to the mausoleum at Charlottenburg. He was not insensible to the horrors of war. He knew how the heart of the Empress Eugénie would bleed and break like his mother's. He knew how the ceded countries would mourn, and how France would struggle under her pecuniary burdens; but out of all the sorrow had come that for which Louise longed and labored, — German unity.

He worshipped the memory of his mother. When he was eighty, and her statue was unveiled in the Thiergarten at Berlin, he said, "In my childhood and in my youth I could not understand what she foreboded, and yet God in his grace chose me to carry to completion what she foresaw, when I myself had scarcely a premonition of what was to happen. It is clear to me that God selects his instruments to do his will. And this inspires me with the deepest humility and the deepest thankfulness."

August Kluckhorn, in his memorial of Louise, translated by Elizabeth H. Denio, of Wellesley College, gives these touching words of the gifted queen: "Even if posterity does not mention my name among illustrious women, yet, when it learns the sorrows of the time, it will know what

I have suffered through them, and will say: She endured much, she remained patient in the midst of suffering. Then I could wish that at the same time they might say: She gave birth to children who were worthy of better times; she endeavored to lead them on, and at last her care has borne rich fruit."

The wish has been fulfilled. Her care has indeed "borne rich fruit." Gracious and beautiful, kind to the lowest and the highest, the cultivated friend of poets and statesmen, a devoted wife and mother, brave and able to lead, yet gentle and lovable, she was, and is, the inspiration of a great nation.

MADAME RÉCAMIER, THE BEAUTIFUL.

"TO be beloved was the history of Madame Récamier. Beloved by all in her youth for her astonishing beauty; beloved for her gentleness, her inexhaustible kindness, for the charm of a character which was reflected in her sweet face; beloved for the tender and sympathizing friendship which she awarded with an exquisite tact and discrimination of heart; beloved by old and young, small and great, by women, — even women, so fastidious where other women are concerned; beloved always and by all from her cradle to the grave, — such was the lot, such will be the renown, of this charming woman! What other glory is so enviable?"

Thus wrote Madame de Hautefeuille in her lament over this celebrated woman.

What gave Madame Récamier her extraordinary power, her charm over all with whom she came in contact? What has made her memory fragrant for half a century?

The cry of every heart is to be loved; to her, love was given in the fullest measure. Every person desires to have influence; she swayed, as by magic, each of her acquaintances. Beauty counts for much, but she received the same worship when she was old and blind, and from those scarcely half her age. The richest in the realm asked her hand in marriage; the poorest gave her homage.

Literary men sought her counsel, and she inspired them to their best efforts. She had learned, what comparatively few ever learn in this world, the secret of power, the way to win and to hold hearts.

Jeanne Françoise Julie Adélaide Bernard was born at Lyons, Dec. 4, 1777. Her father, Jean, a notary, was a handsome man, but of weak character; her mother, Juliette Manton, was equally handsome, but of great strength of mind and business capacity. She amassed a fortune in speculation, and held it through the horrors of the Reign of Terror. She was not only capable, but vivacious and graceful, finding time to educate her daughter carefully, and to be to her a sister as well as a mother. The two were inseparable.

When Julie, or Juliette as she was usually called, was seven years old, her father having been appointed collector of customs in Paris, she was sent to the home of her mother's sister, Madame Blachette, at Ville-franche. Here she was very happy in the affection of a child of her own age, Renard Humblot, the first of her almost numberless admirers.

After a time she became a pupil at the convent of La Déserte at Lyons, where one of her mother's sisters had become a nun. She left this school with great reluctance, to live in Paris. After her death, this notice of her school life was found among her papers: —

The next day,- bathed in tears, I passed over the threshold of that door, the opening of which to admit me I could scarcely remember. I was put into a carriage with my aunt, and we set off for Paris. From this serene and innocent period of my life I turn with regret to one of turmoil. The former comes back to me sometimes like a vague, sweet dream, with its clouds of incense, its innumerable ceremonies, its processions in the gardens, its chants, and its flowers. . . .

It is doubtless owing to these vivid impressions, received during childhood, that I have been able to retain my religious belief, though coming in contact with persons of such various and contradictory opinions. I have listened to them, understood them, admitted them, as far as they were admissible; but I have never allowed doubt to enter my heart.

In Paris, Juliette went early into the social life of which her mother was fond. Once at Versailles, when Louis XVI., Marie Antoinette, and the whole royal family dined in public, as the crowd passed around the table the beauty of the young Juliette attracted the queen, who sent for her to come to their private apartments. Here she met the princess royal, a girl about her own age, eleven or twelve years old.

Juliette grew to womanhood very graceful, timid, yet elegant in manner, very fond of dancing, and gifted in music. She gave up singing and the harp in later life, but always retained her skill on the piano. When blind, years afterwards, she would play from the old masters at twilight, while the tears rolled down her cheeks.

Twice a week, the mother, Madame Bernard, gave fine suppers at her home, where she welcomed all clever people. Among the visitors was M. Récamier, a rich banker, tall and fair, with blue eyes and regular features. He was well versed in Latin, often quoting Horace and Virgil, and also spoke Spanish fluently. He was a good talker, very hopeful, throwing off care easily, agreeable, without very deep feelings, and generous.

He was forty-two and Juliette fifteen when he asked her in marriage. He had been kind to the child and had given her pretty playthings. He was proud of her girlish beauty, and she regarded him as a father. They were married April 24, 1793.

MADAME RÉCAMIER.

The Reign of Terror was at its height. Beautiful Marie Antoinette went to the scaffold that year. M. Récamier saw her die, expecting daily that he and his family would meet the same fate.

For four years Juliette Récamier lived a quiet, uneventful life, till order was somewhat restored in distracted France. She had become very beautiful. Her complexion was surprisingly fair, her teeth white and regular, her mouth small, her dark eyes brilliant though not large, her hair black and curling naturally, and her face arch and frank, lighting up with an irresistible expression of goodness and interest in those she met. Her head was well poised, and her carriage slightly indicative of pride.

Her presence was solicited at subscription balls and other public places. At St. Roch she was asked to pass the contribution box for a charitable object. So intense was the desire to see her that the church was crowded, and people stood on chairs and altars of the side-chapels to catch a glimpse of the beauty of nineteen. The collection amounted to twenty thousand francs. Crowds gathered to see her in the fashionable drives at Longchamps.

In the summers she and her mother lived at the château of Clichy, its park, abounding in flowers, of which Juliette was passionately fond, extending to the Seine. M. Récamier dined with her every day, but slept at Paris, where his tastes and his business called him.

On Dec. 10, 1797, Napoleon Bonaparte, the young Corsican officer, had returned from his triumphs in Italy, and the Directory were giving a *fête* in his honor in the great court of the Luxembourg palace. Five Directors, dressed in Roman costume, sat at the foot of the statue of Liberty, while the place was thronged with ministers, invited guests, and the people, eager in their hero worship.

Talleyrand, Minister of Foreign Affairs, made a speech of congratulation, and Bonaparte responded in a few simple and strong words. Juliette Récamier, dressed, as was her custom, in white, desiring to see the face of the slender young soldier, rose in her seat to look at him. The eyes of the crowd were attracted in a moment, and a murmur of admiration swept through the audience. Napoleon, though not knowing her, gave her a stern look, and she hastily took her seat. She was to know him later on, receive his admiration, and then feel his severity.

The following year, 1798, M. Récamier bought a house in Paris, in the Rue du Mont Blanc, afterwards No. 7 Chaussée d'Antin. It had been the home of M. Necker, the father of Madame de Staël, and through this transaction the life-long friendship of Madame Récamier and Madame de Staël began.

The mansion was immediately repaired and enlarged. The chairs were mahogany and ormolu, in cloth or silk, and trimmed with gold lace. Juliette's bed was considered the most beautiful in Paris, — mahogany enriched with ormolu and bronze, covered with embroidered muslin, bordered with gold lace. Her bath room was inlaid with satin wood and mahogany, with arabesque patterns in black. No expense was spared to make this abode one of rare elegance and luxury.

Napoleon had become First Consul, and in the winter of 1799 Lucien, his brother, then Home Minister, made a *fête* in his honor. For a year Lucien, twenty-four years old, had been deeply in love with Madame Récamier. She showed his ardent letters to her husband, and wished to forbid him her house, but M. Récamier feared to offend the brother of the First Consul, lest his banking business should be injured.

At the *fête* Madame Récamier appeared in white satin, with necklace and bracelets of pearl,—she never wore diamonds even when possessed of her greatest wealth.

At dinner, Napolean passed alone into the dining-room without offering his arm to any lady present. He sat at the middle of the table, his mother, Madame Letitia, on his right, while no one dared to take the vacant place at his left.

After dinner he said to Madame Récamier, "Why did you not take the seat next to me?"

"I should not have presumed," she replied.

"It was your place," he answered. During the music after dinner, Napoleon's constant gaze made her very uncomfortable.

Five years later, when the First Consul had become Emperor, Fouché, Minister of the Police, was sent by Napoleon to ask Madame Récamier to attach herself to his court as lady of honor. "He has not yet," said Fouché, "met a woman worthy of him; and no one knows what the love of Napoleon might be, if he attached himself to a pure person. Assuredly he would allow her to exert an influence that would be entirely beneficent."

Madame Récamier refused the position. She admired the genius of Napoleon, but she could not forgive him for banishing many of her friends, Madame de Staël, the noble Gen. Moreau, and others.

The execution of the Duke d'Enghien seemed to her a blot upon his character. The duke, a prince of the House of Bourbon, suspected by Napoleon of plotting against him, was arrested, tried by court-martial at four o'clock in the morning, March 21, 1814, and, though not proven guilty, was shot at half-past four at Vincennes, and buried in a grave already dug for him before the trial. Fouché said of this act, "It was worse than a crime; it was a blunder."

M. Bernard, the father of Madame Récamier, had been arrested and deprived of the office of postmaster-general, having incurred the displeasure of Napoleon for allowing Royalist documents to be circulated.

Fouché was angered at Madame Récamier's refusal, and it is probable that his imperial master never forgave her. The emperor, when at St. Helena, dictated this statement: —

"Napoleon, upon first taking the reins of the government, was obliged to sign on trust a number of lists; but he very soon established a strict inspection over every department He discovered that a correspondence with the Chouans was going on, under cover of M. Bernard, the father of Madame Récamier. He was immediately removed, and was in danger of being brought to trial and condemned to death. His daughter hastened to the First Consul, and through her solicitations her father was not tried; but Napoleon was resolute with regard to his dismissal. Madame Récamier, accustomed to obtain everything, aimed at nothing less than the restoration of her father to office. Such was the state of morality of the times, that this severity on the part of the First Consul caused great outcries. People were not used to it. Madame Récamier and her party, which was numerous, never forgave him."

In 1802, Madame Récamier. accompanied by her mother, visited England, the Duke de Guignes, ambassador to London under Louis XVI., giving her enthusiastic letters of introduction. Everywhere she received the greatest attention. The Duchess of Devonshire became her intimate friend. The Prince of Wales showed her every courtesy. The journals vied with each other in descriptions of her. Great crowds gathered on the streets and in Kensington Gardens to catch a glimpse of her. Pictures of her were spread throughout England, and were carried to the isles of Greece.

The celebrated painter, David, had made a portrait of her, with which he was not wholly satisfied, and Gérard had painted his full-length portrait of her. David's picture was sold to the museum of the Louvre for six thousand francs.

Madame Récamier already had formed some devoted friendships which lasted through life. Matthieu Jean Félicité, the Duke de Montmorency, met her when he was thirty-eight and she twenty-three. He had served in the war of the American Revolution under his father, had married early in life Mlle. de Luynes, by whom he had one daughter, and though one of the old aristocracy of France, had embraced liberal ideas, and in the National Assembly had moved to abolish the privileges of the nobility. The execution of his brother, the Abbé de Laval, whom he loved tenderly, led the impetuous and worldly young man to become a devoted Christian.

The duke knew when he first met Madame Récamier that her life was not a happy one. Married to a man nearly three times her own age, without similarity of tastes, without children in the home, her heart was desolate. He admired her tenderness, her purity, and her constant thought for others. He saw her desire to please and her longing for love rather than for admiration, and he feared the results for her. Till his death, through all the cares of state that weighed upon him, he never ceased to watch over her, and write to her in his absence.

"Do all those things that are good and kind, and that will cause no heart-breaks or leave regrets behind," he wrote her. "I am not without fear of the daily effects of a frivolous society which can do you no good, and to which you yourself are superior. . . . I hope you have not forgotten your promise to devote, daily, half an hour to consecutive and serious reading. These two conditions are indispensable; and also a few moments to prayer and meditation. Is this too much to ask for the greatest, one might say the only, interest of life?"

George, Grand Duke of Mecklenburg-Strelitz, brother of the Queen of Prussia, became her sincere friend. He wrote her nearly forty years after the beginning of their friendship, "It [the heart] tells me that the ravishing beauty with which nature had endowed you is only the reflection of an adorable soul, and that such a soul could never forget any one whom it once judged worthy of its esteem and affection. . . . We all look upon you as the embodiment of perfect beauty and perfect goodness."

General Bernadotte, afterwards king of Sweden, was her devoted friend. He wrote her while she was in England, "In the midst of all the attention and homage which you receive, and which you so justly merit, pray do not forget that the being the most devoted to you in the world is Bernadotte."

Madame Récamier did not find her pleasure in society alone. She was foremost in all charities, founding schools for girls, visiting the poor and the afflicted, and giving sympathy and appreciation as fully as she gave money and time.

One Saturday, in the autumn of 1806, M. Récamier

came to his wife much disturbed. His banking-house was embarrassed. If the Bank of France would advance a million, he might not fail.

Invitations were already issued for a great dinner which they were to give. M. Récamier hastened to the country because he could not meet the guests. The wife of twenty-nine years must do it, and do it with all her accustomed grace and cheerfulness. The dinner was given, and Madame Récamier met all with a smiling face, while her heart was aching.

The loan of the million was harshly refused by the government, the resentment of the emperor, doubtless, having something to do with the refusal. The great banking-house of M. Récamier failed, and many smaller houses in consequence. M. Récamier gave up everything to his creditors, his wife sold her jewels to help pay the debts, and their house and valuable plate were disposed of.

Those only who have passed through such an ordeal know the anguish of it. To lose for ourselves is little compared with the fact that others lose through us. To owe and not be able to meet obligations, however honestly incurred, has led to many a heart-break and suicide.

The sympathy for Madame Récamier was universal. Madame de Staël wrote her from Geneva, "How I curse the exile which will not permit me to come to you and press you to my heart! You have lost all that pertains to the ease and luxury of life; but, if such a thing could be possible, you are more beloved and more interesting than ever. . . . If it were possible for me to envy any one whom I love, I would willingly give all I have to be you. Beauty that has no equal in Europe, a spotless reputation, a proud and generous character, — what a wealth of happiness still left in this sad life, in which we are robbed of so many treasures. . . . There is still happiness left, when one is conscious of being so well beloved. . . . Neither death nor the indifference of friends menaces you, and these are eternal wounds. Adieu! dear angel, adieu!"

Gen. Bernadotte wrote her on the eve of battle, "I have not ceased to give you my prayers and best wishes; but, though destined to love you ever, I dared not run the risk of tiring you with my letters. Adieu! if you still think of me, believe that you are my chief thought, and that nothing equals the sweet and tender friendship I cherish for you."

When Napoleon was told by Junot, Duke d'Abrantes, of the sorrow felt for Madame Récamier, he answered impatiently, "They could not have paid more honor to a widow of a Marshal of France, who had lost her husband on the field of battle."

Troubles did not come singly to Madame Récamier. Her mother, from whom she had not been separated since her childhood, had been ill for some time. The financial ruin of M. Récamier, and consequent sorrow for her daughter, caused her death Jan. 20, 1807.

For six months Madame Récamier sought respite from her grief in seclusion, but her health becoming affected, she consented to visit Madame de Staël at Coppet, in the middle of the summer.

No one has ever stood in that gray château with its green blinds, in the room hung with Gobelin tapestry, where Madame Récamier used to sit with Madame de Staël and look out upon placid Lake Geneva, so restful to two troubled lives, without feeling the deepest interest in these two remarkable women.

At the time of Madame Récamier's visit, Prince Augustus of Prussia, the nephew of Frederick the Great, was staying at Geneva. He was but twenty-four, handsome, of fine figure, brave in war, and cultivated and refined in peace. He had been taken prisoner at the battle of Saalfeld, where his eldest brother, Louis, was killed.

Prince Augustus met Madame Récamier at Coppet, and gave her the supreme affection of his heart. He knew her unhappy life, and urged her to free herself from her marriage vows and become his wife. She was touched by his devotion, and encouraged by Madame de Staël, wrote to M. Récamier requesting a dissolution of the union which had been such only in name.

M. Récamier replied kindly that he would consent if she wished it, but he recalled his affection given her from her childhood, his present misfortunes, and his oncoming age. If she persisted in her request, he would go with her outside of Paris, where they would not be subject to remark, and help her obtain a separation.

After such a letter, her heart relented, and the divorce was never more thought of. For years Prince Augustus cherished the hope that her resolution might be shaken. He continued to write her until he saw her again eight years later, in 1815, when the allied armies entered Paris. He was in command of the Prussian artillery, and before he reached the city he besieged successively several fortresses, writing her from each one.

He met her again in Paris, in 1818, when he commissioned Gérard to paint for her the picture of Corinne, "as an immortal souvenir of the passion with which she had inspired him, and of the glorious friendship which united Corinne and Juliette." In exchange for this picture, Madame Récamier sent him her portrait by Gérard.

The prince had it hung in the gallery of his palace at

Berlin till his death, when, in accordance with his last wishes, it was returned to her in 1845. Three months before his death he wrote her, "The ring that you gave me I will carry to the tomb." It was buried with him. However unfortunate this hopeless affection of the prince, it was but one of many illustrations of the fact that no person ever loved Madame Récamier without continuing this love through life.

In the summer of 1811, Madame Récamier determined to visit again her exiled friend at Coppet. Madame de Staël — ten thousand copies of her "Germany" had just been destroyed through the decree of government — begged Madame Récamier not to come to her, fearing that she too would be exiled. Other friends tried to dissuade her, but she decided to take the risk.

The result was what had been expected. Madame de Staël says in her "Ten Years of Exile," "It was with convulsions of tears that I saw her enter the house, where heretofore her arrival had always been welcomed with joy. She left the next day, and repaired to the residence of a relative, fifty leagues from Switzerland. But it was all in vain: the fatal stroke of exile smote her also. . . . Separated from all her friends, she passed whole months in a provincial town, a victim to the saddest and most monotonous solitude. Such was the fate which I had brought upon the most brilliant woman of her day."

Madame Récamier lived in exile, forty leagues from Paris, at Châlons-sur-Marne, with the little niece of M. Récamier, whom she had adopted a few weeks previously. Very few friends dared to visit her. To relieve the monotony, she made the acquaintance of the organist of the parish, and went every Sunday to play the organ at high mass. She resolved never to ask to be returned to France, and requested her friends who were near the emperor never to mention her name in his presence.

After ten months of this lonely life, she was induced, by Madame de Staël, to go to Lyons in June, 1812, and reside at the Hôtel de l'Europe. Here she met the elegant Duchess de Chevreuse, who was dying in consequence of exile. She was the daughter-in-law of the Duchess de Luynes, whose daughter had married Matthieu de Montmorency.

At the home of Madame de Sermésy, the niece of M. Simonard, the old friend of Madame Récamier's father, the lonely exile formed some lasting friendships. Camille Jordan, the distinguished orator, had known her from childhood. She had written to him, when M. Récamier failed: "However unexpected my misfortunes, I have been able to bear them with resignation, and I have had the satisfaction of consoling and alleviating the sufferings of my husband and family; and should I not, also, dear Camille, return thanks to Heaven, who, in reserving for me such bitter trials, has given me friends to aid me in bearing them?"

It was a delight to meet this friend again. He introduced her to the eminent Christian philosopher, M. Ballanche, a member of the French Academy and of the Academy of Lyons. Ballanche had loved a young lady of noble birth, but without fortune, had aided her father, and had expected to win the daughter, but had been disappointed in his hopes.

When introduced to Madame Récamier, M. Ballanche talked to her upon philosophy, and literary and political subjects. Though not a great talker, she had so improved her mind by wide reading, that in her communion with men of intellect she could listen, as Sainte-Beuve said, "*avec séduction.*"

From the hour that M. Ballanche met her, he became her devoted friend for life. She was essential to his writing, to his comfort, to his very existence. When it became necessary for her to go to Italy for her health, he selected the books for her to take in her carriage, among them Chateaubriand's "Genius of Christianity."

He wrote her after her departure: "You are the personification of indulgence and pity; you have seen in me an exile from happiness, and have had compassion on me. . . . Allow me to entertain for you the feelings of a brother for a sister. I long for the time when I shall be able to offer you, along with these fraternal sentiments, all the humble homage in my power. My devotion will be entire, and without reserve. I would sacrifice my own happiness to yours. There is justice in this, for you are of more value than I."

Later he wrote: "My one absorbing thought is my warm feeling of friendship for you. I have need to be assured by you, and that as often as possible, that this sentiment shall not end in unhappiness for me. I confess, that every time I think of it I feel a kind of terror that I cannot master. The idea often occurs to me that you think you are attached to me, but that it is not really so; this thought is an agony."

After visiting Parma, Modena, Bologna, and Florence, she arrived at Rome in Holy Week, 1813, and soon took lodgings on the first floor of the Fiano Palace on the Còrso.

One of her first visits was to the studio of Canova. He was delighted to see the "most beautiful woman in Europe," and she in turn to meet genius, which she always worshipped. He returned her visit that evening, and from that time, while she remained in Italy, he never failed to pass the evening with her. He came early, and went away a little before ten o'clock. Every morning he sent her a pleasant note. Her appreciation became a necessity, and her friendship an inspiration.

When summer came, Canova invited Madame Récamier to his home at Albano, in the Hotel Emiliano. He reserved for himself and his brother, the abbé, the rooms facing the square, and gave to Madame Récamier and her niece those commanding a view of the Campagna. J. B. Bassi, a Roman artist, painted a picture of this residence with Madame Récamier seated near the window reading. Canova sent her the picture in 1816. At Albano, as at Châlons, she played the organ every Sunday at high mass and vespers.

In December, 1813, she visited Naples, and received great courtesy from King Joachim Murat and Queen Caroline, the sister of Napoleon. Murat had been a faithful ally of Napoleon, but the Neapolitans declared in favor of separation from France. He signed the treaty which bound him to the Allies Jan. 11, 1814.

While absent with his troops, Caroline was regent. When about to sign a death warrant, Madame Récamier, who was present, begged for the life of the accused. She said to the queen, "Since heaven has brought me here at this time, it is a sign that Providence would save this unhappy man." Her request was granted, and the man was pardoned.

On the return of Madame Récamier to Rome, Canova showed her two clay busts which he had made of her, exclaiming, "*Mira, se he pensato a lei*" (See, I have thought of you).

The busts did not satisfy her, though she tried to conceal her feelings. The artist saw it, and added a crown of olives to the bust with a veil, making the well-known figure of the Beatrice of Dante. A copy of this, in marble, was sent to Madame Récamier by Canova's brother, after the death of the sculptor.

Meanwhile Napoleon had fallen and been sent to the island of Elba. Madame Récamier returned to Paris, June 1, 1814, after an exile of nearly three years.

The House of Bourbon came back to power in the person of Louis XVIII. The Restoration brought back to Paris Madame Moreau, the wife of the illustrious general, Madame de Staël, Matthieu de Montmorency, and other noted friends of Madame Récamier. M. Récamier had somewhat regained his fortune, and his wife had come into possession of her mother's property, valued at four hundred thousand francs. Life seemed again joyous and prosperous. Friends as ever gathered to pay her homage.

The Duke of Wellington came often to her salon. Though a Royalist, Madame Récamier received at her home distinguished friends, irrespective of party.

The religious Baroness Krüdener, who exerted such an influence over the mind of the Emperor Alexander, asked for Madame Récamier's presence at her meetings, but deputed the brilliant Benjamin Constant to write her: "Madame Krüdener begs that you will make your appearance with as few charms as possible. She says that you dazzle everybody, and consequently, as all hearts are disturbed, attention is impossible. You cannot divest yourself of your beauty; but, prithee, do not enhance it."

In the summer of 1817 a great sorrow came to Madame Récamier in the death of Madame de Staël. She, too, had lived in a loveless marriage till she wedded the young army officer, Rocca, in 1811, when she was forty-five and he twenty-three. For six years they idolized each other He died seven months after her death. "I hoped," he said, "to have died in her arms."

The loss to Madame Récamier was irreparable. Madame de Staël had loved her with no common affection. She wrote her: "If I could live near you, I should be only too happy. . . . Your friendship is like the spring in the desert, that never fails; and this it is which makes it impossible not to love you. . . . You are, and you will ever remain, an angel of purity and goodness, worshipped by the devout as well as by worldlings."

When absent they corresponded regularly, though Madame de Staël truly said, "There is no such thing as absence for Christians, because they meet each other in the sentiment of prayer."

By the bedside of Madame de Staël, Madame Récamier made the acquaintance of the man to whom she was thereafter to give the first place in her heart, M. de Chateaubriand. He was a man of brilliant talents, a statesman, a person of distinguished bearing, and the foremost French author of the age.

Born at Saint Malo, a quaint old seaport in Brittany, Sept. 4, 1768, René François Auguste, Viscount de Chateaubriand, was nine years the senior of Madame Récamier. His family was one of the most ancient in Brittany. His father destined him for the naval profession, and later he thought of entering the church, but, diverted from this by sceptical books, he became infidel in sentiment and weary of existence. He was tempted to commit suicide, but was saved from this by his brother, the Count de Combourg, who obtained for him a lieutenancy in the regiment of Navarre.

When he was eighteen, after the death of his father,

he returned with his family to Paris. Alarmed at the excesses of the French Revolution, he embarked in January, 1791, for the United States, hoping to find by the support and help of Malesherbes, the eminent statesman, a northwest passage to the Polar Sea.

With a letter of introduction to Gen. Washington, the President, he called upon him, was received with great kindness, and was invited to dine with him. He never saw Washington afterwards, but the visit made a lasting impression upon him. He said, years later, "There is virtue in the look of a great man. I felt myself warmed and refreshed by it during the rest of my life."

After visiting New York, Boston, and other cities, he dressed himself in the garb of an Indian hunter, and travelled through the wilderness, spending weeks in some Indian village, and sometimes sleeping under a great tree beside a camp-fire, "locked," he said, "in the arms of a limitless moonlit silence, broken only by the cries of wild animals, or the stir of the wind-swept leaves, or the distant roar of eternal Niagara."

Finding in an English newspaper, in a Canadian cabin, an account of the arrest of Louis XVI. he hastened back to France to find his family imprisoned and his estates confiscated.

At the request of his sister, he married Mlle. de Lavigne, a lady of considerable fortune. Going to Germany to join some French nobles in defence of his country, he was wounded, and finally made his way to London, where he lived for several years in poverty and exile, spending his days in translating books to gain a livelihood, and his evenings in composing his "Essay on Revolutions."

This was published in 1797, and created a sensation. While it advocated the principles of virtue and natural religion, the author doubted whether the Christian religion was not crumbling away with the institutions of society.

Meantime sorrow was touching his heart. His brother and sister-in-law, with his friend Malesherbes, had perished on the scaffold. His wife and sister had been imprisoned at Rennes, and his aged mother at Paris. She was a woman of marked ability, from whom Chateaubriand inherited his wonderful memory and remarkable imagination. She died in 1798, with a prayer on her lips for the conversion of her son.

"She charged one of my sisters," he said, "to recall me to a sense of that religion in which I had been educated, and my sister made known to me her wish. When the letter reached me beyond the water, my sister also had departed this life, having succumbed to the effects of her imprisonment. Those two voices coming up from the grave, and that death which had now become the interpreter of death, struck me with peculiar force. I became a Christian. I did not yield to any great supernatural light: my conviction came from the heart. I wept, and I believed."

From that time Chateaubriand resolved to consecrate his pen to the service of religion. He wrote and published, five years later, in 1802, his greatest book, "The Genius of Christianity," a work showing profound research and great beauty of diction. It was eagerly read, admired, and also denounced. It was given to a people at a time of their greatest need. Infidelity had swept over the nation. The Sabbath was abolished, the churches were closed, and Reason was enthroned in place of God. Chateaubriand, with all the resources of his genius, attempted to unfold, as he himself said, "all the marvels which religion has wrought in the regions of poetry, morality, politics, history, and public charity."

Napoleon said, "The style of Chateaubriand is not that of Racine; it is that of a prophet; he has received from nature the sacred flame; it breathes in all his works."

When Napoleon had become First Consul, Chateaubriand returned to France under an assumed name and became one of the editors of the *Mercure*. He had already published his great romance, "Atala," the story of an Indian girl, who is pledged by her mother to virginity from her cradle, and when she is older takes the vow never to marry. She falls passionately in love with René, an Indian warrior, who has been made a captive by her tribe. She plans his escape, and succeeds in accomplishing it. Finding her love for him overcoming her, she kills herself rather than break her vow. The disciples of Voltaire wrote pamphlets against the book, but it had an extended reading, and brought its author into prominence.

Napoleon, with the hope of attracting the Bourbon sympathizers to his side, appointed Chateaubriand first secretary to Cardinal Fesch, then ambassador to Rome. Chateaubriand tired of this position, and Napoleon made him minister plenipotentiary to the Valois, the day before the Duke d'Enghien was shot. Chateaubriand, not fearing the new Dictator, as did most others, at once resigned, and refused to accept any position under the consular *régime*.

He visited Madame de Staël at Coppet, and then made a journey to the Holy Land, stopping at Athens, Smyrna, Cyprus, and also Egypt and Spain, writing "Le dernier des Abencerrages" among the ruins of the Alhambra.

He returned to France in May, 1807, and greatly angered Napoleon by an article in the *Mercure*. He was arrested, deprived of his interest in the paper, and Napoleon spoke of having him executed on the steps of the Tuileries. He returned to his possessions near Aulnay, where he wrote three books.

His favorite sister, Lucille, had died in 1804. He said, "There is not a day that I do not weep for her. Lucille loved concealment. I have made a solitude for her in my heart, which she will quit only when I cease to be."

When his "Journey from Paris to Jerusalem," in three volumes, was ready for publication he was informed that it could not be published unless it contained some pages of eulogy of Napoleon. He refused to submit, but learning that his publisher would suffer through the suppression of the work, he inserted some truthful words about the victories of the French soldiers and their able general.

Napoleon still hoped to win his favor, and Chateaubriand was offered the place in the French Academy made vacant by the death of Chénier, and the general supervision of the imperial libraries, with a salary equal to a first-class embassy. It was the custom of the member-elect to pronounce a eulogy over his predecessor. As Chénier had participated in the downfall of Louis XVI., Chateaubriand denounced the crimes of the French Revolution and the despotism of the existing government. The emperor was exasperated, and exclaimed, "Am I, then, nothing more than a usurper?" Chateaubriand, of course, was not admitted to the Academy.

When the Allies entered France, Chateaubriand declared in favor of the ancient dynasty, and published "Bonaparte and the Bourbons," which Louis XVIII. said was worth to him an army of one hundred thousand men.

Under Louis XVIII. Chateaubriand was appointed ambassador to Sweden, but before his departure Napoleon returned from Elba. Later he was made minister of the interior under Louis XVIII., and called to the House of Peers, where he made some memorable speeches. He defended constitutional government in a work published in 1816, " La Monarchie selon la Charte," and established a periodical, the " Conservateur."

While Chateaubriand was leading this brilliant and influential career, he was subject to periods of deep depression. His life was not a happy one. It was not strange, therefore, that in Madame Récamier's calm yet sympathetic nature he should find the rest as well as appreciation which his heart craved.

Some of her best friends were anxious lest this new friendship should bring her unrest, by reason of the tumultuous life led by Chateaubriand. M. Ballanche hoped to divert her attention by urging her to translate one of her favorite poets, Petrarch, a work which she began but did not finish.

" Poetry and music," he wrote her, " will throw a charm over the leisure that you will be able to make for yourself. You will become famous in a new way. You will reveal that side of yourself of which the world as yet does not dream. . . . You have under your command the genius of music, flowers, imagination, and elegance. Lift your charming head, and do not fear to try your hand on the golden lyre of the poets. My mission in this world may consist in so working that some trace of your noble existence may remain on earth."

Duke de Montmorency wrote her urging her not to rivet " with her own hands an unhappy fetter, from which others will suffer as well as yourself."

Madame Récamier had purchased in the Rue d'Anjou a home for her father, his old friend M. Simonard, her husband, her niece and herself, where she hoped to pass the remainder of her life in peace and comfort. Her sweetness of nature was soon to be put to another test. M. Récamier again failed in business, this time losing one hundred thousand francs of his wife's money.

At this juncture she felt that she must lead a separate and personal life, and, with the advice of friends, sought an asylum in the Abbaye-aux-Bois. With the rest of her fortune she supported her husband while he lived, insisting that he should abandon his disastrous speculations. She provided for his wants and those of her father and M. Simonard with filial affection, obtaining a home for the three aged men near the Abbaye.

She lived on the third floor of the Abbaye in a small suite, paved with tiles. Her bed-room was furnished with a book-case, a harp, a piano, a portrait of Madame de Staël and a view of Coppet by moonlight. Several pots of flowers were on the window-sill. At dinner all her family came to the Abbaye to dine with her, including M. Ballanche and M. Paul David, the nephew of M. Récamier.

At the end of six months, Madame Récamier removed to a suite of rooms on the first floor of the Abbaye, which the nuns ceded to her for life.

The Abbaye soon became a centre of meeting for the most distinguished men and women of France. Her financial reverses made no difference in the hearts of those who loved her. Here came, every evening, Duke de Montmorency. Here came also Sir Humphry and Lady Davy, Maria Edgeworth, Alexander von Humboldt, Eugene Delacroix, Augustin Thierry, the brilliant linguist, Prosper Merimée, whose " Letters to an Unknown " have been one of the fascinating puzzles of literature, J. J. Ampère, the Duchess of Devonshire, the Duke of Hamilton, the

Queen of Sweden, Gérard, and many others. Here Lamartine read his "Méditations," and Delphine Gay recited her first poems. Miss Berry, the beloved of Horace Walpole, came often to the Abbaye.

Chateaubriand had been appointed minister to Berlin, from which place he wrote Madame Récamier that he had been "overwhelmed with kindness and respect" by the royal family. The Duchess of Cumberland became his intimate friend. In his "Mémoires d'Outre Tombe" he says, "I visited her frequently. She often said to me that she would like to confide to me her son, the little George, the prince whom, it was said, his cousin Victoria desired to place by her side on the throne of England." To Madame Récamier he wrote, "I shall be absent only a few months. Be tranquil, then. I will pass my life near you to love you."

In 1822 Chateaubriand was sent as ambassador to London. He wrote sadly to Madame Récamier, "I cannot go anywhere here without seeing something that recalls to me my youth and my sufferings, the friends that I have lost, the people that have passed away, the hopes that I have cherished, my first works, my dreams of glory, — everything in fact involved in the future of a young man who feels himself born for some purpose. I have grasped some few of my chimeras, others have escaped me, and none of them have been worth what they cost. One thing is left to me; and while I retain that, I shall be consoled for my gray hairs and all my failures on the long road I have been travelling for thirty years." Chateaubriand was now fifty-four and Madame Récamier forty-five.

In the midst of political life, letters from her were needful for his happiness. "With what joy I recognized that fine hand!" he wrote her. "Every courier that arrived without one word from you broke my heart. . . . Can you believe that I am dazzled, absorbed even, in the part that I am forced to play in spite of myself? If you do, you little know me. I should be sorry, for my part, not to succeed here. I like to do, as well as I am able, all that I undertake. . . . To be loved by you, to live in a little retreat with you, and a few books, is the desire of my heart and the goal of all my wishes."

In the autumn of 1822, Chateaubriand and the Duke de Montmorency, Minister of Foreign Affairs, were sent to the Congress of Verona. Chateaubriand was charmed with the Emperor Alexander. He wrote to Madame Récamier, "He is a prince full of noble, generous qualities. . . . Prince Metternich is a perfect gentleman, agreeable and capable. In the midst of it all I am sad, and I know why. I perceive that places are no longer anything to me. This beautiful Italy has nothing more to say to me. I look at these great mountains that separate me from that which I love, and I think with Caraccioli, that a little chamber on the third floor in Paris is better than a palace in Naples."

Chateaubriand distinguished himself at Verona for his eloquence in the cause of Greece, and in the defence of his country in relation to the Spanish war, and on his return he was made Minister of Foreign Affairs in place of Duke de Montmorency. This naturally produced coldness between the two men, and it required all of Madame Récamier's tact and kind heart to bring about good feeling between them.

She was constantly using her high position to aid somebody. Chateaubriand often interposed for her sake for an impulsive and brilliant friend like Benjamin Constant, saying, "Talent ought to have privileges. It is the oldest aristocracy that I know of."

Chateaubriand was at the height of his power. With all his greatness he was often irritable, cold where he did not care to please, and sometimes thoughtless. "His devotion," says Madame Lenormant, in the life of her aunt, Madame Récamier, "was the same, nor had his friendship grown cold; but Madame Récamier felt that he no longer treated her with that respectful reserve characteristic of those permanent sentiments which she wished only to inspire."

The niece had become ill, and her physicians advised a southern climate. Perhaps Madame Récamier, with her woman's intuition, felt that absence would produce a good effect upon Chateaubriand. They started for Italy Nov. 2, 1823, accompanied by the faithful M. Ballanche.

Letters from Chateaubriand followed her: "When one has courage like you to break up everything, what signifies the future? However, I shall await you. If I am alive, you will find me such as you have left me, — full of you, not having ceased to love you. . . . Salute the mountains for me, and the smiling valleys that I certainly shall never see again."

Madame Récamier met with a most cordial reception in Rome. Her old friend, the Duke de Laval, Ambassador to Rome, put his house, servants, and horses at her disposal. She spent much time in the studios of noted artists. The beautiful Duchess of Devonshire, formerly Lady Elizabeth Foster, wife of the fifth duke, celebrated in England for her beauty, her talents, and the romance of her life, became her intimate friend.

The Duke de Laval said to Madame Récamier: "The duchess has some of your qualities, to which she owes the success of her whole life. She is the mildest of all the women who rule through sweetness, and she commands invariable obedience. What she did in London in her youth, she is doing here. All Rome is at her disposal: ministers, cardinals, painters, sculptors, society, — all are at her feet."

Gibbon said the duchess was " so alluring that no man could withstand her, and if she chose to beckon the Lord Chancellor from the woolsack, in full sight of the world, he could not resist obedience."

She was large and dark, with very brilliant eyes. She was the patron of art and letters. She published, at her own expense, the fifth Satire of Horace, with a versified Italian translation, and also a translation of the "Æneid," by Annibal Caro. These volumes were illustrated by the most renowned artists then living in Italy. At her death, in 1824, she bequeathed Madame Récamier one of the elegant rings which she wore.

Queen Hortense, the mother of Napoleon III., came often to see Madame Récamier while the latter was in Rome. They met usually at the Colosseum, and there had long talks together, it being deemed imprudent that a Bourbon sympathizer should be seen with a Bonapartist. When, however, the queen's brother, Eugène Beauharnais, died, Madame Récamier braved public opinion, and went at once to see her friend. These pleasant relations continued till the death of Queen Hortense at the Château of Arenberg. The Queen was carried back to France and laid beside her mother, Josephine, at Rueil.

Before her death, Hortense wrote to Madame Récamier : " You are among those persons to whom it is not needful to relate one's life or one's feelings ; the heart is the best interpreter, and they who thus read us become necessary to us. . . . Do not entirely forget me ; believe me, your friendship has done me good. You know what a comfort a friendly voice from one's native country is, when it comes to us in misfortune and isolation. Be kind enough to tell me that I am unjust, if I complain too much of my destiny, and that I have still some frends left."

While in Italy Madame Récamier visited Caroline Murat, the sister of Napoleon. Her husband, losing his throne of Naples in the downfall of Napoleon, had attempted to regain it and was arrested and shot. His wife begged to live at Rome, but as it was probably considered too near Naples, she was allowed to live at Trieste.

She welcomed her "dear Juliette" with great joy. "My position is very sad," she said. "I have also the grief of being separated from my two sons. The persecutions to which we have been subjected have forced them to go to America. Achilles has been there two years; my second son left me a fortnight ago. This separation broke my heart."

Madame Récamier spent eighteen months in Italy. Ballanche was studying Roman history, and another friend who lived with them, J. J. Ampère, was indulging his love for travel and study. Ballanche was as ever dependent upon her society. He said, "When you are laid in your tomb of white marble, it will be necessary to dig quickly a ditch for me, in which I shall hasten to lie down in my turn. What should I do upon earth? But I do not think that you will be the first to pass away; in any case, it seems to me impossible that I could survive you."

Ampère was the son of the noted mathematician, André Marie Ampère, young, brilliant, attractive, the life of every gathering. His mother had died when he was three years old, and he was the only joy and hope of his learned father, whom he idolized. The youth, with his delicate organization, love of nature, and poetic temperament, was a charming companion.

At twenty his father brought him to the Abbaye to meet the distinguished company. Madame Récamier was then forty-three. His conversation and his noble qualities delighted her. For thirty years, till her death, he was like a son or brother.

M. Sainte-Beuve, the noted French critic, thus speaks of these first relations of his renowned friend at the Abbaye-aux-Bois: "During this happy, rapturous time, his imagination yielded itself captive to all the charms of a refined and choice companionship, made still more attractive by a setting sun of divine beauty. . . . She talked to him with her usual grace of their charming days, their drives and walks in the valley, of the cheerful intercourse to which the young man's animated conversation had lent an additional charm. Then, touching with her exquisite tact the tender chord, she casually intimated that there had perhaps been opportunities for warmer feelings, that had they staid there much longer she would have been afraid, at least, lest a heart inclined to poetry might have begun to weave a romance, for her young niece was then with her.

"At these words Ampère could not restrain himself, but suddenly bursting out, agitated and sobbing, 'Ah! it is not for her,' he cried, and fell upon his knees. His declaration was made, his confession had escaped him; he had, without intending it, uttered the sacred word, and he would not take it back. . . . From that moment his destiny was sealed. Madame Récamier had only to go on fascinating him, calming him by degrees, but never curing him."

Ampère wrote her ten years after their first meeting:

"I am not, you know, a great lover of forms, but the first day of the year is an epoch for me, the return of which I cannot see unmoved. It was on New Year's day that I saw you for the first time. That moment, when you dawned upon me, dressed in white, with a grace of which, till then, I had no conception, will never be forgotten.

"It was just ten years ago. Between that time and this lies all my youth; and, at every joyous or painful epoch during that interval, you reappear to me with all the charm of that first day, and with even greater, for daily intercourse with you has revealed to me other reasons for loving and admiring you. . . . Will you not send me for my New Year's gift a few of those lines that you alone know how to write? It will take you only a moment, and I, I live long on such moments."

Madame Récamier repaid these ardent affections by a warm heart. She wrote Ampère: "I pass my life in forming projects; it is the malady of those who are not content with their fate. You are included in all my plans; it cannot be otherwise."

Madame Lenormant says of her aunt: "If Madame Récamier was kind to everybody, in her affections she was exclusive; she confined them to a narrow circle. She was fond of saying that there was a certain taste in perfect friendship to which commonplace characters could not attain."

Ampère's father was desirous that he should marry Baron Cuvier's only child, the lovely Clementine, whose early death broke her father's heart. The hesitation of young Ampère was a serious disappointment to his father. She was engaged at the time of her death, by her own choice, to M. Dupargnet.

Ampère gained fame as an author and a lecturer. After a course on literature at the Marseilles Athenæum, M. Lenormant wrote him: "Paris will now be wanting you; your friends will no longer be obliged to answer for you; there is nothing like type for making a man. Print all you can, — the whole course, or, at least, the greater part."

He won a membership in the Academy of Inscriptions by his works on the sources of French literature, and the formation of the language. He was for a long time professor in the College of France. He was an officer of the Legion of Honor, and a member of the French Academy. His "History of Rome," in four volumes, shows great learning, especially on archæological matters.

His soul was full of poetry. He wrote Madame Récamier: "I go and ensconce myself in a dark seat in the beautiful, dimly-lighted church; there I sit; I listen to the chants; with my head bowed in sincere humility I receive the benediction; then I go out and listen by the seashore to another harmony and another prayer, — the concert of the winds, the waves, the stars, the night." He died March 27, 1864, outliving Madame Récamier fifteen years.

Madame Récamier returned to Paris from Rome the last of May, 1825. Charles X., the brother of Louis XVIII., had come to the throne, and both the Duke de Montmorency and Chateaubriand had gone to Rheims to attend the ceremony of coronation. On their return, Chateaubriand hastened to the Abbaye to greet again, with respectful tenderness, her whose life was so closely united to his own.

The following year, Feb. 1, 1826, the niece of Madame Récamier was married to an accomplished scholar, — M.

Lenormant, Inspector of Fine Arts under the Viscount de la Rochefoucauld. This gave Madame Récamier great happiness, as it was a union of affection. "She realized for the child of her adoption," says Madame Lenormant, "that supreme felicity of love in marriage which had been the dream and the regret of her life."

Many times, in after years, she wrote her niece: "I trust that you will be happier than I have been. . . . Your image mingles with all my reveries; it is through you that I have a future. . . . Your griefs are passing ones, and your lot seems so sweet to me that I would willingly give the brightest days of my life for your saddest ones."

This year, 1826, the Duke de Montmorency died in prayer at his parish church, St. Thomas Aquinas, on Good Friday. His wife engaged a room at the Abbaye that she might come there frequently for prayer and seclusion, and to talk with Madame Récamier about her lamented dead.

Chateaubriand was appointed Ambassador to Rome under Charles X., and left for that city September, 1828. He wrote to Madame Récamier: "All my happiness is in talking with you, and in thinking that sometimes our thoughts meet in spite of the space that separates us. . . . Remember that we must end our days together. It is but a sad gift that I present to you, — the remnant of my life: but take it; and, if I have lost some time, what is left is of greater worth, since it will be devoted wholly to you. . . . When shall I rest myself near you? When shall I no longer waste on the highways those days lent me to put to a better use? I recklessly squandered them while I was rich; I thought the treasure inexhaustible. Now, when I see how much it has diminished, how little time there is left to love you, my anguish is great.

"But are there not long years beyond the tomb? If I had the philosophy of Cousin, I would describe to you that heaven, where I shall expect you, where you will find me again, full of grace, beauty, and youth. Poor and humble Christian, I tremble before the 'Last Judgment' of Michael Angelo. I know not where my future abode will be; but if it is where you are not, I shall be very unhappy. . . .

"Never forget me when I am no more. I shall have to leave you some day. I will go to await you. Perhaps I shall have more patience in the other life than in this, where I find three months without you of immeasurable length. . . . I have all that could be desired in the way of success, in kind attentions, and cordial welcome; but I am more than ever convinced that my political and social life is at an end. It is your society, united with the most profound retirement, that I need now. I am only occupied with one thing, — my health; because I have a great desire to live some time longer for your sake. . . . Live long, long years, so that there shall be somebody in the world who thinks of me."

In his excavations in Torre Vergata, near the tomb of Nero, he wrote her: "I only breathed one wish, and that was for you. I would very willingly consent to live with you, under a tent, in the midst of these ruins. . . . The noise of my steps at Torre Vergata will awaken no one; and, when in my turn I am in my grave, I shall not even hear the sound of your voice."

Evidently Chateaubriand was no longer the proud, self-willed man of former years. "The truth is," he wrote her, "that you have metamorphosed my nature, and that I no longer recognize myself."·

Upon the accession of Prince Polignac to the office of

foreign affairs, Chateaubriand resigned, and returned to Paris. From the Tiber he came back to the Rhone; "to the Rhone," he wrote Madame Récamier, "whose waves you brightened with your gaze as a child."

In the year 1830, France was again distracted by the "Revolution of the three days." On the 26th of July the king issued an edict putting an end to the liberty of the press. The people rose in rebellion, and he was obliged to leave France with his little grandson, Henry V., afterwards the Count de Chambord, the child of the murdered Duke de Berri. Before Louis XVIII. died, he put his hand on the head of his four-year-old great-nephew, and said to his brother: "Let Charles X. take care of the crown for this child." But Charles could not believe in the liberty of the people, and fell by his own acts.

Chateaubriand made an eloquent speech in the House of Peers against the exile of the elder branch of the Bourbons, and advocated the reign of the little Henry, and the appointment of a regent, but the people favored the Duke of Orleans, descended from the brother of Louis XIV. Louis Philippe I. became the head of a limited monarchy. Chateaubriand relinquished his dignity as a peer, with his honors and pensions, and retired poor to private life.

This year, 1830, M. Récamier died, nearly eighty years old. Becoming ill, he wished to be carried to the Abbaye, and there he died in his wife's salon, receiving every attention from her and his niece. Her father, M. Bernard, died two years previously.

The following summer Madame Récamier went to Dieppe for her health, and the next year to Switzerland, where she and Chateaubriand visited the ivy-covered grave of Madame de Staël, at Coppet. From 1834 Chateaubriand devoted himself to his literary work, — his "Essay on English Literature," in two volumes, his "Translation of Milton," and his "History of the Congress of Verona," in two volumes.

Chateaubriand sent the "Essay" and the "Milton" to Béranger, who was greatly pleased with the courtesy, writing back: "It is only from you that I have learned anything. In my youth, the 'Genius of Christianity' taught me to appreciate the great works of antiquity; to-day, thanks to you again, I penetrate into English literature, and reconcile myself with 'Milton.' . . . Adieu, sir. Still give some thoughts to a man who daily remembers you, and who will never cease to hope that your happiness may be equal to your glory."

Chateaubriand, in 1836, was working on his "Memoirs," which, much against his pride, he sold during his life that his wife might have enough for her support. "Though I have no heart for the 'Memoirs' after I have finished what relates to you," he wrote Madame Récamier, "I will accomplish one or two pages a day while I live, in order to fulfil the painful conditions of my bargain, and to wile away the time until the arrival of the two hours I pass with you, which are all my life."

Chateaubriand came every day to the Abbaye, between two and three in the afternoon. For an hour they talked alone, and then other visitors were admitted.

In June, 1838, he made a journey to the southern provinces, and received a perfect ovation from the people; but he hurried home, writing Madame Récamier: "Women, men, skies, palm-trees, are not worth one moment passed in your sweet presence. Therein lies the only repose for me."

So disconsolate was he when Madame Récamier was absent that Madame Chateaubriand would urge her return, saying: "What is to become of M. Chateaubriand? What is he going to do if you stay away long?"

With failing health, Madame Récamier continued her receptions that the learned and the great might meet and comfort Chateaubriand. Alexis de Tocqueville, the noted author of "Democracy in America," and Sainte-Beuve came often to the Abbaye. De Tocqueville was a relation of Chateaubriand, and Madame Récamier was especially drawn to him because he had married through affection.

France, as ever, was disturbed by men ambitious to rule. Prince Louis Napoleon, the son of Hortense, had aspired to the throne, and was to be tried by the Chamber of Peers. Madame Récamier visited him at the Conciergerie. He was condemned to imprisonment for life, and was shut up in the fortress at Ham. Two years afterwards he sent her a pamphlet, which he had just published, with his "deep gratitude," and a letter enclosed to Chateaubriand: —

> Some twelve years ago, while walking one day outside of the Portia Pia, at Rome, I followed silently the Ambassador of Charles X., regretting that frigid politics prevented me from testifying to the illustrious author of the "Genius of Christianity" all my admiration for him. . . .
>
> I want to write the history of Charlemagne, and show the influence this great man exercised on the destiny of the world during his life and after his death. When I shall have collected all the necessary materials, I hope, if I submit to you some questions, I shall not trespass upon your extreme kindness.
>
> Receive, Sir Viscount, the assurance of my high esteem and distinguished consideration.
>
> NAPOLEON LOUIS BONAPARTE.

In 1840, Victor Hugo wrote Chateaubriand: "After twenty-five years, there remain only great things and great men, — Napoleon and Chateaubriand"; and dedicated some verses to him.

Chateaubriand wrote back: "No matter how great a man's fame may be, I shall always prefer liberty to glory."

This year, 1840, although Madame Récamier was in poor health, she arranged a subscription-soirée at the Abbaye, in aid of suffering in her native city, Lyons, caused by the overflow of the Rhone and the Saône. The price for tickets was twenty francs, but several persons gave five times that amount. Viardot, Garcia, Rubini, Rachel, and others, gave their services. In less than ten days nearly five thousand francs had been received. At the soirée Madame Récamier was called the most beautiful person present, and she was then sixty-three years of age.

She lost her bloom as she grew older, but she never lost the extreme winsomeness of her smile, her childlike innocence, and her sincere, gracious manner.

Sainte-Beuve said: "She did not struggle. She resigned herself gracefully to the first touch of Time. She understood, that for one who had enjoyed such success as a beauty, in order to seem yet beautiful, she must make no pretensions. A friend, who had not seen her for many years, complimented her upon her looks. 'Ah! my dear friend,' she replied, 'it is useless for me to deceive myself. From the moment I noticed that the little Savoyards in the street no longer turned to look at me, I knew that all was over.'"

Her playful wit, her even temper, her constant desire to please, never changed. She had perfect ease of manner, but a horror of familiarity. She was indulgent, yet firm. She had great discretion and excellent judgment. While sometimes lacking decision in small matters, she never did in great ones. She was not fond of domestic details, but managed her property well.

In 1843 Chateaubriand was induced to try the waters of Bourbonne-les-Bains. He wrote pitifully to Madame Récamier: "I am going out to walk with the lark; she shall sing to you of me; then she will be silent forever in the furrow into which she will have dropped. . . . Is it not wonderful the sympathy between us? I think exactly as you think. . . . I have only one hope graven on my heart, and that is, — to see you again."

After a dictated letter, he wrote: "I wish to finish by two words in my own writing, to prove to you that I am still living for you. It is very sad to be reduced to this. . . . You see how my poor hand trembles, but my heart is firm."

In the fall of 1743, Henry, the Count de Chambord, asked Chateaubriand to visit him in London. He could not help responding to the call of his young prince.

He dictated a letter from London to Madame Récamier: "I have just received the recompense of all my life. The prince has deigned to speak of me, in the midst of a crowd of Frenchmen, with an enthusiasm worthy of his youth. If I had the gift of description, I would give you the details of it; but I shed tears over it, like a fool." Thus devoted was the aged man to the Bourbon dynasty. In the spring of 1845 he visited the count at Venice, for the last time. Chateaubriand said: "I am a Bourbonist in honor; a Monarchist on grounds of rational conviction; but in natural character and disposition, I am still a Republican."

In 1839, six years previously, a cataract began to form on one of Madame Récamier's eyes. She was treated in 1845 for it, but without benefit. It was decided to perform an operation in the summer of 1846, but Chateaubriand having broken his collar bone in stepping from his carriage, Madame Récamier wished to postpone the matter till he had recovered.

He was never able to walk after the accident. When he came to the Abbaye, he was carried to an arm-chair which was placed by the fireplace.

In February, 1847, Madame Chateaubriand died, after a brief illness. Ballanche was soon taken ill, and lodged opposite the Abbaye. As Madame Récamier had just submitted to an operation upon her eyes by an able surgeon, Ballanche would not consent that she should cross the street in the bright light. She would not be refused, however, and stayed by his bedside till his death, "losing in tears every chance of recovering her sight," says her niece. He was buried in her family tomb.

A few months after the death of his wife, Chateaubriand begged Madame Récamier to honor his name by marriage, but she refused. "Why should we marry?" she said; "at our age, there can be no impropriety in my taking care of you. If solitude is painful to you, I am ready to live in the same house with you. The world, I am certain, will do justice to the purity of our friendship, and sanction anything that will render the task of making you, in your old age, happy and comfortable, more easy for me. If we were younger, I should not hesitate, but accept with joy the right to consecrate my life to you. Years and blindness have given me this right. Let us change nothing in so perfect an affection."

Chateaubriand could not console himself for her refusal, though he acknowledged that she was right.

She submitted to a second operation on the other eye, but it was unsuccessful. Her hearing was acute, and those who did not know that she was blind were unconscious of it, from her recognizing persons by their voices, and the unchanged brilliancy of her eyes. She lamented her blindness because it made her less useful to her friends.

In February, 1848, France was again in revolution, and Louis Philippe went into exile as his predecessor had gone.

Chateaubriand died three months later, July 4, 1848. His last illness was but for a few days. Every time that Madame Récamier left the room, overcome with grief, his eyes followed her with an agonized expression as though he might not see her again, but she could not see these looks. He asked for and received the Sacrament, never speaking afterwards, and dying with his steadfast gaze fixed upon her. He had written her eleven years before: "Never talk of what is to become of me without you; I have not done so much evil in the sight of Heaven that you should be called away before me. . . . It is I, remember, who must go first." And his wish was gratified.

He was buried in a granite rock on a little island, Grand Bey, near his birthplace, St. Malo, where the Atlantic Ocean chants a dirge for him in the strains which seemed so mournful to him when a lonely boy. He then imagined that a beautiful being stood beside him, and he used to go into the woods to worship his "Sylphide." He found her in real life when it was too late. In 1875, on the one hundredth and seventh anniversary of his birth, a statue was erected to his memory at St. Malo, by his admiring countrymen.

Madame Récamier shed no tears at Chateaubriand's death. A strange pallor came over her face and never left it. She was calm, and thanked her friends for attentions, but it was evident that she would soon follow him.

She talked of Ballanche and Chateaubriand as though they were only absent for a moment, and when the hour came on which they were wont to visit her, she would tremble as though they had appeared to her in person.

Eight months passed. She had left the Abbaye and gone to live at the home of her niece. On May 10, 1849, while dressing for dinner, she fainted. A physician was called and pronounced her disease cholera, which she had always feared.

For twelve hours she suffered intensely, bearing her pain with the utmost courage and sweetness. "We shall meet again! We shall meet again!" she said to her niece, and when she could no longer speak, she raised her lips to be kissed. At midnight she called for Ampère and her two nephews, Paul David and Charles Lenormant. They came, and she said farewell as though for the night. She died the following day, May 11.

After death she seemed more beautiful than ever, with an angelic expression. She died as she had lived, beloved by all who knew her. If some women's hearts had ached because of her, as Sainte-Beuve says, "which she sacrificed and wounded without knowing it," it must be remembered that she lived in a different country from ours and that her loveless marriage and that of Chateaubriand as well, were most unfortunate.

What was the secret of her power?

She made no enemies. She appreciated the good in each and drew out the best. She was never censorious or indifferent or frivolous. She never lost a friend. She praised where it was deserved, and inspired all to their utmost endeavor. She won confidence. She was absolutely true to friends, — sincere, natural, and universally kind.

She was so intelligent as to be companionable with the brightest minds of France. She enjoyed philosophy with Ballanche, science with Ampère, and politics, history, and poetry with Chateaubriand. She read Tacitus, Thiers, and Mignet, and collected historical matter for Chateaubriand's works.

She was an interested listener. She rested people by her repose of manner, and cheered them by her good nature and freedom from envy. She was extremely gentle, yet dignified, with a low, sweet voice. Aside from her beauty, she had the transcendent charm of self-sacrifice. She lived for others.

Lamartine, in speaking of her, said: "Her whose angelic face could bear no other name, and of whom it was said that one look sufficed to bind your heart to her forever."

Sainte-Beuve said: "France can never forget her"; and he might have said, "the world."

SUSANNA WESLEY.

SUSANNA WESLEY.

ONE of the extremely interesting places in London is Bunhill Fields, completely filled with graves, a quiet, suggestive spot in the midst of the commotion of a great city. John Bunyan has been long sleeping there. Close to his grave is one beside which thousands have stood, and will stand, in the years to come. It is the grave of the mother of John Wesley.

Here he preached at her death one of his most eloquent and impressive sermons. She was his companion, his guide, his ideal woman. He hoped he might find one like her in marriage, but he failed. He hoped he might not survive her, but he was spared many years to do his wonderful work. She was, says Isaac Taylor, " the mother of Methodism in a religious and moral sense; for, her courage, her submissiveness to authority, the high tone of her mind, its independence and its self-control, the warmth of her devotional feelings, and the practical direction given to them, came up and were visibly repeated in the character and conduct of her son."

She was the twenty-fifth, and youngest, child of Dr. Samuel Annesley by his second wife, and was born in London, Jan. 20, 1669. Dr. Annesley was an able and prominent dissenting minister, dignified and handsome, closely related to the Earl of Anglesey. Mrs. Annesley was a lovely woman, the daughter of a member of parliament, who was also one of the Westminster Assembly of divines. Susanna was always a favorite with her father, who gave every attention to her education. "Greek, Latin, and French, and both logic and metaphysics, had formed part of her studies," says Dr. Adam Clarke. She was deeply interested in the absorbing religious discussions of the day. Though her father was a Nonconformist, she was permitted to think for herself, and joined the Church of England when she was thirteen. In these early years a youth, Samuel Wesley, six and a half years older than herself, visited at the Annesley home. His father was the Rev. John Wesley, and his grandfather the Rev. Bartholomew Wesley. They were related to the Duke of Wellington, Sir Robert Ker Porter and his sisters, the novelists, and other distinguished persons.

When Samuel was sixteen, his father died, leaving his widow and children in very poor circumstances. Several persons contributed thirty pounds a year, and sent the lad to school in London, where he met Susanna Annesley, and, doubtless, enjoyed her bright conversation, and admired her beauty.

At twenty-one, he, too, left the Nonconformists and joined the Church of England; possibly he had influenced Susanna in her choice.

Determined to study and enter the ministry, he walked to Oxford one August morning, in 1683, with a little over two pounds in his pocket, and entered Exeter College. He maintained himself by teaching and some literary work, and after graduation became a curate in London, with an income of thirty pounds a year. This he doubled by writing, and on sixty pounds a year the young couple — Samuel, twenty-seven, and Susanna, twenty — began their married life in London lodgings in 1689.

It must have required great faith to marry on this income; it required something more than faith in the years of privation which followed. The young husband was an untiring student, a man of cheerful nature, and devoted to his work. The wife was a person of fine manners and uncommon beauty. Dr. Adam Clarke says: "She was not only graceful but beautiful in person. Her sister, Judith, painted by Sir Peter Lely, is represented as a very beautiful woman. One who well knew both said, 'Beautiful as Miss Annesley appears, she was far from being as beautiful as Mrs. Wesley.'"

The Marquis of Normandy heard of the poverty of the young minister, and obtained for him the position of rector at South Ormsby, where the salary was fifty pounds a year, instead of thirty. Mr. Wesley was not preaching for money; but having a son four months old, named Samuel, after himself, added to his family, he looked upon the twenty pounds' increase as a great blessing.

They left London with its activities, its libraries, and its cultivated people for the little parish of thirty-six houses and two hundred and sixty persons, at South Ormsby. Mr. Wesley tried to make the best of it, and found expression for his loneliness in verse: —

> "In a mean cot, composed of reeds and clay,
> Wasting in sighs the uncomfortable day;
> Near where the inhospitable Humber roars,
> Devouring by degrees the neighboring shores.
> Let earth go where it will, I'll not repine,
> Nor can unhappy be, while Heaven is mine."

The next year, in 1691, a little girl was born to the Wesleys, but died two years later. In January, 1692, Emilia was born, and in 1694 twin boys, Annesley and

Jedediah, who died in infancy. A few months after their death another little girl was born, named Susanna; and then Mary, who, through a fall, became deformed and ill.

Mrs. Wesley's life was already full of cares. Three children had died, and of the four who were living, one was continually ill, while the mother, a slight, frail woman, was not yet twenty-seven years of age.

Besides his parish work, Mr. Wesley was writing his heroic poem in ten books, on "The Life of our Blessed Lord and Saviour, Jesus Christ." The work was dedicated to Queen Mary. Pope and others pronounced it "intolerably dull," but it went through a second edition. It was probably of little pecuniary help to the beautiful wife and four children.

Mr. Wesley thus describes his wife in the volume:—

> "She graced my humble roof and blest my life,
> Blest me by a far greater name than wife;
> Yet still I bore an undisputed sway,
> Nor was't her task, but pleasure, to obey.
> Scarce thought, much less could act, what I denied.
> In our low house there was no room for pride·
> Nor need I e'er direct what still was right,
> She studied my convenience and delight:
> Nor did I for her care ungrateful prove,
> But only used my power to show my love:
> Whate'er she asked I gave without reproach or grudge,
> For still she reason asked and I was judge."

As Mrs. Wesley was a person of very strong will, and could not have been the grand woman that she was without it, perhaps the "undisputed sway" was somewhat imaginary, but seeming real to him was doubtless comforting.

In the latter part of 1696, Dr. Annesley died, and Mrs. Wesley sincerely mourned her gifted father, but believing in the communion of departed spirits with those left on earth, she found great consolation in the thought that he was always near his favorite child.

Early in 1697 the Wesleys removed to Epworth, a small market town of two thousand inhabitants. It is said that Queen Mary, not forgetting the dedication of the life of Christ, shortly before her last illness expressed a wish that Mr. Wesley should have the living of Epworth, worth two hundred pounds.

The house was of timber and plaster, three stories high and thatched with straw, with large grounds attached. Mr. Wesley determined to farm his own glebe, and therefore purchased oxen and the necessary farming implements. He was in debt already, and was obliged to borrow one hundred and fifty pounds to furnish the house, move his family, and begin life in the new parish. These debts he was never able to cancel, and they proved the intolerable burden of his life.

Soon after the family were settled, Mehetabel was born; the next year the ninth child, which soon died, and in the two years following, John and Benjamin, both of whom died in infancy.

In May, 1701, poverty, even worse than usual, stared Mr. and Mrs. Wesley in the face. The latter was feeble, and often confined to her bed for six months at a time. Writing poetry for London publishers brought little remuneration. Coal was needed, and the last six shillings were used to buy it.

It is probable that the parishioners did not inquire whether the rector had any money in his pocket so long as he preached the gospel regularly. Fortunately, Archbishop Sharpe heard of their poverty, spoke to several of the nobility about it, and even appealed to the House of Lords.

The Countess of Northampton, moved to pity, sent twenty pounds to the family, ten of which Mr. Wesley gave to his own widowed mother. The money was received in both families with thanksgiving.

That evening, May 16, a boy and a girl were born in the Wesley home, but soon died, and the next year, 1702, Annie was born.

The children must be educated; but how? There was no money for schooling, and Mr. Wesley had little time to spare from his church and his writing. The educated but delicate mother must do it.

She, therefore, began her household school, and for six hours a day through twenty years she continued it. When her son John had become a noted man, he begged her to write some details of the education of her children, to which she reluctantly consented. She said, "No one can, without renouncing the world in the most literal sense, observe my method; and there are few, if any, that would devote above twenty years of the prime of life in hopes to save the souls of their children, which they think may be saved without so much ado; for that was my principal intention, however unskilfully and unsuccessfully managed."

The children were early taught to obey, and to "cry softly." A child was never allowed to have a thing because he cried for it, and John Wesley used to emphasize this in his talks to parents, urging that if a child obtained a thing because he cried, that he would cry again. Mrs. Wesley says, "That most odious noise of the crying of children was rarely heard in the house."

One cannot help wishing that Mrs. Wesley had lived on through the centuries to teach this doctrine.

"Drinking or eating between meals was never allowed," she says; "unless in case of sickness, which seldom happened. . . . At six, as soon as family prayer was over, they had their supper; at seven the maid washed them, and, beginning at the youngest, she undressed and got them all to bed by eight, at which time she left them in their several rooms awake, for there was no such thing allowed of in our house as sitting by a child till it fell asleep."

The children were taught never to address each other without prefixing "brother" or "sister," a fashion which John Wesley followed through life, as indeed he did thousands of things taught him by his mother. Her will was law with him, her letters through college his oracles, her life his blessed example.

With great firmness she combined great patience. Once, when she repeated the same thing to one child twenty times, her husband said, "I wonder at your patience; you have told that child twenty times that same thing."

"If I had satisfied myself by mentioning it only nineteen times," she replied, "I should have lost all my labor. It was the twentieth time that crowned it."

Psalms were sung every morning and night at the opening and the closing of school. Each elder child took a younger one morning and evening, and read a chapter in the Bible with him or her, after which each went to private devotions. As soon as they could speak the Lord's Prayer was taught them.

They were to be courteous in all things; a servant was never allowed to grant a favor unless the child said, "Pray give me such a thing." If a child confessed a fault and promised to reform, he was not punished. "This rule," says Mrs. Wesley, "prevented a great deal of lying." Nor was he ever reminded of it afterwards. Acts of obedience were commended. Mrs. Wesley had learned early that the world forgets to commend, but rarely forgets to blame. No one could take the property of another, even to the value of a pin. Every promise must be strictly observed, and a gift once bestowed could not be taken back. The children were not taught to read till they were five years old, and then the letters and small words were learned from the first chapter of Genesis.

In 1702 Mr. Wesley had published his "History of the Old and New Testament attempted in verse, and adorned with three hundred and thirty sculptures," but for this money failed to flow in as he had expected. He therefore went on horseback to London and appealed in various quarters for aid. The Dean of Exeter gave him ten pounds, the Archbishop of Canterbury ten guineas, and others to the amount of sixty pounds. Possibly these were subscriptions previously promised.

He had been home but a short time when his house took fire. He wrote to Archbishop Sharpe, "He that's born to be a poet must, I am afraid, live and die poor; for on the last of July, 1702, a fire broke out in my house by some sparks which took hold of the thatch this dry time, and consumed about two thirds of it before it could be quenched. . . . I got one of his horses [a sick neighbor's, whom he was visiting], rode up, and heard by the way that my wife, children, and books were saved, for which God be praised, as well as for what He has taken.

"I find 't is some happiness to have been miserable, for my mind has been so blunted with former misfortunes that this scarce made any impression upon me."

The house was rebuilt with great difficulty. A fifteenth child was born into the home June 17, 1703, old style, or June 28, new style, and this was John Wesley, the founder of Methodism.

A few weeks later Mr. Wesley's crop of flax was set on fire, perhaps by some incendiary. As that was a day of theological conflicts, and Mr. Wesley was not disinclined to be belligerent with his pen, he doubtless made some enemies.

Samuel, the first born, had been sent to Westminster School, where he became distinguished for scholarship. His fond mother wrote him long letters, chiefly about religion, asking him to preserve them till he was older and could better understand them. He seems to have confided in her. Would not anybody in such a mother? She writes: "If you have wasted or misemployed your time, take more care of what remains. If in anything you want counsel or advice, speak freely to me, and I will gladly assist you. I commit you to God's protection. . . . If you can, possibly, set apart the hours of Sunday, in the afternoon, from four to six for this employment [prayer and meditation], which time I have also determined to the same work. May that Infinite Being, whose we are, and whom I hope we endeavor to serve and love, accept us and bless us. . . . I think your health and studies require that you should take a pretty deal of exercise. You know whether your heart be too much set upon it. If it be, I will tell you what rule I observed in the same case when I was young and much addicted to childish diversions, which was this: never to spend more time in any matter of recreation in one day than I spent in private religious duties."

Again, she writes: "I would advise you, as much as

possible in your present circumstances, to throw your business into a certain method, by which means you will learn to improve every precious moment, and find an unspeakable facility in the performance of your respective duties. . . . Appoint so much time for sleep, eating, company, etc., but above all things, my dear Sammy, I command you, I beg, I beseech you, to be very strict in observing the Lord's Day. In all things endeavor to act on principle, and do not live like the rest of mankind, who pass through the world like straws upon a river, which are carried which way the stream or wind drives them. . . . . I am sorry that you lie under a necessity of conversing with those that are none of the best; but we must take the world as we find it, since it is a happiness permitted to a very few to choose their company."

She writes him as "the son of my tenderest love, my friend, in whom is my inexpressible delight, my future hope of happiness in this world, for whom I weep and pray in my retirements from the world, when no mortal knows the agonies of my soul on your account, no eyes see my tears, which are only beheld by that Father of Spirits of whom I so importunately beg grace for you that I hope I may at last be heard."

Mr. Wesley writes earnest letters to his beloved Samuel, and speaks thus beautifully of his noble wife: "You will, I verily believe, remember that these obligations of gratitude, love, and obedience, and the expressions of them, are not confined to your tender years, but must last to the very close of your life, and even after that render her memory most dear and precious to you. . . . You will endeavor to repay her prayers for you by doubling yours for her, as well as your fervency in them; and, above all things, to live such a virtuous and religious life that she may find that her care and love have not been lost upon you, but that we may all meet in heaven.

"In short, reverence and love her as much as you will, which I hope will be as much as you can. For though I should be jealous of any other rival in your heart, yet I will not be of her; the more duty you pay her, and the more frequently and kindly you write to her, the more you will please your affectionate father."

The Epworth household went on as usual, except that financial matters were growing worse. Hard-working Mr. Wesley had written a poem of nearly six hundred lines, "Marlborough, or the Fate of Europe," on the duke who had gained the battle of Blenheim, August, 1704.

The faithful Archbishop Sharpe showed the poem to the duke, who appointed Mr. Wesley to the chaplaincy of Col. Lepelle's regiment, but the Whigs gaining a victory in politics soon after, the rector was deprived of the chaplaincy, and insulted by a mob on account of his Tory sympathies. They fired pistols about his house, and under the window where his wife lay ill. Her infant of three weeks old had been carried across the street to a nurse, who, broken of her rest by the disturbance, smothered the child when she fell asleep; and then, nearly crazed by the accident, carried it dead to the arms of its mother.

Brave Susanna Wesley bore all these things well; for her husband writes to the archbishop, "All this, thank God, does not in the least sink my wife's spirits. For my own, I feel them disturbed and disordered."

Other troubles soon followed. Mr. Wesley owed some money to one of the persons whom he had angered in the recent election, was arrested and sent to Lincoln jail. The archbishop, in deep sympathy, wrote asking how much he owed. Mr. Wesley replied, "Three hundred pounds";

but he cheerfully adds, "I hope to rise again, as I have always done, when at the lowest, and I think I cannot be much lower now."

While in jail he devoted himself to his companions, and wrote Archbishop Sharpe: "I don't despair of doing some good here (and so long I sha'n't lose quite the end of living), and, it may be, do more in this parish than in my old one, for I have leave to read prayers every morning and afternoon here in the prison, and to preach once a Sunday, which I choose to do in the afternoon, when there is no sermon at the minster. And I am getting acquainted with my brother jail-birds as fast as I can, and shall write to London, next post, to the Society for Propagating Christian Knowledge, who, I hope, will send me some books to distribute among them." The cows on his farm were mutilated, and also his house-dog, because he barked; but Mr. Wesley adds, "'T is not every one who could bear these things, but I bless God my wife is less concerned with suffering them than I am in the writing, or than I believe your grace will be in reading them."

The Archbishop of York went to see Mrs. Wesley, and said, "Tell me, Mrs. Wesley, whether you ever really wanted bread."

"My lord," said she, "I will freely own to your grace that, strictly speaking, I never did want bread. But then I had so much care to get it before it was eat, and to pay for it after, as has often made it very unpleasant to me. And I think to have bread on such terms is the next degree of wretchedness to having none at all."

"You are certainly right," said the archbishop, and gave her a generous sum of money.

Mr. Wesley remained in prison for three months. His heart must have been touched when his wife sent him her rings to help cancel the debt, "because she had nothing else to relieve me with," he says. But he returned them. Finally, several persons raised money enough to pay half the debts; and Mr. Wesley joyfully writes, "I feel I walk a deal lighter, and hope I shall sleep better now these sums are paid. . . . I am a bad beggar, and worse at returning formal thanks, but I can pray heartily for my benefactors." He returned to his rejoicing family.

In the latter part of 1706 another child was born, Martha, who closely resembled John, both in looks and character. On Dec. 18, 1707, Mrs. Wesley's eighteenth child was born, Charles, whose hymns have been the delight of thousands. The babe was so delicate that he was wrapped in wool, and "neither cried nor opened his eyes for several weeks," says Eliza Clarke in her "Life of Susanna Wesley."

A most trying calamity was coming to the Wesleys. They had suffered poverty, imprisonment, and the horrors of debt. On the night of Feb. 9, 1709, Epworth Rectory was burned to the ground. Five days afterwards Mrs. Wesley thus describes the desolation to her eldest son, Samuel: "The fire broke out about eleven or twelve at night, we being all in bed, nor did we perceive it till the roof of the corn chamber was burnt through, and the fire fell upon your sister Hetty's bed, which stood in the little room joining upon it. She awaked, and immediately ran to call your father, who lay in the red chamber.

"We had no time to take our clothes, but ran all naked. I called to Betty to bring the children out of the nursery; she took up Patty and left Jacky [John] to follow her, but he, going to the door, and seeing all on fire, ran back again. We got the street door open, but the wind drove the flame with such violence that none could stand against it. I tried thrice to break through, but was driven back. I made another attempt and waded through the fire, which did me no other hurt than to scorch my legs and face.

"When I was in the yard I looked about for your father and the children, but, seeing none, concluded them all lost. But, I thank God, I was mistaken. Your father carried sister Emily, Sukey, and Patty into the garden; then missing Jacky, he ran back into the house to see if he could save him. He heard him miserably crying out in the nursery, and attempted several times to get up-stairs, but was beat back by the flames; then he thought him lost, and commended his soul to God, and went to look after the rest. The child climbed up to the window, and called out to them in the yard; they got up to the casement and pulled him out just as the roof fell into the chamber. Harry broke the glass of the parlor window, and threw out your sisters Matty and Hetty, and so by God's great mercy we all escaped."

And then she adds to this pitiful letter, homeless and penniless as they are, "Do not be discouraged; God will provide for you."

Mr. Wesley writes to the Duke of Buckingham, that when he heard that "killing cry" of his Jacky, and could not help, "I made them all kneel down in the garden, and we prayed God to receive his soul."

John Wesley, who was then six years old, always felt that God had miraculously saved him. He believed that the moment when his father was praying for him in the garden he awoke. "I did not cry, as they imagined," he says, "unless it was afterwards. I remember all the circumstances as distinctly as though it were but yesterday. Seeing the room was very light, I called to the maid to take me up. But none answering, I put my head out of the curtains and saw streaks of fire on the top of the room. I got up and ran to the door, but could get no farther, all beyond it being in a blaze. I then climbed up on the chest which stood near the window; one in the yard saw me, and proposed running to fetch a ladder.

"Another answered, 'There will not be time; but I have thought of another experiment. Here, I will fix myself against the wall, lift a light man and set him on my shoulders.' They did so, and he took me out of the window. Just then the whole roof fell in; but it fell inward, or we had all been crushed at once. When they brought me into the house where my father was, he cried out, 'Come, neighbors, let us kneel down; let us give thanks to God! He has given me all my eight children; let the house go; I am rich enough.'"

The books which had been purchased with the utmost self-denial were all gone; the collection of Hebrew poetry, the papers of the Annesley family, twenty pounds in money, and their clothing. A month after the fire, in March, 1709, Mrs. Wesley's nineteenth and last child was born, Kezia, who, like Charles, was extremely frail.

The fire, for a time, broke up the Epworth household. Susanna and Hetty went to London to stay with their uncles, Samuel Annesley and Matthew Wesley. Emilia, who was seventeen, and fitting herself to be a governess, stayed with her mother for a year in lodgings, caring for her with a peculiar tenderness and sympathy.

The rectory was rebuilt, after a time, in the Queen Anne style of red brick, at a cost of four hundred pounds, and the scattered Wesleys were gathered again into the fold. The rector, though he could ill afford it, journeyed to London for several winters as the representative of the clergy in his diocese, in convocation.

Mrs. Wesley's teaching went on as usual. Sometimes, in the evening, Emilia read to her mother. The latter writes to her husband at London that Emilia has been reading an account of a Danish mission to Tranquebar: "Their labors refreshed my soul beyond measure," she says; "and I could not forbear spending a good part of that evening in praising and adoring the Divine goodness for inspiring those good men with such ardent zeal for His glory. For some days I could think and speak of little else.

"It then came into my mind, though I am not a man nor a minister of the Gospel, yet if I were inspired with a true zeal for His glory, and really desired the salvation of souls, I might do more than I do. . . . However, I resolved to begin with my own children, and accordingly I proposed and observed the following method: I take such a proportion of time as I can best spare every night to discourse with each child by itself, on something that relates to its principal concerns. On Monday I talk with Molly, on Tuesday with Hetty, Wednesday with Nancy, Thursday with Jacky, Friday with Patty, Saturday with Charles; and with Emily and Sukey together on Sunday."

These Thursday talks with John were never forgotten by him, and he wrote her years afterwards when he was a Fellow of Lincoln College: "If you can spare me only that little part of Thursday evening which you formerly bestowed upon me in another manner, I doubt not it would be as useful now for correcting my heart, as it was then for forming my judgment."

Since John had been so wonderfully preserved to her, Mrs. Wesley writes in her private meditations: "I do intend to be more particularly careful of the soul of this child, that Thou hast so mercifully provided for, than ever

I have been, that I may do my endeavor to instil into his mind the principles of Thy true religion and virtue."

Besides Mrs. Wesley's school duties, she prepared for the religious instruction of her children three text-books: "A Manual of Natural Theology," "An Exposition of the Leading Truths of the Gospel, based upon the Apostles' Creed," and "A Practical Exposition of the Ten Commandments," besides sixty pages of manuscript, entitled "A Religious Conference between Mother and Emilia."

Reading of the Danish mission was about to bear fruit, even if Mrs. Wesley was "not a man nor a minister of the Gospel," for in 1710 she began to hold service every Sunday evening in, the rectory kitchen for the benefit of her own children and servants. Others asked permission to come till soon two hundred or more were present, and many were obliged to go away for lack of room. She read a sermon and then held converse with the people. A woman who could write theological books for her children could talk as acceptably, doubtless, as the curate who preached in Mr. Wesley's absence.

This was indeed an innovation, and Mr. Wesley wrote to his godly and intellectual wife remonstrating with her. She replied in a way that must have been convincing if not conclusive: "The main of your objections," she writes, "against our Sunday evening meetings are — first, that it will look particular; secondly, my sex; and lastly, your being at present in a public station and character. . . . As to its looking particular, I grant it does; and so does almost every thing that is serious, or that may any way advance the glory of God or the salvation of souls, if it be performed out of a pulpit, or in the way of a common conversation. . . . To your second, I reply that as I am a woman, so I am also a mistress of a large family. And though the superior charge of the souls contained in it lies upon you, as head of the family and as their minister, yet in your absence I cannot but look upon every soul you leave under my care as a talent committed to me, under a trust, by the great Lord of all the families of heaven and earth. . . . I never durst positively presume to hope that God would make use of me as an instrument in doing good; the farthest I ever durst go was, 'It may be; who can tell? With God all things are possible.'"

To his third objection that he was in a "public station," she replies: "If I and my children went a-visiting on Sunday nights, or if we admitted of impertinent visits, as too many do who think themselves good Christians, perhaps it would be thought no scandalous practice, though, in truth, it would be so.

"Therefore, why any should reflect upon you, let your station be what it will, because your wife endeavors to draw people to the church, and to restrain them, by reading and other persuasions, from their profanation of God's most holy day, I cannot conceive. But if any should be so mad as to do it, I wish you would not regard it. For my part, I value no censure on this account."

When Mr. Inman, the rector, wrote Mr. Wesley asking him to stop his wife's meetings, and saying that more people went to hear her than came to the church to hear him, Mr. Wesley again remonstrated. Mrs. Wesley wrote back that some who had not been inside a church for seven years came to her meetings, and then she wisely puts the responsibility on him: "If you do, after all, think fit to dissolve this assembly, do not tell me that you desire me to do it, for that will not satisfy my conscience; but send me your positive command, in such full and express terms as may absolve me from all guilt and punishment for neglecting this opportunity of doing good, when you and I shall appear before the great and awful tribunal of our Lord Jesus Christ."

John Wesley never forgot these precious services, and felt that if his mother could win souls, other women should not be debarred from such a labor of love. It is not strange that in his great work in after years, women should have been his invaluable helpers, both by word and deed.

Nearly two centuries have come and gone since the mother of Wesley held services in the Epworth rectory. How many noble and educated women since then have prayed and preached! And what human being shall dare to close the door which Susanna Wesley helped to open for her sex?

John had entered Charterhouse School, London, when he was a little over ten years of age, on the nomination of the Duke of Buckingham. Here he studied for six years, and became a favorite with both teachers and pupils. Through the tyranny of the older boys, who took away the food of the younger, he says, "From ten to fourteen I had little but bread to eat, and not great plenty of that." He was ambitious, and necessarily so, if, as Addison says, "Men of the greatest abilities are most fired with ambition."

Of course, letter after letter passed from the devoted mother to her son. Now she wrote of the "knockings" at the rectory which have never been accounted for; now to keep courage in his struggle with poverty, — he had gone to Christ Church, Oxford, on a forty-pound scholarship from the Charterhouse School, — "and to hope for better days."

A rich brother, Samuel Annesley, was coming from India, and he would probably help them all. Mr. Wesley had acted as his agent for a time, but the arrangement had not been satisfactory. He blamed Mr. Wesley, and the loyal wife replied that her husband might not be "fit for worldly business," but added, "Did I not know that Almighty wisdom hath views and ends in fixing the bounds of our habitation, which are out of our ken, I should think it a thousand pities that a man of his brightness and rare endowments of learning and useful knowledge in relation to the church of God should be confined to an obscure corner of this country, where his talents are buried, and he determined to a way of life for which he is not so well qualified as I could wish."

Sukey, who had been led to expect aid from her uncle, becoming discouraged by poverty, married, unwisely, a man from whom she afterwards separated. Mrs. Wesley went to London to meet the brother from India, but he did not come, and was never heard from afterwards. When John learned that his mother was going to London, he wept for joy at the thought of seeing her, but as he had no money, he could not leave Oxford.

On closing his college life, John began to think of becoming a clergyman. He wrote to his father, who counselled him to wait, fearing that he might be inclined to this step merely as a profession, but his mother understood him better, and wrote at once, "I was much pleased with your letter to your father about taking holy orders, and liked the proposal well. . . . I approve the disposition of your mind, and think the sooner you are a deacon the better." Mr. Wesley soon agreed with his wife.

John wrote her, making inquiries about predestination and other doctrines which troubled him, and she, with her superior education, answered with rare ability and clear judgment. She advised what books to read. Thomas à Kempis, on the "Imitation of Christ," and Jeremy Taylor's "Rules for Holy Living and Dying" made a lasting impression upon John Wesley. After reading the latter, he said, "I resolved to dedicate all my life to God, — all my thoughts and words and actions, — being thoroughly convinced there was no medium." What John Wesley would have been with an ignorant mother, it is difficult to conjecture. The old question of ways and means could not be ignored. The expenses of ordination must be met. Poor Mr. Wesley wrote his son, "I will assist you in the charges for ordination, though I am myself just now struggling for life."

John was ordained deacon Sept. 19, 1725, and in the following March was elected Fellow of Lincoln College. His father had interceded for him with Dr. Morley, rector of the college, telling John meantime to "study hard lest your opponents beat you"; and when elected, with a glowing heart, though burdened with debt, writing, "I have done more than I could do for you. . . . The last twelve pounds pinched me so hard that I am forced to beg time of your brother Sam till after harvest to pay him the ten pounds that you say he lent you. Nor shall I have as much as that, perhaps not five pounds, to keep my family till after harvest. . . . What will be my own fate God only knows. Wherever I am, my Jack is Fellow of Lincoln."

For more than a quarter of a century John Wesley held this honorable position. He laid out a plan of work, and closely followed it. Mondays and Tuesdays he devoted to Greek and Roman historians and poets; Wednesdays to logic and ethics; Thursdays to Hebrew and Arabic;

Fridays to metaphysics and natural philosophy: Saturdays to oratory and poetry, chiefly to composing; and Sundays to divinity. He perfected himself in French, and gave considerable time to mathematics and optics.

He wrote to his brother Samuel, "Leisure and I have taken leave of one another. I propose to be busy as long as I live."

In the summer of 1727 John came to Epworth to assist his father who had become somewhat disabled by paralysis. He was now sixty-five years old, and poverty and labor were telling upon the rector of Epworth. Brain work was fatiguing, but poverty a thousand times more so, and the never-to-be-lifted debt was eating like a cancer. Strange that somebody did not lift the burden! And yet we are as blind to-day as were the people of Epworth. To be our "brother's keeper" was, and is, a very difficult part of religion.

All were delighted to have John at home. He seems to have fallen somewhat in love with Betty Kirkham, which he confides to his mother, but he is soon recalled to Lincoln by Dr. Morley to become Greek lecturer and moderator of the classes, with several private pupils, and is so busy that his love matter is neglected or forgotten. When John returned to college he found that his brother Charles, who was at Christ Church, Oxford, had gathered round him a small band of Christian young men who not only studied earnestly, but met frequently evenings to read the Greek Testament together. Charles attributed his increased spirituality to "somebody's prayers, — my mother's, most likely."

John at once joined the little band, and, being older, became the leader. They were all devoted churchmen, visited the poor and the sick, prisoners and debtors, —

the Wesley boys must have had a tender feeling for the latter, — went without all luxuries and many necessities for the sake of doing good; and, living with all the *method* to which they had been trained by Mrs. Wesley, were nicknamed "Methodists."

John Wesley began to rise at four o'clock in the morning for his work, and continued in this habit for sixty years. In the first six years the number of Methodists grew to fourteen. Who supposed then that it would ever grow to over fourteen millions?

John wrote his father of the work they were doing, and the good old man wrote back, "I have the highest reason to bless God that He has given me two sons together at Oxford, to whom He has granted grace and courage to turn the war against the world and the devil."

A curacy was offered to John eight miles from Oxford, at thirty pounds a year, which he accepted in addition to his other work. When he had thirty pounds a year, he lived on twenty-eight pounds, and gave away two. The next year, receiving sixty pounds, he lived on twenty-eight, and gave away thirty-two. The third year he received ninety, and gave away sixty-two.

One cold winter's day, a young girl whom the Methodists were keeping at school, called upon John Wesley. She looked nearly frozen. "You seem half starved," said Wesley; "have you nothing to wear but that linen gown?"

"Sir, this is all I have," said the girl.

Wesley put his hand in his pocket, and found it nearly empty. Then he looked at the pictures on his walls. "It struck me," he says, "will thy Master say, 'Well done, good and faithful steward'? Thou hast adorned thy walls with the money which might have screened this poor creature from the cold! O justice! O mercy! Are not these pictures the blood of this poor maid?"

This habit of giving he continued through life. When he was an old man he wrote in his journal, "For upwards of eighty-six years I have kept my accounts exactly. I will not attempt it any longer, being satisfied with the continual conviction that I save all I can, and give all I can: that is, all I have."

In one of his last impassioned sermons, he says, "Leave children enough to live on, not in idleness and luxury, but by honest industry. And if you have not children, upon what scriptural or rational principle can you leave a groat behind you more than will bury you? . . . Oh, leave nothing behind you! Lend all you have before you go into a better world! Lend it, lend it all unto the Lord, and it shall be paid to you again."

In the spring of 1731, Mr. Matthew Wesley, of London, came to Epworth to visit his brother, and on his return wrote a very stern letter to the rector, because he was rearing his family in such poverty. He did not realize that it cost more to support and educate the rector's eight children than it did his only child.

Mrs. Wesley, as ever, was enduring trials. Several of her daughters, tired of the struggle with poverty, had married unfortunately, and increased their troubles. The bright and beautiful Hetty, who read Greek at eight, married against her will a drinking man, who ill-treated her. Martha, a woman of unusual loveliness of character, married a curate who led a most unworthy life. When he was dying, after he had made her unhappy for forty years, he said, "I have injured an angel, — an angel that never reproached me." Kezia died at thirty-two, her affections having been won by the man who was already engaged to Martha.

Mary, the deformed girl, was married to a young man whom the Wesleys educated, and then gave him the living at Wroote, a part of Mr. Wesley's parish. The young couple had fifty pounds a year to live on. Mary and her infant child died a year after her marriage. Mrs. Wesley took this death very much to heart.

In 1734 Mr. Wesley made his last visit to London to see his "Dissertations on the Book of Job," dedicated to Queen Caroline, through the press. Five hundred copies were printed, and Samuel and John, as well as their father, obtained all the subscriptions possible.

Mr. Wesley was growing old, seventy-two, — the wonder was that he was not growing discouraged, — and how to leave his family provided for was a serious question. He wrote pitifully to Samuel, urging him to become rector of Epworth, and thus care for his mother at her home: "As for your aged and infirm mother, as soon as I drop she must turn out unless you succeed me, which, if you do, and she survives me, I know you'll immediately take her then to your own house, or rather continue her there, where your wife and you will nourish her till we meet again in heaven; and you will be a guide and a stay to the rest of the family."

Samuel did not wish to live at Epworth, and John was urged to come, but he gave twenty-six reasons against it. As ever, through life, Mr. Wesley's hands seemed tied, and he could do no more.

Mrs. Wesley saw that the end was approaching, and wrote John and Charles to come to Epworth. They arrived in time to talk with their father. He longed to see his "Job" through the press and his debts paid, but both these comforts were denied him. Mrs. Wesley came into the room but seldom, for she fainted each time and had to be carried out. At sunset, April 25, 1735, the debt-burdened, devoted Samuel Wesley passed away, while John was praying. Mrs. Wesley was comforted, because she believed that her prayers were answered in his easy death.

The day after the burial in Epworth churchyard, the landlady seized all Mrs. Wesley's "quick stock," Charles wrote to his brother Samuel, valued at forty pounds, for the fifteen pounds which his father owed her. "It will be highly necessary," he adds, "to bring all accounts of what he owed you, that you may mark all the goods in the house as principal creditor, and thereby secure to my mother time and liberty to sell them to the best advantage. . . . Let the Society [which gave aid to the widows of clergymen] give her what they please, she must be still in some degree burdensome to you, as she calls it. How do I envy you that glorious burden, and wish I could share it with you! You must put me in some way of getting a little money, that I may do something in the shipwreck of the family, though it be no more than furnishing a plank."

Mrs. Wesley moved away from Epworth, the place of so many joys and sorrows to her, and went to live with Emilia, who had been helped by her brothers to establish a school at Gainsborough.

A short time after the death of Mr. Wesley, John and Charles were invited by Gen. James Edward Oglethorpe, a member of Parliament who had founded the State of Georgia, to go to the New World and help Christianize the natives as well as minister to the colonists. John declined to leave his aged mother. On being urged to go if she would consent, he visited her, determining to abide by her decision. When asked her advice, the brave woman replied, "Had I twenty sons, I should rejoice that they were all so employed, though I should never see them more."

This, of course, was decisive, and the two young men bade her farewell, and sailed Oct. 14, 1735, for America.

In her first letter to her beloved John, she mourns that she "does not long to go home, as in reason I ought to do. This often shocks me; and as I constantly pray (almost without ceasing) for thee, my son, so I beg you, likewise, to pray for me, that God would make me better, and take me at the best." One does not wonder that she desired to live, if only to see brighter days if possible! After spending a year or more with Samuel, she went to live with her daughter, Martha.

On the voyage to America the two young ministers used every hour well. Wesley studied German, Spanish, and Italian, when not talking with the passengers or holding service. He found the Indians ready to hear the Gospel, though "they would not be made Christians as the Spaniards make Christians," one of the chiefs said. After two years or more, Wesley decided to return to England, not satisfied with his success, though Whitefield said, "The good Mr. John Wesley has done in America is inexpressible. His name is very precious among the people."

Early in 1738 Wesley met Peter Böhler from Germany, an educated Moravian, who "preached justification through faith in Christ, and of freedom by it from the dominion and guilt of sin." Böhler taught that a man may be converted in an instant from sin to joy in the Holy Spirit. Wesley felt that there was a peace in believing and an assurance of pardon which he did not then possess, and was determined to find it through prayer.

He was troubled for many days, till, on the evening of May 24, 1738, he experienced a great change. "I felt my heart strangely warmed," he says. "I felt I did trust in Christ, Christ alone, for salvation; and an assurance was given me that He had taken away my sins." His joy and peace were not unbroken, but from that time onward he knew no rest in his marvellous work. His message forever after was, "By grace are ye saved, through faith."

"Christians are called to love God with all their hearts, and to serve Him with all their strength," he said, "which is precisely what I apprehend to be meant by the scriptural term, *perfection.*"

He began to preach with renewed ardor. He talked to the felons in Newgate; he spoke in churches and before societies, and the congregations grew larger every day. Soon the church doors began to be closed against him and Whitefield, and they preached in the open air.

"At first," he says, "I could scarce reconcile myself to this strange way of preaching in the fields; having been all my life, till very lately, so tenacious of every point relating to decency and order, that I should have thought the saving of souls almost a sin if it had not been done in a church."

During the last eight months of 1739 Wesley delivered five hundred discourses, only eight of which were given in churches. At Blackheath, from twelve to fourteen thousand persons gathered to hear him, and quite as many at Moorfields, Kennington Common, and elsewhere. Good Mrs. Wesley was seeing the fruit of her labors.

Persecutions had begun in earnest. John Wesley was forbidden by the sheriff to speak at Newgate, the last place where prohibition was to be expected! The Methodists were called "crackbrained enthusiasts, profane hypocrites, and mad dogs."

In Staffordshire a crowd surrounded Wesley, struck him with clubs on the breast and mouth till the blood flowed, and one seized him by the hair. The slight, sweet-faced John Wesley said, "Are you willing to hear me speak?"

"No, no; down with him; kill him at once!"

"What evil have I done? Which of you all have I wronged in word or deed?"

"Bring him away, bring him away!" cried the mob.

Wesley began to pray, when the ringleader said, "Sir, I will spend my life for you; follow me, and no one shall hurt a hair of your head."

"From the beginning to the end," says Wesley, "I found the same presence of mind, as if I had been sitting in my own study. But I took no thought for one moment before another; only once it came into mind, that, if they should throw me into the river, it would spoil the papers that were in my pocket. For myself, I did not doubt but I should swim across, having but a thin coat and a light pair of boots."

Sometimes cattle were driven among the congregations; stones were thrown, one of which struck Wesley between the eyes, but wiping away the blood, he continued preaching. Women were kicked and dragged by the hair, and their clothes set on fire by rockets. Men were knocked down and thrown into the gutters. The houses of those who were called Methodists were torn down and the furniture was broken into fragments.

Thousands of conversions were reported, and many marvellous answers to prayer. Samuel Wesley had become alarmed at such strange doings, and the more so that he had heard that his mother had attended one of these gatherings. He wrote her: "John and Charles are now become so notorious, the world will be curious to know when and how they were born, what schools bred at, what colleges, if in Oxford, and when matriculated, what degrees took, and where, when, and by whom ordained; what books they have written and published. I wish they may spare so much time as to vouchsafe a little of their story. For my own part, I had much rather have them picking straws within the walls, than preaching in the area of Moorfields.

"It was with exceeding concern and grief I heard you had countenanced a spreading delusion, so far as to be one of Jack's congregation. Is it not enough that I am bereft of both my brothers, but must my mother follow too?"

Two weeks later Samuel Wesley was called away from such earthly distractions as John was engaged in. He died suddenly, Nov. 5, 1739, at the age of forty-nine. Mrs. Wesley bore the death of her first-born and dearly loved Samuel with composure, saying, "He is now at rest. . . . He hath reached the haven before me, but I shall soon follow him."

A month later she wrote to Charles: "Your brother, whom I shall henceforth call Son Wesley, since my dear Sam is gone home, has just been with me and much revived my spirits. . . . I want either him or you; for, indeed, in the most literal sense, I am become a little child and want continual succor."

Shortly after Samuel's death, in 1739, John Wesley purchased the old Foundry, near Moorfields, London. It had been used by the government for casting cannon, till in 1716 an explosion left it in ruins. He had no income save the Oxford fellowship, but friends loaned and gave money, some four, six, and ten shillings a year,-so that at an expense of about eight hundred pounds a plain chapel to accommodate fifteen hundred persons was built, with a house for lay preachers, and a band-room, large enough for three hundred, where the classes met, and where five o'clock morning service was conducted. The north end of the room was used for a school, and the south end for a book-room where Wesley's publications were sold and the proceeds devoted to Gospel work. During his long ministry he wrote hundreds of pamphlets and books which had an extensive sale.

Besides his own works, he prepared about fifty volumes of the "Christian Library," which were made up of extracts from the best writers, grammars of five languages, natural philosophy, history, memoirs, etc. His object was "that peasants and persons of neglected education might have the means of acquiring useful knowledge at the smallest expense of time and money."

He used to say, "It cannot be that the people should grow in grace unless they give themselves to reading. A reading people will always be a knowing people."

Over this band-room were the rooms of John Wesley, and thither he brought his idolized mother to live with him. He was then thirty-six. These must have been happy days for tired, trusting Susanna Wesley. She and her son talked together of theological matters. When Thomas Maxfield, one of the first lay preachers, was almost insensibly led from praying with the converts to preaching, and John was disturbed at this new departure, Mrs. Wesley said, "John, take care what you do with respect to that young man, for he is as surely called of God to preach as you are. Examine what have been the fruits of his preaching, and hear him yourself."

Wesley was convinced, and said, "It is the Lord; let Him do what seemeth Him good. What am I, that I should withstand God?"

A little later, Emilia, who had married an impecunious apothecary, was left a widow, and came to live at the Foundry.

Wesley was drawn into some Calvinistic disputes with Whitfield and others, but, in the main, his life was devoted to the one purpose of winning souls. He was punctual, always kept his word, would ride all night rather than fail to meet an appointment, and was careful in the use of time. Once, when he was kept waiting, he exclaimed sadly, "I have lost ten minutes forever!"

Meetings were being held all over Great Britain. The persecutions continued, and so did the conversions. Charles, too, as well as John, was becoming known and loved for his hymns. During his life it is said that he composed not far from six thousand six hundred. The Wesleys collected and furnished the tunes for their people. John said to his preachers, "Exhort every one in the congregation to sing, not one in ten only."

In 1742, when John was thirty-nine, he visited his old home at Epworth. He offered to assist Mr. Romley, the curate, either by preaching or reading prayers; but the offer was declined, and a sermon preached against enthusiasts. At six o'clock, therefore, Wesley preached in Epworth churchyard, standing on his father's grave, to the largest congregation ever gathered in the town. He remained eight days, every evening preaching on the grave. The effect was magical. On one occasion the people on every side wept aloud, and then broke into praise and thanksgiving. Men who had not been inside a church for thirty years were deeply moved. The "brand plucked from the burning," when he was six years old, had kindled such a fire at Epworth as would never go out. The fifteenth child of the patient Susanna Wesley was paying her a thousandfold for all her care and sacrifice.

Wesley was building more chapels in London; one had just been opened by him in Seven Dials; visiting the sick, going among the poor, preaching several times a day, — never weary, never despondent, never fretting, he said, "I dare no more fret than curse and swear."

Wesley preached without notes. As he was about to preach in Allhallow's Church, London, when he was eighty-five, he said to his attendant, "It is above fifty years since I first preached in this church. I came without a sermon; and going up the pulpit stairs, I hesitated, and returned into the vestry, under much mental confusion and agitation. A woman who stood by noticed my concern, and said, 'Pray, sir, what is the matter?' I replied, 'I have not brought a sermon with me.' Putting her hand on my shoulder, she said, 'Is that all? Cannot you trust God for a sermon?' This question had such an effect on me that I ascended the pulpit, preached extempore, with great freedom to myself and acceptance to the people, and have never since taken a written sermon into the pulpit."

Wesley's style was always simple and clear — two characteristics of all good writing or speaking. He said, "When I transcribe anything for the press, I think it my duty to see that every phrase be *clear*, *pure*, *proper*, and *easy*."

Feeling that relief for the needy and Christian consolation should go hand in hand, Wesley divided London into twenty-three districts, and appointed visitors to call upon the sick three times a week, and relieve the wants of the poor. One rule he especially emphasized: "Be mild, tender, and patient." Those who asked relief were to receive "neither an ill word nor an ill look." He carried this out in his own life.

Once, when he was eighty, on leaving Norwich, a crowd of poverty-stricken people gathered about him. He had given so much that he had just enough left to take him to London. He said, somewhat sharply, "I have nothing for you. Do you suppose I can support the poor in every place?"

At the moment he was stepping into his carriage, his foot slipped and he fell to the ground. Feeling that God had rebuked him, he said to a friend near by, "It is all right; it is only what I deserved; for if I had no *other* good to give, I ought, at least, to have given them good words."

Wesley said, and with truth, "Money never stays with *me*; it would burn me if it did. I throw it out of my hands as soon as possible, lest it should find a way into my heart."

When asked by the Commissioners of Excise to pay a tax on his silver plate, he replied by letter, "I have two silver teaspoons at London, and two at Bristol. This is all the plate I have at present, and I shall not buy any more while so many around me want bread."

When he was eighty-four years old, the white-haired preacher spent five days in traversing the streets of London, often ankle-deep in mud and melting snow, to collect funds for the poor. This he did each year.

An eminent artist once asked Wesley to have a cast of his face taken, and he would pay him ten guineas. He refused, but finally consented and took the money. On leaving the house, he saw an excited crowd surrounding an auctioneer who was selling the furniture of a poor debtor; even the bed upon which the man was dying. Wesley rushed into the crowd, and asked the amount of the debt.

"Ten guineas," was the answer. "Take it," said Wesley, "and let the man have his furniture again. I see why God sent me these ten guineas," said the devoted preacher.

Two small houses were added to the Foundry for needy and deserving widows. A school was opened with about sixty children, most of them so poor that they were taught and clothed gratuitously. A lending society was also started, Mr. Wesley begging from the London people fifty pounds, to be loaned in sums not to exceed twenty shillings, payable within three months. With this small sum two hundred and fifty persons were helped in one year. Mr. Wesley said, "If this is not lending unto the Lord, what is?" The capital was increased later to one hundred and twenty pounds, and the maximum loan was five pounds. And all this time Mr. Wesley was preaching day and night to assembled thousands, and organizing societies of Christians in the various chapels. He had no thought of separating from the Church of England, and, indeed, never did leave the church; his one desire being, as he said, "Church or no church, I must save souls."

The blessed work of Susanna Wesley was about to end; no, not to end, for it was to be carried forward by millions after her. What must have been her feelings as she saw societies and schools springing up throughout the land? Books and tracts scattered by thousands; people sitting up all night in the chapels for fear they might not be awake in time for the five o'clock service before the great preacher left the town!

While preaching in Bristol on Sunday evening, July

18, 1742, John Wesley heard of his mother's illness. He hastened to the Foundry in London. "I found my mother on the borders of eternity," he writes in his journal; "but she has no doubt or fear, nor any desire but, as soon as God should call her, to depart and be with Christ."

On the morning of Friday, July 23, as she awakened from sleep, she cried, "My dear Saviour! art Thou come to help me at my last extremity?"

"About three in the afternoon," writes Mr. Wesley, "I went to my mother, and found her change was near. I sat down on the bedside. She was in her last conflict, unable to speak, but, I believe, quite sensible. Her look was calm and serene, and her eyes fixed upward, while we commended her soul to God. From three to four the silver cord was loosing, and the wheel breaking at the cistern; and then, without any struggle or sigh or groan, the soul was set at liberty. We stood round the bed, and fulfilled the last request uttered before she lost her speech: 'Children, as soon as I am released, sing a psalm of praise to God.'" The poverty and the struggle were over at seventy-three. These last days must have been the best and brightest.

Mrs. Wesley was buried on Sunday, Aug. 1, in Bunhill Fields. John records in his journal: "Almost an innumerable company of people being gathered together, about five in the afternoon, I committed to the earth the body of my mother, to sleep with her fathers. The portion of scripture from which I spoke was, 'I saw a great white throne, and Him that sat on it, from whose face the earth and the heaven fled away; and there was found no place for them. And I saw the dead, small and great, stand before God; and the books were opened; and the dead were judged out of those things which were written in the books, according to their works.' It was one of the most solemn assemblies I ever saw, or expect to see this side eternity."

Mrs. Wesley's tombstone having become defaced by time, eighty-six years afterward, in 1828, a new monument was set up over her grave, and in December, 1870, an obelisk of Sicilian marble was erected to her memory opposite the City Road Chapel, fronting Bunhill Fields.

The triumphant words of Charles Wesley, "God buries his workmen, but carries on His work," were true, and though the remarkable mother had gone, the remarkable sons went forward in their untiring labors.

Seven years after Mrs. Wesley's death, Charles, then forty-two, was married to Sarah Gwynne of South Wales, a young lady twenty-three, of excellent family, musical, and well educated. The union proved a happy one. She survived him thirty-four years, he dying at eighty and she at ninety-six.

The year of Charles's marriage, John, who was then forty-six, expected to marry Grace Murray, an attractive widow of thirty-three. She was devoted to Wesley's work, was gifted in speaking, nursed him during an illness, and was offered marriage by him. She accepted, replying, "This is too great a blessing for me; I can't tell how to believe it. This is all I could have wished for under heaven."

She was also loved by a lay preacher, John Bennett. Charles, believing that Grace Murray was not the one for his brother, not being his equal socially, and thinking that his work would be injured, influenced her to marry Bennett.

It was a great blow to John Wesley. Four days after her marriage he wrote a friend: "Since I was six years old, I never met with such a severe trial as for some days past. For ten years God has been preparing a fellow-laborer for me, by a wonderful train of providences. Last year I was convinced of it; therefore I delayed not, but, as I thought, made all sure beyond a danger of disappointment. But we were soon after torn asunder by a whirlwind.

"In a few months the storm was over; I then used more precaution than before, and fondly told myself that the day of evil would return no more. But it too soon returned. The waves rose again since I came out of London. I fasted and prayed, and strove all I could; but the sons of Zeruiah were too hard for me. The whole world fought against me; but above all, my own familiar friend. Then was the word fulfilled, 'Son of man, behold, I take from thee the desire of thine eyes at a stroke; yet shalt thou not lament, neither shall thy tears run down.'

"The fatal, irrevocable stroke was struck on Tuesday last. Yesterday I saw my friend (that was), and him to whom she is sacrificed. I believe you never saw such a scene."

For thirty-nine years Wesley did not see Grace Bennett. In 1788, when her son was officiating in a chapel in Moorfields, she expressed a wish to see Mr. Wesley. He was then eighty-five and she seventy-two. Her husband had been dead twenty-nine years, and Mr. Wesley's wife, whom he married two years after his disappointment, had been dead seven years. The meeting was brief and affecting. He was never heard to mention her name afterwards. She survived Mr. Wesley twelve years, dying at the age of eighty-seven. Her last words were, "Glory be to Thee, my God: peace Thou givest."

Wesley's marriage to Mrs. Vazeille, when he was forty-eight, proved a most unfortunate union. She was jealous, left him several times, and at her death gave her money, five thousand pounds, to her own family, with only a ring to her husband. He had desired somebody like his mother, and the disillusion must have been a great disappointment. His habits of life were formed, and mutual concessions were perhaps difficult. For thirty years Mr. Wesley did his work from this unhappy home. He repeatedly said that he believed the Lord overruled this painful business for his good; and that, if Mrs. Wesley had been a better wife, he might have been unfaithful in the great work to which God had called him. He outlived her ten years.

The amount of Mr. Wesley's work seems almost incredible. During the fifty years of his itinerant ministry it is estimated that he travelled a quarter of a million miles, usually on horseback, reading poetry, philosophy, and history, while the bridle hung loosely on the horse's neck. He loved poetry and sometimes wrote it, but his mother said, "Make poetry your diversion and not your business," and he accepted her advice. He delivered more than forty thousand sermons, a large part of these in the open air, and sometimes preached four and five times a day; he wrote books, he superintended churches and schools, he carried on a vast correspondence; he was accessible to the highest and the lowest.

"When you met him in the street of a crowded city," said Southey, "he attracted notice, not only by his band and cassock, and his long hair — white and bright as silver — but by his face and manner, both indicating that all his minutes were numbered, and that not one was to be lost."

Wesley said, "Though I am always in haste, I am never in a hurry; because I never undertake any more work than I can go through with perfect calmness of spirit."

When Wesley was sixty-seven his beloved Whitefield died in Newburyport, Mass., Sept. 30, 1770. The latter had intended to be buried in Tottenham Court Chapel, London, and wished the Wesley brothers to lie beside him. He said, "You refuse them entrance here while living. They can do you no harm when they are dead."

According to a promise made between the two men, Wesley preached the funeral sermon in Whitefield's church to an immense multitude. On the same day he preached in Whitefield's Tabernacle in Moorfields. The hour appointed was half-past five, but the place was filled at three. Wesley's text at both places was, "Let me die the death of the righteous, and let my last end be like his!"

When Wesley was eighty, he said, "I find no more pain or bodily infirmities than at five-and-twenty. This I still impute: 1, To the power of God, fitting me for what He calls me to; 2, To my still travelling four or five thousand miles a year; 3, To my sleeping, night or day, whenever I want it; 4, To my rising at a set hour; 5, To my constant preaching, particularly in the morning."

He wrote to a friend at this time, "I am afraid you want the grand medicine which I use,—exercise and change of air."

Three years later he writes that he is working on the "Life of Mr. Fletcher." "To this I dedicated all the time I could spare till November, from five in the morning till eight at night. These are my studying hours; I cannot write longer in a day without hurting my eyes." Fifteen hours, and he eighty-three years of age! When Wesley was eighty-five, his brother Charles died. A fortnight afterwards, when at Bolton, in reading the hymn, —

> "My company before is gone,
> And I am left alone with Thee,"

Mr. Wesley burst into tears, and sat down in the pulpit, covering his face with his hands.

On his eighty-eighth birthday, he wrote in his journal: "For above eighty-six years, I found none of the infirmities of old age; my eyes did not wax dim, neither was my natural strength abated; but, last August, I found almost a sudden change. My eyes were so dim that no glasses would help me. My strength likewise now quite forsook me, and probably will not return in this world. But I feel no pain from head to foot; only it seems nature is exhausted; and, humanly speaking, will sink more and more, till 'the weary springs of life stand still at last.'"

A little before this, Henry Crabbe Robinson describes John Wesley preaching in the great round meeting-house at Colchester. "He stood in a wide pulpit, and on each side of him stood a minister, and the two held him up, having their hands under his armpits. His feeble voice was barely audible, but his reverend countenance, especially his long white locks, formed a picture never to be forgotten. There was a vast crowd of lovers and admirers."

On Feb. 23, 1791, Wesley arose at four o'clock as usual, and set out for Leatherhead, eighteen miles from London, where he preached in the dining-room of a magistrate from the words: "Seek ye the Lord while He may be found, call ye upon Him while He is near." This was his last sermon.

The next day he wrote his last letter to Wilberforce on the abolition of slavery. "Unless God has raised you up for this very thing, you will be worn out by the opposition of men and devils; but, if God *be for you, who can be against you?* Are all of them together stronger than God? Oh, *be not weary in well doing.* Go on in the name of God, and in the power of His might, till even American slavery, the vilest that ever saw the sun, shall vanish away before it."

Each day he was failing. On Tuesday, March 1, he said, "I want to write." A pen was put in his hand, but he could not use it. "Let me write for you," said a friend; "tell me what you wish to say." "Nothing," he replied, "but that God is with us."

He tried to speak, but it was difficult to understand him. He was able to communicate to them that he wished his sermon on "The Love of God to Fallen Man" given to everybody. And then, with great effort, he said, "The best of all is, God is with us!" And after a pause, while lifting his arm in triumph, he reiterated, "The best of all is, God is with us!"

During the night he repeated scores of times, "I'll praise! I'll praise!" In the morning, at ten o'clock, the friends present knelt around his bed, while one prayed. "Farewell!" said the dying man, and passed away March 2, 1791. Remembering the dying words of his mother, "Children, as soon as I am released, sing a psalm of praise to God," they sang beside the body of her beloved John, —

> "Waiting to receive thy spirit,
>   Lo! the Saviour stands above;
> Shows the purchase of His merit,
>   Reaches out the crown of love."

The excitement was so great when it was learned that Wesley was dead, that it was decided to have the funeral at five in the morning. He was buried March 9, behind the chapel in City Road.

He left "six pounds, to be divided among the six poor men, named by the assistant, who shall carry my body to the grave; for I particularly desire there may be no hearse, no coach, no escutcheon, no pomp, except the tears of those that loved me, and are following me to Abraham's bosom."

A great multitude came notwithstanding the early hour, and sobbed aloud when their precious dead was buried from their sight.

Eighty-five years afterwards, in 1876, a mural tablet was unveiled in Westminster Abbey by the lamented Dean Stanley, bearing the faces of John and Charles Wesley, with these words of John, "I look upon all the world as my parish"; his dying words, "The best of all is, God is with us"; and the words of Charles, "God buries His workmen, but carries on His work."

Southey said, "I consider Wesley as the most influential mind of the last century; the man who will have produced the greatest effects, centuries, or, perhaps, millenniums hence, if the present race of men should continue so long." Theodore Parker said, "John Wesley was the greatest organizer a thousand years have produced."

Wonderful son of a wonderful mother! Both educated, both saving every moment, both cheerful. Wesley said, "I do not remember to have felt lowness of spirits for one quarter of an hour since I was born." Both brave to meet every trial; both consecrated to the winning of souls.

"The world is my parish!" Thus it has proved. What have been the results of that godly training at Epworth

Rectory, and of the little band of Methodists at Oxford in 1729?

One hundred years have passed away since Wesley died in 1791. This year, 1891, the Second Methodist Ecumenical Council, with five hundred delegates in attendance, has been held at Washington, D. C. The following statistics were there given: Methodist churches in the United States, fifty-five thousand, — more than one-third of all the churches in our country; thirty-six thousand Methodist ministers, besides thirty thousand local preachers; five million communicants, and twenty million adherents, with a church property worth two hundred million dollars.

What a record since Francis Asbury, the son of peasant parents, came to this country in 1771, without a cent in his pocket! "His daily rides," says Rev. Luke Tyerman in his "Life of Wesley," "were often from thirty to fifty miles over mountains and swamps, through bridgeless rivers and pathless woods, his horse frequently weary and lame, and he himself wet, cold, and hungry. For forty-five years, when steamboats, stage-coaches, railways, and almost roads, were utterly unknown, Asbury made a tour of the American States, travelling never less than five thousand, and often more than six thousand, miles a year, and this generally on horseback. . . .

"Usually, he preached at least once every week day, and thrice every Sunday; delivering, during his ministry in America, more than twenty thousand sermons. . . . Most of his life was spent on horseback, in extemporized pulpits, or in log-cabins crowded with talking men and noisy women, bawling children, and barking dogs, — cabins which he was obliged to make his offices and studies, and where, with benumbed fingers, frozen ink, impracticable pens, and rumpled paper, he had to write his sermons, his journals, and his letters." He died in 1816, and was followed to his grave, in Baltimore, by twenty-five thousand of his friends.

Besides this grand record in the New World, what have been the results of Wesley's work in the Old? "The total for the world, one hundred years after the death of Wesley," says the Rev. D. H. Muller, D. D., of Cleveland, Ohio, to whom I am indebted for the above figures, "is forty-two thousand itinerant Methodist ministers, eighty-seven thousand local preachers, six million (6,147,000) members, with twenty-five million adherents."

Dr. Dobbin might well say: "A greater poet may arise than Homer or Milton, a greater theologian than Calvin, a greater philosopher than Bacon, a greater dramatist than any of ancient or modern fame, but a more distinguished revivalist of the churches than John Wesley, never."

It was a blessing to the world that Susanna Wesley ever lived, and the work of her and her noble son is only in its beginning. What shall it be centuries from now?

HARRIET MARTINEAU.

ONE of my greatest pleasures in a walking trip through the English lake district was a visit to the home of Harriet Martineau, "The Knoll," at Ambleside. The distinguished woman and author had gone out of it by death six years before, but the sunny rooms, and books, and vines were as she left them.

The gothic, gray stone cottage was a mass of exquisite color from the green ivy, the white clematis, the purple passion flower, the red Virginia creeper, the yellow honeysuckle, and roses, many of these flowers in abundant bloom, and clambering to the very top of the house.

Here were the trees which Wordsworth, Macready, and other visitors had planted. Here were the narrow stone steps leading to the garden, where I gathered, at the suggestion of the courteous owner of "The Knoll," flowers of many varieties, which the woman who belonged to America as well as to England had planted. Here was the gray granite sun-dial, in the shape of a gothic font, with its motto, "Come, Light! visit me!" sent her by Miss Sturch of London, in remembrance of a dial in the garden of her maternal grandfather, which she loved when a child.

The house was cheery and homelike. On the right of the hall was the drawing-room, full of sunlight through

HARRIET MARTINEAU.
(1833.)

its long windows, and rich in gifts of pictures, statuary, and books from celebrated friends, — Florence Nightingale; Charles Darwin, Jacob Bright, H. Crabbe Robinson, Lady Byron, Mrs. Carlyle, and others.

When the mother of the noble Col. Robert G. Shaw, the first white colonel of the first black regiment raised during our Civil War, sent her son's picture to Miss Martineau, it was hung in a conspicuous place. "It always melts my heart to look at it," she said; "and think of that great deed that proved two races worthy of each other, and helped to save your land for both!"

Col. Shaw fell in the attack upon Fort Wagner, on the night of July 18, 1863. As his regiment, the Fifty-Fourth Massachusetts Infantry, rushed on the double-quick to the charge, his last words were, "We shall take the fort or die there." He was shot through the heart. The next morning the dead and dying were found piled three feet deep upon each other. Col. Shaw was buried among the black soldiers, who showed that day that they were brave enough and true enough to stand among the free forever.

Opposite this drawing-room was the study, used also as a dining-room, the walls covered with books on art, education, political economy, philosophy, theology, and general literature; dictionaries, encyclopedias, annuals, hand-books, — in short, whatever a gifted and unusual mind could need for its work.

Back of these two rooms was the only other room on the ground floor, the large, sunny kitchen, with its library for servants — a feature which wisely might be copied in other homes.

Above, the sleeping rooms were as airy and cheerful as those below. Here George Eliot, Emerson, Charlotte Brontë, and other noted men and women had been her guests. From here the brilliant, lonely genius from Haworth, the author of "Jane Eyre," wrote to her sister Emily: "Her [Miss Martineau's] visitors enjoy the most perfect liberty; what she claims for herself she allows them. I rise at my own hour, breakfast alone. . . . I pass the morning in the drawing-room, she in her study. At two o'clock we meet, talk and walk till five, — her dinner hour, — spend the evening together, when she converses fluently and abundantly, and with the most complete frankness. I go to my room soon after ten, and she sits up writing letters. She appears exhaustless in strength and spirits, and indefatigable in the faculty of labor: she is a great and good woman."

Why do thousands, year after year, visit the home of Harriet Martineau? Because she was, as Thomas Wentworth Higginson truly says, "in many respects the ablest and most helpful woman whom this century or any century has produced."

Americans will always owe her gratitude and honor for her attitude on slavery — a system which the South now disbelieves in not less than the North — and for her deep interest and aid in the time of our Civil War. The Hon. W. E. Forster, in his great speech at Bradford, England, said that "it seemed as if she alone was keeping the country straight in regard to America."

Harriet Martineau, born June 12, 1802, was descended from the Huguenots, a party of whom, after the Revocation of the Edict of Nantes in 1688, settled in Norwich, England. Her father, Thomas Martineau, a manufacturer of bombazines and camlets, was a gentle, refined, peace-loving man who, failing in business, died under the stress of pecuniary troubles. "Humble, simple, upright, self-denying, affectionate to as many people as possible, and kindly to all," said Harriet in after years, "he gave no pain and did all the good he could."

The mother, Elizabeth Rankin, the daughter of a sugar refiner of Newcastle-on-Tyne, was a woman of strong will, dominant temperament, probably rendered less amiable by her husband's losses and the care of eight children, for whom she and her husband, says Harriet in her autobiography, "exercised every kind of self-denial to bring us up qualified to take care of ourselves. They pinched themselves in luxuries to provide their girls, as well as their boys, with masters and schooling; and they brought us up to an industry like their own; — the boys in study and business, and the girls in study and household cares."

Harriet was the sixth child, rather plain and sickly. Her childhood was not a happy one. System and duty seemed to be the watchwords of the home. There was little time, and apparently no inclination, for words of endearment or appreciation. The father was too heavily weighted with cares, and the mother too busy teaching her family how to sew and to cook, and to spend every minute in work. Time for everything but love!

Mrs. Martineau was devoted to her children as far as working for them was concerned, but instead of caresses, she used that sharpest of all weapons, sarcasm, which cuts both ways, the user and the one on whom it is used.

When Harriet was sent with sarcastic messages to the maids, such as "Bid them not to be so like cart-horses overhead," she says, "It was impossible to give such an one as that: so I used to linger and delay to the last moment, and then deliver something civil, with all imaginable sheepishness, so that the maids used to look at one another and laugh."

Harriet was very susceptible to kindness, and was unhappy because she felt that nobody loved her. "A friend asked me," she says, "why my mother sat sewing diligently for us children, and sat up at night to mend my stockings, if she did not care for me; and I was convinced at once;—only too happy to believe it, and being unable to resist such evidence as the stocking-mending at night, when we children were asleep."

Once when she had a severe earache, Mrs. Martineau took the little girl on her lap and laid the ear against her breast. "I was afraid of spoiling her starched muslin handkerchief with the tears which *would* come; but I was very happy, and wished that I need never move again," she wrote in middle life.

At another time, when she was sent twice to find some cravats in a drawer, with the usual remark that "she was more trouble than she was worth," and they were at last found in another place, her mother kissed her, and said, "And now, my dear, I have to beg *your* pardon." The girl answered with tears, but the words cheered her for long afterwards.

A wretched habit seems to have prevailed in the Martineau home, that of "taking down" any member who showed any self-appreciation. Self-conceit is one thing, but a true self-appreciation is quite another. Let a child be told repeatedly that he or she is awkward, plain, unlovely, or stupid, and he is very apt to become so. The whole world loves and needs encouragement. We are not told that the habit of whipping was indulged in, that form of brutality, happily, having passed away from most schools, and the better class of homes in England and America.

Harriet Martineau said years later in her book, "Household Education": "It should never be forgotten that the happier a child is the cleverer he will be. This is not only because in a state of happiness the mind is free, and at liberty for the exercise of its faculties instead of spending its thoughts and energy in brooding over troubles, but also because the action of the brain is stronger when the frame is in a state of hilarity; the ideas are more clear, impressions of outward objects are more vivid, and the memory will not let them slip."

The sternness in the Martineau household bred deception. Neither children nor adults give their confidence when they know they will be blamed. "In my childhood," says Harriet Martineau, "I would assert or deny anything to my mother that would bring me through most easily. . . . This was so exclusively to one person that, though there were remonstrance and punishment, I was never regarded as a liar in the family."

The child used often to long for heaven, which she thought was a place "gay with yellow and lilac crocuses," and sometimes meditated suicide as a way of getting there. She was always fond of color. She tells this incident of her childhood : —

"One crimson and purple sunrise I well remember, when James [her youngest brother] could hardly walk alone, and I could not therefore have been more than five. I awoke very early, that summer morning, and saw the maid sound asleep in her bed, and 'the baby' in his crib. The room was at the top of the house. . . . I crept out of bed, saw James's pink toes showing themselves invitingly through the rails of his crib, and gently pinched them to wake him. With a world of trouble I got him over the side and helped him to the window and upon a chair there. I wickedly opened the window, and the cool air blew in; and yet the maid did not wake. Our arms were smutted with the black on the window-sill, and our bare feet were corded with the impression of the rush-bottomed chair; but we were not found out. The sky was gorgeous."

When Harriet was seven a peculiar and unexpected happiness came to her. One Sunday when the family had gone to church, she found on the table an old calf-bound volume of "Paradise Lost." She read it eagerly, and went to sleep at night repeating it, till she knew the book almost by heart.

At nine years of age the frail child was sent into the country in exchange for a girl who wished to come to Norwich for study. This brought never-to-be-forgotten days. Long afterwards she said, "I never see chestnuts bursting from their sheaths, and lying shining among the autumn leaves, without remembering the old manor-house where we children picked up chestnuts in the avenue, while my hostess made her call at the house. I have always loved orchards and apple-gatherings since, and blossomy lanes."

The youngest child, Ellen, was born in the Martineau home in the year 1811, much to the delight of the young reader of Milton, who informed a friend that she, then nine years old, "should now see the growth of a human mind from the very beginning!"

The baby Ellen was a great joy to Harriet, with her repressed affections. She hurried through her lessons to get time to watch the infant, kissed her eagerly, and, when she was vaccinated, "locked her door and prayed long and desperately" that Ellen might soon recover.

Thomas, the oldest brother, taught his sisters Latin; Henry taught them writing and arithmetic, while Harriet also took music lessons and French. She thinks she was indolent naturally, but if so, she overcame it wonderfully.

She was an inquisitive child, like her brother James, afterwards the well-known minister. When she was ten, and he about eight, having heard that the round earth "swims in space," they determined to prove it by digging in their garden till they reached the other side. After digging through two feet of soil, they came upon a mass of rubbish, broken bricks and pottery, which stopped their progress. They then altered their plan, dug graves and lay down in them, to learn "what dying was like."

At eleven Harriet and her sister Rachel went to a school for boys and girls, taught by the Rev. Isaac Perry. Harriet read Cicero, Virgil, and Tacitus, taking great delight in the latter, especially, and in mathematics. "In an intellectual life I found then," she says, "as I have found since, refuge from moral suffering, and an always unexhausted spring of moral strength and enjoyment."

At the end of two years, Mr. Perry's school closed because he could not make ends meet, and Harriet went back to the old, unhappy life. At thirteen she had begun to grow deaf. At first it seemed an almost unbearable sorrow. It was such a privation as those only know who have experienced it. But she made a "vow of patience"—"that I would smile in every moment of anguish from it; and that I would never lose temper at any consequences from it. . . . With such a temper as mine was then, an infliction so worrying, so unintermitting, so mortifying, so isolating as loss of hearing must 'kill or cure.' In time, it acted with me as a cure."

She thought late in life that her great sorrow was about the best thing that had ever happened to her; "the best, in a selfish view, as the grandest impulse to self-mastery; and the best in a higher view, as my most peculiar opportunity of helping others."

In 1834 she published her valuable "Letter to the Deaf," which had a wide circulation. In it she says, "We can never get beyond the necessity of keeping in full view the worst and the best that can be made of our lot. The worst is either to sink under the trial or be made callous by it. The best is to be as wise as possible under a great disability, and as happy as possible under a great privation."

Harriet spent fifteen months at a school in Bristol, and then her education was considered as finished. She used to rise early and study Italian and Latin before breakfast, and philosophy in hours stolen from sleep, but the days were spent in sewing, — making fancy work when there were no clothes to be made, — as this was supposed to constitute the proper work for women. Even Jane Austen kept her manuscript covered with a large piece of muslin, so that "genteel people," when they called, would not think she was stepping outside of her sphere.

Harriet Martineau, though fond of needle work, regretted through life having spent such "a frightful amount of time in sewing," and wasting her nerve power. "No one," she says in her "Household Education," "can well be more fond of sewing than I am, and few, except professional seamstresses, have done more of it, and my testimony is that it is a most hurtful occupation, except when great moderation is observed. . . . There is something in prolonged sewing which is remarkably exhausting to the strength, and irritating beyond endurance to the nerves."

At nineteen, the unsatisfied life was to be somewhat changed. James was going back to college, and, seeing that she was so unhappy at his absence, he advised her to try authorship. As whatever James said was law with her, she began at seven one bright September morning, an article for a small Unitarian journal, the *Monthly Repository*, on the subject, "Female Writers on Practical Divinity." She told no one what she was doing, and when the article was completed, signed it "Discipulus," and carried it to the post-office.

To her surprise the article appeared in the next number. On Sunday evening her brother Thomas, a physician, she having gone to his house to tea, proposed to read to the family the new *Monthly Repository*. "They have got a new hand here," he said. "Listen." And after reading a while, he added, "Ah! this is a new hand; they have had nothing so good as this for a long while."

As Harriet said nothing in praise, he was surprised and finally exclaimed, "What is the matter with you? I never knew you so slow to praise anything before." She replied in confusion, "The truth is, that paper is mine." He laid his hand upon her shoulder, and said gravely, "Now, dear, leave it to other women to make shirts and darn stockings; and do you devote yourself to this."

"I went home," she says, "in a sort of dream, so that the squares of the pavement seemed to float before my eyes. That evening made me an authoress."

The literary work was continued. In 1823 a little volume of hers was published anonymously, called "Devotional Exercises," which were reflections and prayers for young persons. A year or two later, another book, which was a great comfort to her father, was published, entitled "Addresses, Prayers, and Hymns."

Dr. Thomas Martineau, the oldest brother, to whom Harriet was much attached, died in 1824, and her father, losing nearly all his property in the bank failures of 1825, died the following year.

With these sorrows had come one great joy. Mr. Worthington, a classmate of James's, and like him fitting for the Unitarian ministry, had spent his vacation at Norwich, and had fallen in love with Harriet. As he was poor, and Harriet was supposed to have property, he had hesitated to offer himself, though his affection was known and reciprocated. James did not favor the union, as he feared Harriet's strong nature would clash with Mr. Worthington's more gentle; but love has powers of which James Martineau, at that time of life, knew nothing. The love affair did not at that time end in an engagement, and both were anxious and dissatisfied.

After the death of the father, and it was found that his family were left poor, Mr. Worthington offered himself and was accepted. He was associated in the charge of a large church in Manchester, broke down from overwork and previous worry, and had brain fever, by which his mind became unbalanced. The physician recommended that Harriet be sent for, as her presence might help to effect a cure.

The mother of the young minister sent for Harriet, but Mrs. Martineau forbade her daughter to go. Accustomed to obey, though well-nigh heartbroken, the girl of twenty-four waited for some weeks, till Mr. Worthington's death made a visit no longer necessary. His family were embittered by her apparent neglect, and had been given to understand, by some mischievous person, that Harriet was engaged to another. It was evident that somebody deserved a lifelong remorse, and possibly had it.

What this love and death were to Harriet, she has shown in various portions of her writings. In an essay in the

Monthly Repository, entitled "In a Death Chamber," she says: "In watching by the couch of another, there is no weariness; but this lonely tending of one's own sick heart is more than the worn-out spirit can bear. . . . What is aught to me, in the midst of this all-pervading, thrilling torture, when all I want is to be dead? . . . Since the love itself is wrecked, let me gather up its relics, and guard them more tenderly, more steadily, more gratefully. . . . Oh, grant me power to retain them — the light and music of emotion, the flow of domestic wisdom and chastened mirth, the lifelong watchfulness of benevolence, the thousand thoughts — are these gone in their reality? . . . If I were to see *my* departed one — that insensible, wasted form — standing before me as it was wont to stand, with whom would I exchange my joy?"

To Harriet Martineau love beautified and transfigured commonplace life. She says, "In a Hermit's Cave," "Where this flame, the glow of human love, is burning, there is the temple of worship, be it only beside the humblest village hearth. . . . Would that all could know how, by this mighty impulse, new strength is given to every power; how the intellect is vivified and enlarged; how the spirit becomes bold to explore the path of life, and clear-sighted to discern its issues."

Later she says in her "Tale of the Tyne," in a conversation between a young husband and wife: "Do you really think there are any people that have passed through life without knowing what that moment was, that stir in one's heart on being first sure that one is beloved? It is most like the soul getting free of the body and rushing into Paradise, I should think," says the wife. And then, in most expressive language, the husband voices his experience: "I felt as if I could have brought the whole world nearer to God, if they would have listened to me. I shall never forget the best moment of all — when my mind had suddenly ceased being in a great tumult, which had as much pain as pleasure in it. When I said distinctly to myself, 'She loves me.' Heaven came down round about me that minute."

After the joys and the sorrows, Harriet worked harder than ever. She wrote a "Life of Howard" for the Diffusion of Knowledge Society, for which she was promised thirty pounds. The Society claimed that the manuscript was lost, though she found afterwards that portions of it were used to adorn another life of Howard! She never received a penny for it.

To make matters worse, the reduced business left by her father became bankrupt, and the family were left with the merest pittance. Harriet had, she says, "precisely one shilling in my purse." She did not regard the losses as a calamity. "Many and many a time since," she writes, "have we said that, but for that loss of money, we might have lived on in the ordinary provincial method of ladies with small means, sewing and economizing, and growing narrower every year: whereas, by being thrown, while it was yet time, on our own resources, we have worked hard and usefully, won friends, reputation, and independence, seen the world abundantly, abroad and at home, and, in short, have truly lived instead of vegetated."

It was arranged that two of the sisters should teach, but what could the deaf Harriet do? She could sew, and at once she began to make fancy work to sell. All day long she worked with her needle, and at night with her pen, earning very little in both ways.

"The quantity I wrote, at prodigious expenditure of

nerve, surprises me now, after my long breaking-in to hard work. Every night that winter, I believe, I was writing till two, or even three in the morning, — obeying always the rule of the house, — of being present at the breakfast table as the clock struck eight. Many a time I was in such a state of nervous exhaustion and distress that I was obliged to walk to and fro in the room before I could put on paper the last line of a page, or the last half-sentence of an essay, or review."

These days of anxiety wore upon her. She said, twenty years afterwards, that people who knew her in the early years did not recognize her or her portraits later. "The frown of those old days, the rigid face, the sulky mouth, the forbidding countenance, which looked as if it had never had a smile upon it, told a melancholy story which came to an end long ago."

She sold a ball-dress — she had no more need of it — for three pounds, and thus had a little spending money. For two years she lived on fifty pounds a year.

She told Mr. Fox, the editor of the *Monthly Repository*, that she could no longer write for him gratuitously, so fifteen pounds a year were given her for her monthly contributions, — book reviews, poems, and essays. The wear and tear of literary life had but just begun. She was yet to travel over the old road so familiar to most writers. She offered her sketches to editors of magazines and publishers, and they were scarcely looked at. She had no literary friends or acquaintances. In despair, the sketches were sent at last to the *Monthly Repository*, which brought no fame, and little money. She had used three stories in the *Repository*, which had been so much liked that she determined to bring them out in a little book, under the title of "Traditions of Palestine."

When these were going through the press, she went to London, staying with a relative. Mr. Fox, knowing how desirous she was to earn her living by her pen, obtained for her an offer from a printer to correct proof if she desired to remain in London, thinking that she would get journalistic work after a time. She was overjoyed, and wrote to her mother of her wish to remain.

Meantime the relative had written to Mrs. Martineau that Harriet would earn little by writing, and that she would better return to Norwich, where it seemed evident that she did not starve by sewing. Mrs. Martineau was convinced, and at once wrote to Harriet, then twenty-seven, a peremptory letter to return home. The relative gave Harriet some lilac, blue, and pink pieces of silk, and advised her to make little bags and baskets for sale.

Harriet went back to Norwich with "grief and desolation in her heart." The mistaken mother, who thought she was doing the best for her daughter, was so distressed by her pale and anxious face, that she made Harriet go to bed, while she sat beside her and talked with her.

At this time the Central Unitarian Association had advertised for prize essays, by which Unitarianism was to be presented to Catholics, Jews, and Mohammedans. Always deeply interested in theology, Harriet determined to try for *all* the prizes. The prizes were ten, fifteen, and twenty guineas.

The first essay was written in a month, and copied, so as not to be seen in her handwriting, by a poor-school boy, to whom she gave a sovereign, which she could ill afford. Then she wrote "Five Years of Youth," two hundred and sixty-four pages, for which she received twenty pounds. After this came the essays to the Jews and the Mohammedans.

"The task became very onerous before it was done," she says. "I was by that time nearly as thin as possible, and I dreamed of the destruction of Jerusalem, and saw the burning of the Temple almost every night."

To her astonishment, and that of her mother, Harriet, though there were many learned competitors, received all the prizes, forty-five guineas! The prize-money enabled the tired woman to go to Dublin on a visit to her brother James and his wife.

Four years previously, in 1827, in reading Mrs. Marcet's "Conversations on Political Economy," she had become more than ever interested in the science, — her two stories, "The Rioters" and the "Turn-Out," having been in that vein, — and felt that she might diffuse practical ideas among the people by a series of stories on this subject. She felt that the people needed lessons in economy, about property, taxes, wealth, and all that pertains to good citizenship.

She thought out her plan carefully, — that of writing a series of brief books, - and wrote to some London publishers, offering the series. She received refusals by return of mail. Finally, with a brave heart, the unknown author started for London in the beginning of December, to seek personal interviews with publishers.

Day after day, for three long weeks, in the mud and fog, she visited strangers, the indifferent publishers all saying "No" into her ear-trumpet. They made substantially the same excuse, — "Considering the public excitement about the Reform Bill and the cholera, they dared not venture." "I was growing as sick of the Reform Bill," she says, "as poor King William himself."

Night after night she worked till long after twelve o'clock, determined that the first two numbers should be written, because she believed that the people wanted the books. If the people did, it was evident that the publishers wanted no stories on political economy.

She kept up as bravely as she could. She says, "I was resolved, in the first place, the thing should be done. . . . Next, I resolved to sustain my health under the suspense, if possible, by keeping up a mood of steady determination, and unfaltering hope. Next, I resolved never to lose my temper in the whole course of the business. I knew I was right; and people who are aware that they are in the right need never lose temper."

Finally, she took one day's rest at the house of Mr. Fox, and touched by the sympathy of the family, she spent nearly the whole night crying. Help came at last, as it usually comes,—through friendship. Mr. Fox got his brother, Mr. Charles Fox, a young and poor bookseller, to make Miss Martineau a proposition.

It was not a generous one, as it saved him from all risk, but it was something that he was willing to touch the matter at all, where others had refused. First, five hundred subscribers must be obtained for the works. Second, Mr. Fox was to have half the profits, after the usual bookseller's commission; and, third, a thousand must be sold in the first fortnight after issue, or he would withdraw from the contract.

Her pride rose against soliciting subscriptions for her own books, as she knew that the whole labor would fall upon her. But there was no alternative. She made ready her circulars and sent them out. By the advice of Mrs. Martineau, a prospectus was sent to each member of Parliament, but without request to buy. Some kind words and orders came, but slowly. The husband of a cousin sent her two sovereigns, gave her a lecture on her rashness in undertaking authorship, and recommended "a family subscription to eke out her earnings with her needle." She returned the two sovereigns. After she was famous, the gentleman apologized.

One night, while the circulars were being sent out, she became well-nigh discouraged. She had finished the preface to her "Illustrations of Political Economy" at two o'clock at night; had cried before the open fire till four; cried in bed till six; fell asleep, but was at the breakfast-table at half-past eight, ready for the daily drudgery again.

The first edition printed was fifteen hundred copies. At the end of ten days, Mr. Charles Fox sent her a letter, with a copy of her book. A postscript informed her that he should need three thousand copies; a second postscript, four thousand; and a third postscript, five thousand!

She says, "I remember walking up and down the grass-plot in the garden (I think it was on the tenth of February), feeling that my cares were over. And so they were. From that hour, I have never had any other anxiety about employment than what to choose, nor any real care about money."

The whole press seemed to speak in Miss Martineau's favor. The Society for the Diffusion of Knowledge, which had refused one of her stories ("Brooke and Brooke Farm"), now begged to bring out the whole series. Lord Brougham, who was one of the committee, "tore his hair," she says, "unable to endure that the whole society, 'instituted,' as he said, 'for the very purpose, should be driven out of the field by a little deaf woman at Norwich.'"

Mr. Hume, on behalf of a new society, offered her any price she would name for the whole series. She was besought on every side to take up various subjects for treatment, under the guise of fiction. Members of Parliament sent blue-books through the post-office, till the postmaster sent her word "that she must send for her share of the mail, for it could not be carried without a barrow."

It soon became evident that Miss Martineau must live in London to be near the libraries. She moved thither at thirty years of age, and a life of fame and honor in the great world began.

"I have had no spring," she said, some years later; "but that cannot be helped now. It was a moral disadvantage, as well as a great loss of happiness; but we all have our moral disadvantages to make the best of; and 'happiness' is *not*, as the poet says, 'our being's end and aim,' but the result of one faculty among many, which must be occasionally overborne by others if there is to be any effectual exercise of the whole being. . . . I had now, by thirty years of age, ascertained my career, found occupation, and achieved independence. . . . Any one to whom that happens by thirty years of age may be satisfied; and I was so."

She had promised to produce a book a month, of from one hundred and twenty to one hundred and fifty pages. Besides writing her story, she had to read carefully upon every topic.

Her daily life was regular. She rose at seven, made her own coffee, and began work immediately, remaining at her desk till two. Till four, she received visitors, who came on all possible pretexts, — she could not return calls for lack of time, — and after four took her daily walk till dinner, when a carriage was always in waiting to take her to some distinguished home.

She met and enjoyed the most noted people of her time.

Hallam was a valued friend. At the breakfasts of Rogers, the poet, she met Dean Milman, Lord Jeffrey, Southey (then growing old), and others. The inimitable Sydney Smith came often to her home, — he was as fast a talker as she or Macaulay, and full of wit. It was always his boast that Miss Martineau needed no trumpet when he talked with her. She said "his voice was to her like the great bell of St. Paul's."

Hawthorne said of Miss Martineau: "She is the most continual talker I ever heard. It is really like the babbling of a brook, and very lively and sensible, too; and all the while she talks, she moves the bowl of her ear-trumpet from one auditor to another, so that it becomes quite an organ of intelligence and sympathy between her and yourself."

Richard Monckton Milnes (Lord Houghton), whom Sydney Smith called "The Cool of the Evening," came often to see her. Mr. Grote, the historian, then the leading member of the radical section in Parliament, came with Mrs. Grote. Eastlake was home from Italy, and most interesting. Landseer was an agreeable companion. Barry Cornwall, modest and kind, was a delightful acquisition to any circle. Mary Russell Mitford came to the Martineau home, — Mrs. Martineau had come to live with her daughter, — and Letitia E. Landon, before she went to the Cape Coast to meet her pitiful fate.

Browning she met and liked. "He is a real genius," she said. "Mr. Macready put 'Paracelsus' into my hand when I was staying at his house, and I read a canto before going to bed. For the first time in my life, I passed a whole night without sleeping a wink."

She frequently visited at the homes of Mrs. Somerville and Carlyle, in Chelsea. She said of the latter, "His excess of sympathy has been, I believe, the master-pain of his life. He does not know what to do with it and with its bitterness, seeing that human life is full of pain to those who look out for it; and the savageness which has come to be a main characteristic of this singular man, is, in my opinion, a mere expression of his intolerable sympathy with the suffering."

Miss Martineau arranged several courses of lectures for him at a time when the money from them was most acceptable. But he was obliged to discontinue them from his nervousness. "Yellow as a guinea," she says, "with downcast eyes, broken speech at the beginning, and fingers which nervously picked at the desk before him, he could not for a moment be supposed to enjoy his own effort; and the lecturer's own enjoyment is a prime element of success."

She met Coleridge, who told her he waited for her books from month to month. "He is not sixty and looks eighty. . . . He is most neatly dressed in black; has perfectly white hair; the under lip quivering with the touching expression of weakness which is sometimes seen in old age; the face neither pale nor thin; and the eyes — I never saw such! glittering and shining so that one can scarcely meet them."

Her thirty-four volumes were written in about two years and a half. She never believed in waiting for inspiration in writing. She says, "I have suffered, like other writers, from indolence, irresolution, distaste to my work, absence of 'inspiration,' and all that; but I have also found that sitting down, however reluctantly, with the pen in my hand, I have never worked for one quarter of an hour without finding myself in full train; so that all the quarter hours, arguings, doubtings, and hesitation as to whether

I should work or not which I gave way to in my inexperience, I now regard as so much waste, not only of time but, far worse, of energy."

She worked without stimulants. When told by a physician that she had better "keep a bottle of hock and a wine-glass in the cupboard, and help herself when she felt that she wanted it," she replied, "No, thank you. If I took wine, it should not be when alone; nor would I help myself to a glass. I might take a little more and a little more, till my solitary glass might become a regular tippling habit. I shall avoid the temptation altogether." Again she said, "Fresh air and cold water are my stimulants."

Her books were read and talked about everywhere. Archbishop Whately thought "The Parish" the best of them. After the "Guide to Service" was written, at the request of the Poor-Law Commissioners, so graphic was it, that it was reported that Miss Martineau had been in service as a "maid-of-all-work." After "A Manchester Strike" appeared, the people were positive that she had worked in a cotton mill. After "Vanderput and Snoek," the favorite of Hallam, a story on Bills of Exchange, it was said that she surely must have lived in Holland.

Some of her works gave offence, as the "French Wines and Politics," laid in the time of the French Revolution. Louis Philippe, who had read the series and wished to have them introduced into the national schools, now objected. Miss Martineau was apprised of his disaffection and replied, "I wrote with a view to the people, and especially the most suffering of them; and the crowned heads must, for once, take their chance for their feelings."

The Tsar of Russia had also been delighted with the series, and by his orders great numbers had been bought for the schools. When "The Charmed Sea" appeared, the characters, exiled Poles in the mines of Eastern Siberia, — the question discussed being the origin of the currency, — the Tsar ordered every copy of her works burnt, and forbade that she should ever set foot upon Russian soil. Evidently there were some matters in Siberia, then as now, that the Tsar preferred should not come to light. Austria was also disturbed to have any sympathy excited for the Poles, and forbade her entering the country.

Some of her own nation were hurt at the plain but needed words on over-population and consequent poverty, in her "Weal and Woe in Garveloch." But Harriet Martineau was not one to be afraid, wherever she thought duty called her.

"Sowers not Reapers" is an Anti Corn-Law story; "The Loom and the Lugger" is upon Free Trade; "Demerara" on Slavery; five of the stories were written at the request of Lord Brougham and Mrs. Fry, on Pauperism and Its Remedies.

Nearly twenty years after this time Miss Martineau had received about two thousand pounds as her share from the little books. "I got a hearing," she says; "which was the thing I wanted."

Worn with her arduous work, she determined to travel; but where? Lord Henley, a friend who was deeply interested in philanthropy, said, "Will you not go to America? Whatever else may or may not be true about the Americans, it is certain that they have got at principles of justice and mercy in their treatment of the least happy classes of society, which we should do well to understand. Will you not go, and tell us what they are?"

The more Harriet Martineau thought upon the new

world, the stronger grew her desire to see it and its people. She sailed for America early in August, 1834. After forty-two days on the Atlantic, she and her friend, whose expenses she paid in America, except the passage money, arrived in New York.

Miss Martineau's fame had preceded her. For nearly two years she travelled East, South, and West. In Washington she met socially the most distinguished persons, like Webster and Clay. Chief Justice Marshall gave her " a general letter of introduction," asking " aid and protection" for " two English ladies of distinction," and stating that " he individually should feel himself under obligations" to anybody who could be useful to them. In Boston and New York she was entertained in homes of elegance and culture.

She came to America for rest, and yet such a woman could not help studying our institutions and our people. She found both North and South exercised over the terrible evil of slavery. She saw Garrison dragged through the streets of Boston by a mob composed of gentlemen!

Desiring to learn all that was possible she attended, with some friends, a meeting of anti-slavery women. She was asked if she would give a word of sympathy. She knew how the Abolitionists were despised, but she felt that she must be true to her convictions, whatever the result to herself.

She rose and said, "I will say what I have said through the whole South, in every family where I have been; that I consider slavery as inconsistent with the law of God, and as incompatible with the course of his providence. I should certainly say no less at the North than at the South concerning this utter abomination — and I now declare that in your *principles* I fully agree."

At once she met the usual opprobrium of press and people given to all leaders in an unpopular cause. The world has never been tolerant, though fortunately the despised of to-day becomes the idol of to-morrow, if the cause be just and right.

Miss Martineau was called "a foreign incendiary," and her life was threatened, so bound hand and foot was the nation by the slave power. She was told in 1835 by leading statesmen, "that the abolition of slavery would never be named in Congress," to which she replied that when they "could hedge in the wind and build out the stars from their continent, they might succeed in their proposed exclusion." Twenty-five years later it was not only named, but its very name wiped out in blood.

After two years Harriet Martineau returned to England, not saying good-by to her many friends, as she believed that she should return and perhaps die in America. Emerson and a host of others remained her friends to the last, visiting her at Ambleside in later years, and, at her request, an American lady, Mrs. Maria Weston Chapman, received all her papers after her death, and wrote her life.

As soon as Miss Martineau reached home she was besought to write a book on America. The leading London publishers called upon her, and were eager to outdo each other in their offers. She must have recalled those days when she visited them only a few years before when the "Reform Bill and Cholera" prevented their even looking at her manuscripts!

She finally accepted the offer of Messrs. Saunders & Otley to pay her three hundred pounds per volume — there were to be three volumes — for the first edition of three thousand copies. She completed in six months her work called "Society in America," in which she showed a wonderful knowledge of our plan of government, our politics, our charities, indeed our whole country, with its unsolved problems.

She had high hopes for our future: "The democratic party are fond of saying that the United States are intended to be an agricultural country. It seems to me," said she, "that they are intended for everything. The Niagara basin, the Mississippi valley, and the South will be able to furnish the trading world with agricultural products forever, — for aught we can see. But it is clear that there are other parts of the country which must have recourse to manufactures and commerce."

She believed that the time would come when the South would find free labor more profitable than slave labor — a thing now demonstrated.

"The manners of the Americans (in America)," she said, "are the best I ever saw: and these are seen to the greatest advantage in their homes; and as to the gentlemen, in travelling, if I am asked what is the peculiar charm, I reply with some hesitation, there are so many! but I believe it is not so much the outward plenty, or the mutual freedom, or the simplicity of manners, or the incessant play of humor, which characterize the whole people, as the sweet temper which is diffused like sunshine over the land. They have been called the most good-tempered people in the world; and I think they must be so. . . . I imagine that the practice of forbearance requisite in a republic is answerable for this pleasant peculiarity." Again she said, "The Americans may always be trusted to do right *in time*."

She saw and deplored the fact that we lacked some things along the line of education: "There is not even any systematic instruction given on political morals," she said; "an enormous deficiency in a republic." It is only in recent years that we have felt the necessity and the wisdom of teaching children how our country is governed, cultivating a patriotic spirit, giving lessons upon good manners and, in our higher institutions, upon social ethics, so that the student shall be fitted to act upon the great questions of the time.

In her "Society in America," she advocated suffrage for women. "That woman has power to represent her own interests, no one can deny till she has been tried. . . . The principle being once established, the methods will follow easily, naturally, and under a remarkable transmutation of the ludicrous into the sublime. The kings of Europe would have laughed mightily, two centuries ago, at the idea of a commoner, without robes, crown, or sceptre, stepping into the throne of a strong nation. Yet who dared to laugh when Washington's super-royal voice greeted the New World from the presidential chair, and the old world stood still to catch the echo?

"The principle of the equal rights of both halves of the human race is all we have to do with here. It is the true democratic principle which can never be seriously controverted, and only for a short time evaded."

She said, in her autobiography: "Let women be educated, — let their powers be cultivated to the extent for which the means are already provided, and all that is wanted or ought to be desired will follow of course. Whatever a woman proves herself able to do, society will be thankful to see her do, — just as if she were a man. If she is scientific, science will welcome her, as it has welcomed every woman so qualified. If capable of political thought and action, women will obtain even that.

"The time has not come, which certainly will come, when women who are practically concerned in political life will have a voice in making the laws which they have to obey; but every woman who can think and speak wisely, and bring up her children soundly in regard to the rights and duties of society, is advancing the time when the interests of women will be represented, as well as those of men. I have no vote at elections, though I am a tax-paying housekeeper and responsible citizen; and I regard the disability as an absurdity, seeing that I have for a long course of years influenced public affairs to an extent not professed or attempted by many men."

She was deeply interested in opening up new avenues for women to earn a living. She said in the "Edinburgh Review" for April, 1859, in an article on "Female Industry," that "three millions out of six of adult English women work for subsistence. . . . With this new condition of affairs, new duties and new views must be adopted . . . to provide for the free development and full use of the power of every member of the community."

At the suggestion of her publishers she wrote another work on America, with more incidents of persons and descriptions of scenery, called "Retrospect of Western Travel:" This was in three volumes, for which she was paid six hundred pounds. When she read the proof she said, "I wish I could write a review of my book, I see so many faults in it. There is no education like authorship for ascertaining one's knowledge and one's ignorance."

The manuscript of this work has been presented this year (1892), in his valuable collection, by Mr. George W. Childs, to the Drexel Institute of Art, Science, and Industry in Philadelphia. The librarian of the Institute writes me, concerning this manuscript, "The work is in three volumes, bound in four, in full crushed levant. The size is square quarto, and it contains portraits of her taken in 1833 and 1850. It is closely written in a legible handwriting, and is much corrected with erasures and insertions. It is in excellent condition, and is one of the important manuscripts in the collection."

The Rev. James Freeman Clarke said that both these works on America " were, perhaps, the best then written by any foreigner except De Tocqueville. They were generous, honest, kind, and utterly frank — they were full of capital descriptions of American scenery. She spoke the truth to us, and she spoke it in love. The chief faults in these works was her tone of dogmatism and her *ex cathedra* judgments."

After the books on America were finished, she wrote some valuable articles for the " Westminster Review," — " Domestic Service," and "The Martyr Age of the United States" ; and on her thirty-sixth birthday, June 12, 1838, began her first novel, "Deerbrook," and finished it in the following February. The book went through two large editions, but was criticised as to plot and characters.

In the midst of this work she had domestic trials, — her mother, now nearing seventy, was becoming blind, and her brother Henry, who lived with them, had become intemperate ; and worn with her book and her cares, she started for Switzerland and Italy. She became so ill by the time she reached Venice that she was obliged to abandon her journey, and was brought back to her sister's at Newcastle-on-Tyne, to be under the medical care of her brother-in-law, Dr. Greenhow.

In the fall, she went to Tynemouth, overlooking the sea, nine miles from Newcastle, not willing to be a care to her sister, and here she was a constant sufferer for five years. She could not go out of the house, only passing from her bed to a couch in an adjoining room.

And yet, through all these years, while enduring bodily pain, she kept on writing. Her first work was an article in behalf of Oberlin College, where, happily, nobody is debarred from study by reason of sex or color of skin.

Then, believing in the possibilities of the negro race in the way of education and good citizenship, when freed from bondage, she wrote "The Hour and the Man," a novel founded on the brave and able President of the Republic of Haiti, Toussaint l'Ouverture.

Lord Jeffrey, formerly editor of the "Edinburgh Review," was greatly moved, and said, "The book is really not only beautiful and touching, but *noble;* and I do not recollect when I have been more charmed, whether by very sweet and eloquent writing and glowing description, or by elevated as well as tender sentiments. . . . I would go a long way to kiss the hem of her garment, or the hand that delineated this glowing and lofty representation of purity and noble virtue."

Carlyle wrote to Emerson, "It is beautiful as a child's heart, and in so shrewd a brain!"

Later on, Wendell Phillips, by his eloquent lecture, made known, through the length and breadth of America, the courage and the nobility of the hero of San Domingo.

Often needing ready money in these days, as she had tied up her funds in deferred annuities, she refused to receive a pension, as she twice refused later in life. When unable to give money to the anti-slavery cause in America, she did fancy work to be sold at its fair, — one table-cover of Berlin wool, wrought in flowers and fruits, brought one hundred dollars, — wrote for its newspapers, and a long article in support of the society, when a number of persons left it because women were permitted to become members! This reads strangely, a half century later, when educated women work with men in all philanthropic efforts.

In 1841, Miss Martineau began a series of children's stories, four in number: "Settlers at Home," "The Prince and the Peasant," "Feats on the Fjord," and "The Crofton Boys." In 1843, she wrote, in six weeks, "Life in the Sick Room," a book greatly praised by Wordsworth. A little later, she wrote a little one-hundred-page story, "Dawn Island," sold for the benefit of the anti-corn league, in their great bazaar, in 1845.

All through these five years of illness, she received numerous testimonials of friendship. Sydney Smith said that "everybody who sent her game, fruit, and flowers was sure of heaven, provided always that they punctually paid the dues of the Church of England." Lady Byron sent her one hundred pounds to use in benevolence, in any way which she chose. Some other friends raised a testimonial fund of fourteen hundred pounds, and invested it for her.

In 1844, she was restored to perfect health through mesmerism, — Lord Lytton, Hallam, and others, had urged her to try it, — a fact which created widespread discussion, much disbelief in the reality of the cure, a cessation of friendly intercourse between her sister's family and herself, but the greatest joy in her own heart that she could walk again, and live, when day by day she had expected death. Her "Letters on Mesmerism" were published in the "Athenæum" in 1845. The same old intolerance came to the front, because she had not been cured in the usual way. Some were wise enough to be courteous and open to conviction. Mr. Hallam said, "I have no doubt that mesmerism, and some other things which are not mesmerism, properly so called, are fragmentary parts of some great law of the human frame which we are on the verge of discovering."

Harriet Martineau longed to see trees. She had not seen a tree for five years, "except a scrubby little affair which stood above the haven at Tynemouth." She repaired to the English lake district, and took lodgings close to Lake Windermere for six months. The view from her windows was beautiful; "one feature being," she says, "a prominent rock, crowned with firs, which so projected into the lake as to be precisely reflected in the crimson, orange, and purple waters when the pine-crest rose black into the crimson, orange, and purple sky at sunset. When the young moon hung over those black pines the beauty was so great that I could hardly believe my eyes. . . . The meadows were emerald green, and the oaks were just exchanging their May-golden hue for light green, when the sycamores, so characteristic of the region, were growing sombre in their massy foliage."

In 1845, Miss Martineau bought two acres of land, and built her pretty graystone cottage, half a mile from Ambleside, where she lived until her death. She felt great pleasure in building. Wordsworth came often to give advice about the new house. He said, mindful of the economy which most poets are obliged to practise, "When you have a visitor, you must do as we did; you must say, ' If you like to have a cup of tea with us, you are very welcome, but if you want any meat, you must pay for your board.'"

She loved to take long walks at sunset, such walks as Longfellow used to take from Boston to Cambridge, walking always towards the gorgeous light. It was a great pleasure in these walks to meet the aged poet Wordsworth. She says, "In winter, he was to be seen in his cloak, his Scotch bonnet, and green goggles, attended perhaps by half a score of cottagers' children, the youngest pulling at his cloak, or holding by his trowsers, while he cut ash switches out of the hedge for them. After his daughter's death I seldom saw him, except in his phaeton, or when I called. He gave way sadly (and inconsiderately, as regarded Mrs. Wordsworth) to his grief for his daughter's loss, and I heard that the evenings were very sad."

During the winter of 1845 she wrote three volumes of "Forest and Game-Law Tales," Mr. John Bright, from his committee on the game laws, furnishing her the evidence. The books did not have as large a sale as her other works. They were, of course, not cared for by the hunters of game who found pleasure in killing animals, but some poor persons whose crops were spoiled by the ruthless hunters, brought a load of sods one night — these were difficult to get — and left them under her window, with a dirty note on the pile, stating that the sods were "a token of gratitude for the *game-law tales*, from a poacher."

April 7, 1846, she moved into her new home, and a happy domestic life began at forty-two. She never wished to live in London. "She had always been alive," says John Morley in his "Miscellanies," "to the essential incompleteness, the dispersion, the want of steadfast self-collection, in a life much passed in London society. And we may believe that the five austere and lonely years at Tynemouth, with their evening outlook over the busy waters of the harbor-bar into the stern far-off sea, may have slowly bred in her an unwillingness to plunge again into the bustling triviality, the gossip, the distracting lightness of the world of splendid fireflies."

In the autumn of 1846 she enjoyed a journey with friends, at their expense, through the East. They studied Thebes and Philæ, Cairo, Palestine, and after eight months returned to England. They had the rare tact " to leave her perfectly free. We were silent when we chose without fear of being supposed unmannerly," a good lesson for persons who feel that they must constantly "entertain" their company.

In 1848, she wrote and published her "Eastern Life, Past and Present," which, Mr. Higginson, thinks " will for many years retain a distinctive value, however thoroughly the same scenes may be explored. More than any other of her books, it possesses a quality approaching genius in its ready grasp of details, its picturesque unrolling, its reverential appreciation of mighty symbols."

From the first year's proceeds of this book, Miss Martineau paid for her home. Her share in the second edition she gave to reducing the cost of the book. During the year 1847 she wrote "Household Education," and in the following year began a very important work for Mr. Knight, the publisher, the "History of the Peace," between the years 1815 and 1845. She shrank from the labor, as does every writer, probably, in beginning a new piece of work. " When I had laid out my plan for the history, and began upon the first portion, I sank into a state of dismay. I should hardly say 'sank,' for I never thought of giving up or stopping; but I doubt whether, at any point of my career, I ever felt so oppressed by what I had undertaken as during the first two or three weeks after I had begun the history."

She rose very early in the morning, in the winter before daylight, and took a long walk. In summer, she started on her walk about six, and returned to her breakfast at half-past seven. From eight till three she sat at her desk, stopping to read her mail at half-past ten. In the afternoon, she walked again, and read in the evening, either for her work, "or Montaigne, or Bacon, or Shakespeare, or Tennyson, or some dear old biography." Of course, she read the newspapers; how can any woman be intelligent as to the world's work without these?

The first volume of the "History" was ready for the press in six months, — she averaged seven manuscript pages a day, — and the second volume in about the same time. John Morley regards this as "an astonishing example of rapid industry." He thinks that Miss Martineau showed her good sense in not spending years over a piece of work, which in the nature of things must be supplanted by later historians.

"Literature," he says, "is no doubt a fine art — the finest of the arts — but it is also a practical art; and it is deplorable to think how much stout, instructive work might and ought to be done by people who, in dreaming of ideals in prose or verse beyond their attainment, end, like the poor Casaubon of fiction, in a little pamphlet on a particle, or else in mediocre poetry, or else in nothing. By insisting on rearing nothing short of a great monument more durable than brass, they are cutting themselves off from building the useful little mud-hut, or some of the other modest performances by which alone they are capable of serving their age. It is only one volume in a million that is not meant to perish, and to perish soon, as flowers, sunbeams, and all the other brightnesses of the earth are meant to perish." The "History of the Peace" was so successful that Miss Martineau wrote an introductory volume, covering the first fifteen years of the century.

While all this hard work was going forward, each winter she gave free courses of lectures to the working and trades people of Ambleside. There was a course on sanitary matters, — the last two of the course being on intemperance, — on her travels, on the history of England, on the history and constitution of the United States, and on the Crimean War and Russia. She was an admirable speaker, clear, interesting, and eloquent.

The amount of good to those persons who, through lack of time or mental training, do not read and inform themselves, cannot be estimated. Few, like Miss Martineau, could or would do all this work without compensation. It is cause for congratulation that in many cities in America funds have been provided for such courses to the people, as in the Lowell Institute, Boston; Cooper Institute, New York; the Peabody Institute, Baltimore; the White Fund at Lawrence, Mass., and elsewhere.

She organized a Building Society among the people, and showed them how " they were paying away, in rent, money enough to provide every head of a household with a cottage of his own in a few years." She demonstrated this by building some cottages which the workingmen could buy, a lady loaning her five hundred pounds to begin the work.

What she did in a small town is now being done in the cities of both Great Britain and America by Building and Loan Societies, and there seems now to be a possibility for most laboring men, who are willing to live without the wastefulness of drink, to own a home. She loaned her library freely to the people, and those who value their books will know what kindness of heart it requires to do this!

In 1851, Miss Martineau published "Letters on the Laws of Man's Nature and Development," really a set of questions asked by her and answered by Henry George Atkinson, F. G. S. He was a scholarly man of means, much younger than herself, not known to the public, "her dearest friend in all the world," says Mrs. F. Fenwick Miller, in her admirable life of Miss Martineau, and doubtless overrated by her. The book was agnostic in sentiment, though asserting a great First Cause. It created much bitter feeling, estranging permanently her brother, the Rev. Dr. James Martineau, who reviewed the book somewhat harshly, putting most of the blame upon Mr. Atkinson.

Lord Houghton wrote her after reading the "Letters": "I am less and less troubled about theories which I disapprove when adopted by the good and true. *You* can hold them, and hold your moral judgment and sensibilities, too. You are unharmed by what would be death to me."

Her next work was a translation and condensation into two volumes of the "Positive Philosophy" of Auguste Comte, in six volumes. The work was so well done that Comte adopted it for use among his students, and her book was retranslated into French. A friend gave her five hundred pounds for doing a work which he had long wished to see undertaken. She used over half the money in paying the whole expense of publication, and shared the profits with M. Comte.

A volume of her short stories was published in 1856, and descriptions of manufactures under the title, "Health, Husbandry, and Handicraft" in 1861. She received before her death about ten thousand pounds from her books.

She had already been asked to do an unusual work for a woman — to write "leaders" for one of the large London newspapers, the *Daily News*. During the summer of 1852 she wrote two leading editorials each week. In the autumn of this year she spent two months in Ireland, and wrote letters to the *Daily News* almost every other day. These were brought out in book form later.

During 1853 she wrote four articles each week, and then six, one each day, for the paper. Besides this she wrote long articles for the "Westminster Review" on the struggle between England and Russia in the Crimean War, on "The Census of 1851," on "Ireland," and other topics. She wrote also a "Complete Guide to the Lakes."

In 1854, her health failed, and her physician told her that she could live but a short time. She went to London for a time, the next year. She lived for twenty-one years after this, however, but during most of that period, she was a great sufferer, it was supposed from heart disease; but after her death it was found to have been from a tumor. She never left her home again in all these years, but with patience and cheerfulness she did her great work. Sometimes she was well enough to go out upon the terrace, or sit in the porch among her vines.

"On my terrace," she said, "there were two worlds extended bright before me, even when the midnight darkness hid from my bodily eyes all but the outlines of the solemn mountains that surround our valley on three sides, and the clear opening to the lake on the south. In the one of those worlds, I saw now the magnificent coast of Massachusetts in autumn, or the flowery swamps of Louisiana, or the forests of Georgia in spring, or the Illinois prairie in summer; or the blue Nile, or the brown

Sinai, or the gorgeous Petra, or the view of Damascus from the Salahiey; or the Grand Canal under a Venetian sunset, or the Black Forest in twilight, or Malta in the glare of noon, or the broad desert stretching away under the stars, or the Red Sea tossing its superb shells on shore, in the pale dawn. That is one world, all comprehended within my terrace wall, and coming up into the light at my call.

"The other and finer scenery is of that world, only beginning to be explored, of Science. . . . Wondrous beyond the comprehension of any one mind is the mass of glorious facts, and the series of mighty conceptions laid open; but the shadow of the surrounding darkness rests upon it all. The unknown always engrosses the greater part of the field of vision; and the awe of infinity sanctifies both the study and the dream."

She continued her "leaders" for the *Daily News*, sixteen hundred and forty-two in all, before she was obliged to resign in 1866, after fourteen years of labor. Her articles were on America, the Southern Confederacy, Indian Famines, Drainage in Agriculture, Syrian Improvement, The Morrill Tariff, French Free Trade, India and Cotton, Loyalty in Canada, and the like; in short, what an educated and broad-minded statesman would write.

A series of articles on "The History of British Rule in India" for the *Daily News*, were republished in a book; also a series of articles on "The Endowed Schools of Ireland." In 1859 she published a volume on "England and Her Soldiers," to aid her friend, Florence Nightingale, in her work for the army. This year and the two succeeding years she sent over ninety long articles to America for the anti-slavery publications.

She wrote also, for *Once a Week*, articles on "Representative Men," historical stories, which she called "Historiettes," and on a variety of other topics. She had also written many stories for Dickens's "Household Words."

During all the years of our Civil War she wrote for four leading English papers, keeping the people informed of the real condition of affairs, and molding opinion in favor of a whole-hearted support of our Union. She kept up an extensive correspondence with statesmen and leading persons in both countries. The *Daily News* was so warmly our friend, all through the struggle, that George William Curtis declared in *Harper's Weekly*, which he edited, " our children's children may well gratefully remember this course of the London *Daily News*." Everybody knew whose clear head and brave heart had helped to make its course what it was.

She stimulated and aided the Lancashire workers who were impoverished for lack of our cotton. She wrote for the " Atlantic Monthly " a series of articles on " Military Hygiene " to help the Northern soldiers, for whom she felt such deep sympathy. She wrote for the " Edinburgh Review" an article on "The Progress of the Negro Race," expressing her constant belief in their better future. Her history of the American Compromises, which came out in the *Daily News*, was circulated by the thousands in book form. She nullified, as far as it was possible, the influence exerted by the London *Times*. She wrote to her friend, Mrs. Chapman, " I am abundantly disgusted with Club and *Times* insolence and prejudice, and I speak and write against them with all my might. . . . I call everybody I know to witness that if we have war with the United States the *Times* may be considered answerable for it. It seems to me to be a sort of crazy malignity."

She deplored hasty words from either nation. "One insulting word," she said, "is sometimes more dangerous to nations than even a hostile deed; and always more disgraceful to him who utters it."

She knew what most of us learn in middle life, that the people who cry out for war are very often willing to stay at home and cheer on those who go to battle!

She never lost her deep concern for America. She wanted to see our best men interested in politics: "What a fine spectacle it is," she wrote Mrs. Chapman, "the higher order of citizens, the men of culture, trained tastes, and gentle manners, repairing to the field of political action because it is the field of patriotic duty!"

She was living in accordance with her oft-repeated statement, "The real and justifiable and honorable subject of interest to human beings, living and dying, is the welfare of their fellows surrounding them or surviving them." She and Florence Nightingale took an active part in the repeal of Acts ostensibly against vice, passed by Parliament in 1866 and 1869. The "Westminster Review" of 1870 helped to bring about this repeal. In 1868, through the courtesy of the *Daily News*, her "Biographical Sketches," published in that paper, were put into a book, and went through four editions in England. The book was reprinted in America.

The articles were graphic, analytic, and interesting, though occasionally they seemed harsh; but she meant always to be just. "I had a devouring passion for justice," she said of her youth; "justice first to my own precious self, and then to other oppressed people. Justice was precisely what was least understood in our house, in regard to servants and children." She said of Charlotte Brontë that she had, "in addition to the deep intuitions of a gifted woman, the strength of a man, the patience of a hero, and the conscientiousness of a saint."

Macaulay, she thought, as a talker, "perhaps unrivalled." His life was mainly intellectual, "brilliant, and stimulating," but wanting heart. Those who have read Trevelyan's life of him can scarcely agree with her.

The last years were drawing nigh. Her nieces, one or more, always lived with her, and were very dear to her. To her servants she was tenderly attached, and they in turn idolized the gifted woman. The life was still a busy one. "I should think there never was such an industrious lady," said the maid who lived with her during the last eleven years of her life; "when I caught sight of her, just once leaning back in her chair, with her arms hanging down, and looking as though she was n't even thinking about anything, it gave me quite a turn. I felt she *must* be ill to sit like that!"

She loved her work, though she recognized that authorship "is the most laborious effort that men have to make; for I have never met a physician who did not confirm this conviction by his ready testimony." She used to say to her mother, when she had written ten hours a day for six weeks, "Never be uneasy about my writing so much. It is impossible to give you an idea of the increasing facility and delight which come with practice. It is the purest delight to me when there is a fair prospect of usefulness, and it is easier than the mere manual act once was. How I once marvelled at the manufacture of a volume! Now I wonder that those who once write do not always write."

Later she said, "How I love life in my study, — all alone with my books and thoughts! Books are not sufficient companions if one only reads. If one adds writing, one does not want the world, though it is wholesome to have some of it." All her middle life she never allowed herself more than five or six hours of sleep at night.

She still kept up her reading. When she was seventy-two, she said, "I am reading again that marvellous 'Middlemarch,' finding I did not value it before." After reading "Adam Bede" twice, she said of George Eliot, "A singular mind is hers, I should think, and truly wonderful in power and scope." She was a great admirer of Jane Austen, having read "Persuasion" eleven times, which she thought "unequalled in interest, charm, and truth." She enjoyed Thackeray's "Esmond," having read it three times. "It appears to me *the* book of the century," she said, "in its department." She never tired of Scott's novels.

When she thought she was going out of life, twenty years before, she wrote, "The world, as it is, is growing somewhat dim before my eyes; but the world as it is to be looks brighter every day."

Her last work was the knitting of a blanket for a neighbor's baby which was brought to see her one sunny day in March, 1876. She left a second blanket unfinished. She loved children, and felt that it was, perhaps, wise that she had none of her own, as she would have idolized them.

She waited cheerfully for the last change. "Under the weariness of illness I long to be asleep; but I have not set my mind in any state," she wrote to a friend. She thought "annihilation" was our possible future. At sunset, June 27, 1876, she sank peacefully into the rest of death. "During that last night that she lay at the Knoll," says Mrs. Chapman, "before being removed for her funeral in Birmingham, her coffin was heaped with flowers by unknown hands, even as she had filled the place with multiplied blessings." She was buried in Birmingham among her kindred, with her name and dates of birth and death graven on the stone.

Mrs. Chapman thus describes her friend: "She had rich, brown, abundant hair, folded away in shining waves from the middle of her forehead. . . . It was worn low over the eyes, like the Greek brows; and embossed rather than graven by the workings of thought. [Her hair became white before her death.] The eyes themselves were light and full, of a grayish, greenish blue, varying in color with the time of day or with the eye of the beholder. They were steadily and quietly alert, as if constantly seeing something where another would have found nothing to notice. Her habitual expression was one of serene and self-sufficing dignity — the look of perfect and benevolent repose that comes to those whose long, unselfish struggle to wring its best from life has been crowned with complete victory. You might walk the livelong day in any city streets, and not meet such a face of simple, cheerful strength, with so much light and sweetness in its play of feature."

Miss Martineau's death caused mourning in thousands of hearts. Florence Nightingale, with her sublime faith, said, "I know what her opinions were, and for a long time I have thought how great will be the *surprise* to her, — a glorious surprise. She served the Right, that is, God, all her life. How few of those who cry, 'Lord, Lord,' served the Lord *so well* and so wisely! . . . She is gone to our Lord and her Lord. Made ripe for her and our Father's house."

On this side the ocean the sorrow was not less genuine and the honor not less universal. The *Nation* said, "One looks in vain, indeed, for a parallel to this remarkable woman as a molder of public opinion through the press and through printed works."

Americans did not forget her noble efforts in their behalf. The citizens of New York sent her, while living, a set of the "Rebellion Record," published by Putnam. The Hon. Henry Wilson sent her his "Slave Power in America," "with the gratitude of the author for her friendship for his country, and her devotion to freedom."

After her death, funds were raised by public subscription in America for a statue of her in white marble, which has been executed by the sculptor, Anne Whitney, of Boston. It represents Miss Martineau seated, with her hands folded over a manuscript on her knees.

The statue was unveiled in the Old South Church, Dec. 26, 1883, Mary A. Livermore presiding, and William Lloyd Garrison, Jr., and Wendell Phillips making addresses. It proved to be the last public speech of Mr. Phillips, who died six weeks later.

He spoke with his usual fervor and unsurpassed grace. "When a moral issue is stirred," he said, "then there is no American, no German, we are all men and women. . . . In an epoch fertile of great genius among women, it may be said of Miss Martineau, that she was the peer of the noblest, and that her influence on the progress of the age was more than equal to that of all the others combined. . . . It is easy to be independent when all behind you agree with you, but the difficulty comes when nine hundred and ninety-nine of your friends think you wrong. Then it is the brave soul who stands up, one among a thousand, but remembering that one with God makes a majority. This was Harriet Martineau. . . .

"She was always the friend of the poor. Prisoner, slave, wage-serf, worn out by toil in the mill, no matter who the sufferer, there was always one person who could influence Tory and Liberal to listen. . . . We want our children to see the woman who came to observe, and remained to work, and, having once put her hand to the plough, persevered until she was allowed to live when the pæan of the emancipated four millions went up to heaven, sharing the attainment of her great desire."

JENNY LIND.

"GREAT as was the wonder of seeing a whole population thus bewitched by one simple Swedish girl, it sinks into nothing before the wonder of herself.

"You have seen her, and therefore you can appreciate the grace, the dignity, the joyousness, the touching pathos of her entrance; her attitude, her courtesies, her voice. . . .

"You must conceive a character corresponding to all this, and transpiring through a thousand traits of humility, gentleness, thoughtfulness, wisdom, piety. The manners of a princess with the simplicity of a child, and the goodness of an angel. . . . She came on Tuesday night, and is gone this evening; and it seems quite a blank, as if a heavenly visitant had departed."

Thus wrote Arthur Penrhyn Stanley, afterwards Dean of Westminster, to a friend, Sept. 22, 1847.

Mendelssohn said, "I have never in my life met so noble, so true and real an art nature as Jenny Lind is. I have never found natural gifts, study, and sympathetic warmth united in such a degree; and although one or the other quality may have appeared more prominently in this or the other case, I do not believe that they have ever been found united in such potency."

Mendelssohn told Hans Andersen, "There will not be born, in a whole century, another being so gifted as she."

JENNY LIND.

To Andersen, Jenny Lind was an inspiration. He said, "Through Jenny Lind I first became sensible of the holiness of Art. Through her I learned that one must forget one's self in the service of the Supreme. No books, no men, have had a more ennobling influence upon me, as a poet, than Jenny Lind. . . . She is happy — belonging, as it were, no longer to the world. A peaceful, quiet home is the object of her thoughts; yet she loves Art with her whole soul, and feels her vocation in it. A noble, pious disposition like hers cannot be spoiled by homage."

Frederika Bremer called her "a great artist, but still greater in her pure, human existence."

Jenny Lind fills a unique place among the world's great artists. She was gifted to a marvellous extent in voice. She was not beautiful in face, though Sir Julius Benedict said that when she was inspired with her theme, "her whole face lighted up and became perfectly beautiful." She was the idol of the public, not simply on account of her talent, for many are talented, but also because she was a veritable prince among givers, and the guardian angel of the poor and the unfortunate.

She was born in Stockholm, Sweden, Oct. 6, 1820. Her father, the son of a lace-maker, was a good-natured but weak man, unable to provide for his wife and child. He had a good voice, and enjoyed music of "a free and convivial kind."

Her mother was a woman of great energy and determination, who, being obliged to care for the child of a former unhappy marriage, and in addition the husband and child of a second marriage, by teaching school, had lost much of her natural sweetness of disposition through stern contact with poverty.

The mother could not care for the child and teach, so Jenny was boarded for three years with a church organist a few miles out of Stockholm. At this early age she showed a love for the country, a passion for the singing of birds, and for trees and wild flowers, which continued through life.

After her return to Stockholm she attended the school kept by her mother, and found much comfort and companionship in her grandmother. The latter first discovered that Jenny had a voice for singing.

Having heard some military bugles in the street, the child crept to the piano one day, thinking that she was alone in the house, and picked out the air which she had heard the soldiers play.

The grandmother, hearing the music, called out the name of the half-sister, Amalia, supposing that it was she. Jenny hid under the piano in terror. When her grandmother found her, she exclaimed, astonished, "Child, was that you?" The girl confessed in tears. When the mother returned, the grandmother said, "Mark my words, that child will bring you help."

Fru Lind's school did not pay — it was the old struggle of the poor to make ends meet — and she determined to become a governess, taking Amalia with her. The grandmother went to the Widow's Home, taking Jenny with her.

The child was not old enough to realize much about privation, and as she said in after life, "sang with every step I took, and with every jump my feet made." She had a pet cat, with a blue ribbon around its neck, to which she sang almost constantly.

Jenny Lind, at Cannes, in 1887, a little before her death, thus spoke of these early days to her eldest son: "Her favorite seat with her cat was in the window of the steward's rooms, which look out on the lively street leading up to the Church of St. Jacob's, and there she sat and sang to it; and the people passing in the street used to hear, and wonder; and amongst others the maid of a Mademoiselle Lundberg, a dancer at the Royal Opera House; and the maid told her mistress that she had never heard such beautiful singing as this little girl sang to her cat.

"Mademoiselle Lundberg thereupon found out who she was, and sent to ask her mother, who seems to have been in Stockholm at the time, to bring her to sing to her. And, when she heard her sing, she said, 'The child is a genius; you must have her educated for the stage.' But Jenny's mother, as well as her grandmother, had an old-fashioned prejudice against the stage, and she would not hear of this.

"'Then you must, at any rate, have her taught singing,' said Mademoiselle Lundberg; and the mother was persuaded, in this way, to accept a letter of introduction to Herr Crœlius, the court secretary and singing-master at the Royal Theatre.

"Off with the letter they started, but as they went up the broad steps of the Opera House, the mother was again troubled by her doubts and repugnance. She no doubt had all the inherited dislike of the burgher families to the dramatic life. But little Jenny eagerly urged her to go on, and they entered the room where Crœlius sat; and the child sang him something out of an opera composed by Winter.

"Crœlius was moved to tears, and said he must take her in to Count Puke, the head of the Royal Theatre, and tell him what a treasure he had found. And they went at once, and Count Puke's first question was, 'How old is she?' and Crœlius answered. 'Nine years old.' 'Nine!' exclaimed the count; 'but this is not a *crèche!* It is the king's theatre!' And he would not look at her, she being, moreover, at that time, what she herself (in her letter to the 'Biographical Lexicon') calls 'a small, ugly, broad-nosed, shy, *gauche*, under-grown girl!'

"' Well,' said Crœlius, 'if the count will not hear her, then I will teach her gratuitously myself, and she will one day astonish you!' Then Count Puke consented to hear her sing; and, when she sang, he too was moved to tears; and from that moment she was accepted, and was taken and taught to sing, and educated, and brought up at the Government expense."

Nearly twenty years later, when her name was on every lip, and the good Crœlius was near his death, he wrote in answer to a letter of gratitude from her, "My interest in you is, and will always remain, the most genuine. Your honor, your success will be the comfort of my old age and a balm for my sufferings."

For ten years Jenny studied and acted at the Royal Theatre. The pupils boarded at various homes in the city, the theatre paying for food and clothes, and as Fru Lind had given up her position as governess and returned to Stockholm, she took her own child, among others, to board. At the theatre the girl was taught singing, elocution, dancing, and other matters necessary for her profession, while her mother agreed to see that she was taught the piano, French, history, geography, and other studies.

German she did not learn till she was twenty-four, but she pronounced it beautifully, and N. P. Willis said, when she was in America, "She is a perfect mistress of French, and speaks English very sweetly."

These early years, full of hard work, were not very happy ones for the young girl. The mother, with her burdens and discouragements, was probably irritable, and Jenny, unable to bear the friction of home life any longer, ran away. After a law-suit between the impecunious Linds, who needed the board-money, and the directors of the theatre, the child was returned to her parents, to whom, unfortunately, she legally belonged.

Still the girl was fond of her mother, and when she died in 1851, when Jenny was in America, the latter wrote to a friend in Sweden: "My mother's death I have felt most bitterly; everything was now smooth and nice between us; I was in hopes that she would have been spared for many a long year; . . . and that, now that she was quieter and more reasonable, I might have surrounded her old age with joy, and peace, and tender care. But the ways of the Lord are often not our ways."

Jenny began to act almost as soon as she was admitted to the Royal Theatre. At ten she played the part of Angela in "The Polish Mine." The next year she was Johanna in "Testamentet." The press spoke of her acting as showing "fire and feeling far beyond her years."

The year she was thirteen she appeared in twenty-two performances. The press said the child showed "unnatural cleverness," but regretted that she had to take parts full of "coquetry, boldness, and heartlessness." From twelve to fifteen she sang in concerts, and the Swedes were becoming very proud of her. At seventeen, when she had appeared on the stage one hundred and eleven times for her board and clothes, it was decided that it was time to give her a salary of about sixty pounds a year.

During her seventeenth year she appeared on the boards

ninety-two times in twelve new characters. It was fortunate that she had a good memory and great versatility, otherwise the work required of her would have broken her constitution. The state had not proved an easy taskmaster, but the life was more enjoyable than if it had been passed in the poverty of the Lind home.

When about seventeen she began to study the part of Agatha in Weber's "Der Freischütz." One day she thought, to satisfy her teacher, Madame Erikson, of whom she was very fond, she would put her whole soul into her part. She did so, and the teacher met the effort with silence. "Am I, then, so incapable?" thought the girl, till she saw the tears on her teacher's face. "My child, I have nothing to teach you; do as nature tells you," she said.

On the day of her *début*, March 7, 1838, she was extremely nervous and worried, but after the first note on the stage all fear disappeared. The people were surprised and delighted, and she most of all, for she had learned her ability.

She often said afterwards, "I got up that morning one creature; I went to bed another creature. I had found my power." All through life the 7th of March was kept with grateful remembrance; it was a second birthday.

In 1839 her most effective part was Alice in Meyerbeer's "Robert le Diable," which she played twenty-three times to enthusiastic audiences. So popular was she in this piece that she gave it sixty times in the same theatre during the next four years.

Bournonville, eminent in Copenhagen and at Stockholm as a composer, said later, her voice even then "possessed the same sympathy, the same electric power, which now makes it so irresistible. She was worshipped." He said, three years afterwards, when she sang in Denmark, "Jenny Lind discovered that she could get her living out of Sweden; and also she learned that the artist, in reality, should not settle down on the native soil, but, like the bird of passage, should go there only in search of rest."

Jenny was able to take a brief rest in the summer of 1839 at Gothenburg, and her mother went with her to enjoy the country air. Fru Lind wrote back to her husband: "Our Jenny recruits herself daily, now in the hay-stacks, now on the sea or in the swing, in perfect tranquillity, while the town people are said to be longing for her concert and greatly wondering when it will come off. Once or twice she has been singing in rather good circles, the divine air of 'Isabelle' from 'Robert le Diable.' Nearly everybody was crying, — one lady actually went into hysterics from sheer rapture; this has got abroad already. Yes, she captivates all, all! It is a great happiness to be a mother under such conditions." Poor, tired Fru Lind had gained courage in the struggle, and was evidently looking forward to better days.

Towards the close of 1839 Jenny removed from her home to the house of the chief of Swedish song-writers, Adolf Fredrik Lindblad. In this family she found companionship and quiet for study. " I have to thank him," said Jenny Lind, forty years later, "for that fine comprehension of art which was implanted by his idealistic, pure, and unsensual nature into me, his ready pupil. Subsequently Christianity stepped in to satisfy the moral needs, and to teach me to look well into my own soul."

Lucia in Donizetti's "Lucia di Lammermoor" became one of her famous rôles. After her thirteenth performance of Lucia on June 19, 1840, a number of the actors serenaded her, and on her return home she was presented with a silver tea and coffee service which she always valued highly, and, at her death, willed to her eldest son.

The girl was as lovely in character as she was gifted in song. The poor home and the hard work had not soured her nature, but had made her more tender to the suffering, and more considerate of others.

She began to win friends among the distinguished people of her country. Erik Gustaf Geijer, the noted author and popular Professor of History in the University of Upsala, wrote several songs for her. One, especially, stirred her with ambition. It was found after her death among her papers, with this line in her own hand on the bottom of the page: "On these words I was launched into the open sea."

> "Oh! if from yon Eternal Fire,
>   Which slays the soul that sets it free,
> Consuming them, as they aspire,
>   One burning spark have fallen on thee, —
>
> "Fear not! though upward still it haste,
>   That living fire, that tongue of flame!
> *Thy* days it turns to bitter waste;
>   But ah! from heaven — from heaven it came!"

When Jenny sang in Upsala before the enthusiastic students, she must have enjoyed the lovely home and garden of the gifted Geijer. He died April 23, 1847. Forty years later I counted it a privilege to gather from that garden some beautiful pink roses which I still preserve.

The daughter of Baron L. thus describes the singer at a party in the baron's home: "On the threshhold stands the host and by his side, shaking hands with him, a young girl, with an abundance of curls round the pale cheeks; a gown in simple style softly clings round the maiden figure and there is a dreamy, half-absent, and fascinating look in the deep-set eyes.

"The hum is increasing still more when the old nobleman leads the visitor into the midst of his guests; but he has not time to pronounce her name, it is already on everybody's lips, and is now flying round the room with a subdued sound: Jenny Lind! Jenny Lind!

"The beauties of the season are forgotten and, what is more, they forget all about themselves; flirtation is suppressed; . . . a crowd of the high assembly gathers round the plain-looking young girl, thus for once justly conceding the preference of genius to birth — of beauty of soul to beauty of features."

Jenny Lind was about five feet and three to four inches in height, with "dove-like blue eyes" and light hair, a face which expressed every emotion, a quick and alert mind which, said N. P. Willis, "comprehended everything by the time it was half expressed," a dislike of the "small talk" of society and of compliments, and a natural, frank, sincere manner. While vivacious, there was an undertone of melancholy in her nature, as perhaps there must always be in those who think deeply, and are conversant with the world's woes.

"She has the simplicity of genius," said Mrs. Stanley, the wife of the Bishop of Norwich and the mother of Dean Stanley, some years later. "She never speaks of herself, never appears to think of herself." She moved on the stage with all its perils, true to whatever was best in womanhood.

Conscious that she had great talents, the "Swedish

Nightingale," as she was called, felt that she must put forth every effort for their cultivation. She was ambitious and rightly so. To develop every talent, however small, and use it to the fullest extent possible, is the duty of every human being. Indolence makes thousands of mediocre lives; Jenny Lind won her place in part, as she used to say, "by incredible labor."

When she was twenty she was made a member of the Royal Swedish Academy of Music, and was appointed court singer by his Majesty, Carl Johan. She had determined to go to Paris to study, feeling that she had the Eternal Fire of which Geijer had written. The directors of the theatre tried to dissuade her by the offer of a salary of one hundred and fifty pounds, which she declined.

In the summer of 1840, Jenny Lind made a provincial tour, thereby earning enough money, with what she had saved, to study in Paris for a year. The provincial concert tour was a fatiguing one. She wrote a friend, "The roads were so bad that the wheels, now and then, sank a foot deep into the mud, and it was very horrid sitting about in the atrocious weather; but as soon as I arrive in a town, and see the exceeding great kindness and friendliness the people have for me, then I feel it wicked to grumble. You cannot think to what an extent they all vie with each other in serving me. It is quite astonishing!"

Already she had begun the generosity which was forever to make her name honored and beloved. She writes again to the same friend "to visit Bruhn the painter, a poor sick man, ill in bed these last fourteen years; I forgot to bring him his monthly allowance before coming away; will you be good enough to give him, on my behalf, eight riksdaler banco, and to tell him this is for the months of July and August."

'Through life she felt that the money she earned was only hers, in trust, as well as her voice. "Every morning when she got up, she told me," writes Mrs. Stanley, "she felt that her voice was a gift from God, and that, perhaps, that very day might be the last of its use."

Through the autumn of 1840 and spring of 1841 her labors were incessant. Twenty-three times she gave Lucia; fourteen times Alice in "Robert"; nine times Agatha in "Der Freischütz"; seven times Bellini's "Norma," besides other plays and concerts. On June 19, 1841, she appeared for the four hundred and forty-seventh time on the stage of the Royal Theatre, since, when a child of ten, she had played Angela in "The Polish Mine."

Two weeks later she started for Paris, spending the whole last night before her departure, says Madame Lindblad, in writing letters, "coming occasionally into our rooms to have a good cry."

On leaving Sweden, Jenny Lind took a letter of introduction from Queen Desirée (the wife of Maréchal Bernadotte, who became King of Sweden and Norway in 1818, under the title of Carl XIV., Johan) to her relative, Madame la Maréchale Soult. At the house of the latter Jenny sang before Signor Manuel Garcia, the greatest singing-master of the century. Later, Jenny called upon him, desiring to take lessons. She sang in "Lucia," in which she had appeared thirty-nine times in Stockholm the previous year, and broke down. He said to the frightened girl, who had nearly worn herself out by her hard work, "It would be useless to teach you, Mademoiselle; you have no voice left."

She told Mendelssohn years afterward that the agony of that moment exceeded all she had suffered in her whole life.

She asked Garcia, with tears in her eyes, what she was to do. Evidently moved by her sorrow, he said she must give her voice a complete rest for six weeks, not singing at all, and talking very little. At the end of that time she might come to him again. At once she began diligently to perfect herself in the French language.

On her return to Garcia her voice had so improved that he was willing to give her two lessons a week. She began to practice the scales and exercises four hours or more daily. For ten months she studied almost continuously. Garcia's help was valuable, but she knew that her power came from another source.

She wrote, years afterward: "The greater part of what I can do in my art, I have myself acquired by incredible labor, in spite of astonishing difficulties. By Garcia alone have I been taught some few important things. God had so plainly written within me what I had to study; my ideal was, and is, so high, that I could find no mortal who could in the least degree satisfy my demands. Therefore 'I sing after no one's method; only, as far as I am able, after that of the birds; for their Master was the only one who came up to my demands for truth, clearness, and expression."

Her voice had increased in depth of tone, in clearness in the upper register, and in sympathetic adaptation to the words of every song. She had also learned to fill the lungs with such dexterity that it was impossible to detect when the breath was renewed. Unlike Henrietta Sontag, she had naturally limited sustaining power, and this increase of sustaining power was gained by practice.

In May, 1842, Jenny Lind returned to Stockholm, the directors of the theatre giving her about one hundred and fifty pounds, with extra-service money, and costumes provided. She sang in "Norma," "Lucia," Mozart's "Le Nozze di Figaro," and won additional fame as Amina, in Bellini's "La Sonnambula." In nine months she appeared one hundred and six times in thirteen different parts.

Her first duty and pleasure was to purchase a little home in the country for her father and mother, and then she transferred her guardianship to Herr Henric M. Munthe, a judge of high position and character. To the end of his life he was her helpful friend.

When she was sixty years old, she wrote his son Carl in appreciation of his noble father. She states that she had intended to write her autobiography, as her experience had been so varied, but later she abandoned it after the public so criticised the "Reminiscences" of Carlyle.

In the summer of 1843, Jenny Lind sang in Finland to delighted audiences. Topelius, the poet and historian, remembering the welcome of the people, wrote in 1888, after her death: —

> "I saw thee once, so young and fair,
>   In thy sweet spring-tide, long ago;
> A myrtle wreath was in thy hair,
>   And, at thy breast, a rose did blow.
>
> . . . .
>
> "Poor was thy purse, yet gold thy gift;
>   All music's golden boons were thine:
> And yet, through all the wealth of art,
>   It was thy soul which sang to mine.
>
> "Yea! sang, as no one else has sung,
>   So subtly skilled, so simply good!
> So brilliant! yet as pure, and true
>   As birds that warble in the wood!"

She sang next in Denmark. "All Copenhagen was in raptures," said Hans Andersen. "Jenny Lind was the first artist to whom the students ever offered a serenade! The torches flashed round the hospitable villa where the song was sung. She expressed her thanks by a few more of the Swedish songs, and I then saw her hurry into the darkest corner, and weep out her emotion. 'Yes, yes,' she said, 'I will exert myself; I will strive; I shall be more efficient than I am now, when I come to Copenhagen again!'"

In this city, having heard that a young man who was ill felt greatly disappointed because he had not heard her, she visited his home, and sang to him and his young wife, notwithstanding she was to sing in "Norma" that afternoon. Hans Andersen tells of another act of kindness on a second visit to Copenhagen. Every hour was occupied, but having heard of a society which took children out of the hands of bad parents, and provided for them, she desired to help raise funds.

"Have I not still a disengaged evening?" said she. "Let me give a performance for the benefit of these poor children, and we will have doubled prices."

The concert was given, and the proceeds were large. When told how many poor children would be helped, her eyes filled with tears, as she said, "Is it not beautiful that I can sing so?"

From October, 1843, to July, 1844, she made sixty-six appearances in Stockholm; gave concerts to raise money for the Swedish composer, Josephson, that he might study abroad, and found occasional rest in her "cosey little home."

She writes to Hans Andersen, describing it: "Cheerful, sunny rooms, a nightingale and a greenfinch; the latter, however, is greatly superior as an artist to his celebrated colleague, for, while the first remains on his bar, grumpy and moody, the other jumps about in his cage, looking so joyous and good-natured, as if, to begin with, he was not in the least jealous, but, instead of that, supposes himself created merely for the purpose of cheering his silent friend! And then he sings a song, so high, so deep, so charming and so sonorous, that I sit down beside him, and, within, lift up my voice in a mute song of praise to Him whose 'strength is made perfect in weakness.' Ah! it is divine to feel really good."

At this time she was invited by Meyerbeer to sing in his new opera, "Das Feldlager in Schlesien," to be given at the opening of the new Royal Opera House in Berlin. When she left Stockholm in July, 1844, to go to Dresden to study the German language, the queen gave her portrait-medals of herself and the late king, with a watch, which, she said, is "to remind you not to forget the time of your return to us."

As ever, she was homesick at leaving Sweden, but her ambition sustained her. In Dresden she lived quietly, refusing to enter society, devoting herself methodically to her study. Recalled to Sweden to assist, as court-singer, at the coronation of King Oscar I., she was offered about four hundred and twenty pounds, annually, for eight years, with a pension for life, by the theatre directors, if she would remain in Sweden. She was inclined to accept the offer, but was dissuaded by friends.

In the fall of 1844, she went to Berlin. Through Meyerbeer she was privately presented to the royal family. Before appearing in opera, she was asked to sing at a small party given by Augusta, afterwards empress. The Countess of Westmoreland, whose husband, the earl, was the English ambassador to Prussia, and a noted musician as well, the founder of the Royal Academy of Music in London, was at the party given by Augusta. Lady Westmoreland thus describes the event, as told her by her mother, the countess: " She went in, full of curiosity, and saw sitting by the lamp a thin, pale, plain-featured girl, looking awkward and nervous, and like a very shy country schoolgirl. She could not believe her eyes, and said that she and her neighbors, among whom was Countess Rossi (Henrietta Sontag), whose fame as a singer and a beauty was then still recent, began to speculate whether Meyerbeer was playing a practical joke on them; and when he came up to speak to them, my mother asked him if he was really serious in meaning to bring that frightened child out in his opera. His only answer was, '*Attendez, Miladi.*'

"When the time came for her song, my mother used to say it was the most extraordinary experience she ever remembered. The wonderful notes came ringing out; but over and above that was the wonderful TRANSFIGURATION — no other word could apply — which came over her entire face and figure, lightening them up with the whole fire and dignity of her genius. The effect on the whole audience was simply marvellous.

"When she reached home, my father asked her, 'Well, what do you think of Meyerbeer's wonder?'

"She answered, 'She is simply an angel.'

"'Is she so very handsome?'

"'I saw a plain girl when I went in, but when she began to sing her face simply and literally shone like that of an angel. I never *saw* anything, or *heard* anything, the least like it.'

"My mother used to say that she thought her dramatic

power was quite as great as her musical genius, and that if she had had no voice she might still have been the greatest of living actresses."

The gifted Henrietta Sontag called her afterwards, "the first singer of the world."

Jenny Lind did not sing in Meyerbeer's new opera, because a prima donna who had sung for years at the theatre, declared it to be her right to sing. The public were, of course, disappointed. But jealousies are not confined to the stage!

Jenny Lind's first appearance in Berlin was in "Norma." She interpreted the character differently from Madame Pasta, for whom it was written, or from Madame Grisi, who was playing it nightly in London and Paris, with less of passion, but more of true womanhood. Meyerbeer was charmed with Jenny Lind, and determined that she should appear in his new opera. "He is a most polite man," wrote Josephson; "something of the courtier; something of the man of genius; something of the man of the world; and has, in addition, something fidgety about his whole being. Before reproducing the opera with Jenny Lind, he called upon her, to the best of my belief, at least a hundred times to consult about this, that, or the other."

Before she appeared as Vielka in "Das Feldlager in Schlesien," she was exceedingly nervous, and kept practising the whole afternoon and before the beginning of the opera. Her reception was most enthusiastic. After the fourth performance, an attempt was made to secure her for London. She unwisely signed a contract with Mr. Alfred Bunn, of Drury Lane Theatre, which, from disagreement, ended in a lawsuit, with damages against her of twenty-five hundred pounds.

Every evening was an ovation to the singer. When

"La Sonnambula" was given, the prices asked and paid were unprecedented. Meyerbeer wrote her, urging her to overcome her diffidence; but added, "Whether heaven grants you or not this little supplement to your other precious qualities, you will always be, for me, my dear Mademoiselle, one of the most touching and noble characters that I have ever met with during my long artistic wanderings, and one to whom I have vowed for my whole life the most profound and sincere admiration and esteem."

Her farewell concert was in aid of the "Asylum for Blind Soldiers."

Though constantly meeting such distinguished persons as Tieck, Brockhaus, the head of the great publishing firm in Leipzig, and Frau Bettina von Arnim, — Goethe's Bettina, — she wrote to Judge Munthe: "In the midst of all these splendors, my whole soul goes out in longing for Sweden. There is an inexplicable home-sympathy in the depths of my soul, and I look upon its possession as an unspeakable happiness; for to feel so warmly as this for one's country is a divinely elevating sentiment."

On her way back to Sweden she sang in Hanover and in Hamburg. She was serenaded and escorted home by torchlight processions. "She was the first in Hamburg," says Dr. Hermann Uhde, "whose whole figure had ever been so completely bestrewn with flowers that she stood upon an improvised carpet of blossoms." On her return to Sweden, though it was midnight, the streets were completely blocked by those who had come to welcome her home.

She was soon recalled to Prussia to sing at an entertainment given by King Frederick William IV., — the son of the immortal Louise, — in honor of Queen Victoria and

Prince Albert, who had come to Prussia to be present at the unveiling of a bronze statue at Bonn to the incomparable Beethoven.

Queen Victoria was charmed with Jenny Lind, and showed her many attentions through life.

During this visit she met George Grote, the historian of Greece, and his wife, who were ever after her cherished friends. She confided to Mrs. Grote that the stage was distasteful to her, and that she should leave it as soon as she was pecuniarily independent, adding, "My wants are few, my tastes simple, a small income would content me." She also wrote her old friend, Madame Erikson, "Connection with the stage has no attraction for me; my soul is yearning for rest from all these persistent compliments and this persistent adulation."

She sang for nine nights at Frankfort. At Darmstadt, when she was called before the curtain, she was received with "a gentle shower of flowers."

In the last week of October, 1845, Jenny Lind returned to Berlin, and in the following five months sang twenty-eight times, taking the part of Donna Anna in Mozart's "Don Giovanni," Agatha in "Der Freischütz," Julia in Spontini's "Die Vestalin," Valentine in Meyerbeer's "Les Huguenots." The house of Prof. Ludwig Wilhelm Wickmann, the friend of Thorvaldsen and the favorite pupil of Schadow, was her home. Here the great singer met the choicest spirits of Germany. Hans Andersen came to see her. One day a poor tailor, who was also a poet, came to call upon the gifted Dane. Andersen had little to offer him, but suggested that he might arrange for him to hear Jenny Lind.

"I have heard her," said the man. "I could not afford to buy a ticket; so I went to the man who provides the 'supers,' and asked him if I could not go as a 'super' one evening in 'Norma.' To this he agreed. So I was dressed up as a Roman soldier, with a long sword at my side, and in that guise appeared upon the stage; and I heard her better than any one else, for I stood close beside her. Ah! how she sang! and how she acted! I could not stand it; it made me weep. But they were furious at that. The manager forbade it, and would never permit me to set foot upon the stage again, for one must not weep upon the stage."

Mendelssohn came now and then to Berlin, for while his devoted family lived there, his duties called him to Leipzig, where he had founded the Conservatorium in 1843, and as leader of the orchestra of the Gewandhaus. Jenny Lind wrote to Judge Munthe, "Felix Mendelssohn comes sometimes to Berlin, and I have often been in his company. He is a *man*, and, at the same time, he has the most supreme talent. Thus should it be."

Mendelssohn took Jenny Lind to Leipzig to assist in his famous Gewandhaus Concerts, the finest in Europe. The rush for tickets was so great that not one fourth of the applicants could be accommodated. Herr Brockhaus said, "Soul and expression so intimately associated with so beautiful a voice and so perfect a method will never be met with again. . . . One can only wonder, and love her. And this affectionate appreciation is universal, — the same with young and old, with men and with women."

Instead of giving a benefit for herself, she gave a concert for the widows of deceased members of the Gewandhaus Orchestra. After the concert the grateful musicians gave her a serenade, and a beautiful silver salver.

The Brockhaus children were delighted with the lovable guest — she was staying with Frau Friedrich Brockhaus, a sister of Richard Wagner — because she made herself one with them; looked at their pictures, and showed them a bracelet given her by the King of Prussia, on the top of which were three large pearls on a cover, and beneath the cover a cylinder watch, a little larger than an English sixpence.

After this, Mademoiselle Lind sang at Weimar, visiting, with great feeling, the graves of Goethe and Schiller.

While at Prof. Wickmann's, she commissioned Prof. Magnus to paint her portrait, as a gift to the former and his wife. This admirable likeness remained in the Wickmann family till 1877, when, at the request of the Berlin National Gallery, the son sold it to the nation for twelve thousand thalers.

She was cheered in the midst of her hard work by letters from Mendelssohn. He, too, was working beyond his strength. He wrote: "You ask how things go with me. On the days when I was so quiet in my room, writing music without interruption, and only going out from time to time for a walk in the fresh air, they went very well indeed with me — or, at least, I thought so. . . . I, like yourself, rejoice very much indeed in thinking of the time when I shall be able to put aside the duty of conducting music and promoting institutions, and quit this so-called 'sphere of activity,' and have no other 'sphere of activity' to think of than a quire of blank music-paper, and no need to conduct anything that I do not care for, and when I shall be altogether independent and free. It will, indeed, be a few years before this can take place, but I hope *not more than that.*" He died the next year.

Early in April, 1846, Mademoiselle Lind started for Vienna, by the way of Leipzig, helping Mendelssohn in his last concert, save one, in the Gewandhaus. He played

Beethoven's "Sonata in C sharp minor" as no one else could play it. His last performance in the Gewandhaus was on July 19, 1846, when he played the pianoforte part of Beethoven's "Kreutzer Sonata."

Mademoiselle Lind was more than ever impressed with the remarkable devotion of Mendelssohn to his family. Brockhaus says in his diary: "I am convinced that she would gladly exchange all her triumphs for simple, homely happiness. She sees that in Mendelssohn's house, where the wife and children make his happiness complete."

Mendelssohn helped to make Vienna pleasant for her by letters to his friends. He wrote the singer, Herr Franz Hausen, later the director of the Conservatorium in Munich, to receive her "not as a stranger, but as one of ourselves." "She pulls at the same rope with all of us, who are really in earnest about that; thinks about it; strives for it; and, if all goes well with her in the world, it is as pleasant to me as if it went well with me; for it helps me, and all of us, so well on our road."

Madame Birch-Pfeiffer, a well-known author, wrote a friend in Vienna: "She speaks little, and thinks deeply. She is full of perception, and the finest tact — a mixture of devotion and energy, such as you have probably never before met with. Free, herself, from the slightest trace of coquetry, she regards all coquetry with horror. In short, she stands alone of her kind, from head to foot."

Mademoiselle Lind had promised to sing at the "Theater an der Wien," at that time the largest in Vienna. It had been built by Emmanuel Schickaneder, who, when in financial difficulties, was given "Die Zauberflöte" by Mozart, with the promise that the score should not pass out of his hands. He accepted the gift, but broke his word, and sold a copy to every provincial manager who was able to buy. Mozart died soon after in extreme poverty, without having received a cent for his great work, while Schickaneder became rich, and built his theatre.

Mademoiselle Lind feared that her voice would not fill the hall, but was finally persuaded by her friends to make the attempt, and received the same ovation as in Berlin. She wrote Madame Birch-Pfeiffer that at the close of "Norma," "I was called back sixteen times, and twelve or fourteen before that. Just count that up! And this reception! I was quite astounded!"

Mendelssohn wrote her cheering letters: "To-morrow, or the day after to-morrow," he said, "the first part of my oratorio ["Elijah"] will be quite finished; and many pieces out of the second part are already finished also. This has given me immense pleasure during these last weeks. Sometimes, in my room, I have jumped up to the ceiling, when it seemed to promise well. But I am getting a little confused, through writing down, during the last few weeks, the immense number of notes that I previously had in my head, and working them backwards and forwards upon the paper into a piece, though not quite in the proper order, one after another."

He wrote to Herr Hausen: "I sit, over both my ears in my 'Elijah,' and if it turns out half as good as I often think it will, I shall be glad indeed. I like nothing better than to spend the whole day in writing the notes down, and I often come so late to dine that the children come to my room to fetch me, and drag me out by main force."

As ever, Mademoiselle Lind was pining for Sweden,— writing to the wife of Prof. Wickmann: "I have been so homesick, that I scarcely knew whether I should live or die."

Despite the homesickness, the enthusiasm of the people must have been most gratifying. When "La Sounambula" was given at the farewell — when flowers were falling in showers upon the stage — the empress mother dropped a wreath at the singer's feet. Such a favor was unknown in Vienna. The audience insisted on a few words from Mademoiselle Lind, who said in German, "You have well understood me. I thank you from my heart."

The crowd outside the theatre was so great that it was deemed wise for her to wait before going to her apartments. Thirty times the people summoned her to the window, shouting, "Jenny Lind, say you will come back again to us!" She stood sobbing like a child, and throwing them flowers from the mass of bouquets piled before her.

Hour after hour passed, till, as morning dawned, she took her departure. The crowd even then so surged about the carriage that her man-servant was badly injured.

In May, 1846, Jenny Lind assisted at the "Lower Rhine Musical Festival," Mendelssohn conducting it, at Aix-la-Chapelle. The two principal songs in Haydn's "Creation," "On Mighty Pens" and "With Verdure Clad," and the solo and chorus, "The Marvellous Work," displayed Jenny Lind's powers admirably. Her greatest success, however, was at the "Artists' Concert" in Mendelssohn's "Auf Flügeln des Gesanges" and "Frühlingslied." Here, as at various other places, she was presented with a poem, printed in black and gold, on white satin. After this, she sang at Hamburg and other German cities for the poor, and for Orchestra Pension Funds.

In the fall of 1846 she sang in Munich, making her

home with the family of Prof. Wilhelm von Kaulbach. At Stuttgard she earned for the poor about one hundred and thirty pounds by a concert; at Carlsruhe two hundred gulden were set apart for the chorus; at Nuremburg a medal was struck in her honor.

On her return to Vienna she sang thirteen times in "Vielka," — another name for "Das Feldlager in Schlesien," — Meyerbeer superintending. So distrustful was she of her own powers that at the close of the first performance of "Vielka," when Meyerbeer came to thank her and tell her she "had sung divinely," he found her in tears, exclaiming, "Oh! Herr Director! forgive me for singing so badly, and spoiling your opera."

Moscheles thought her song with two flutes in this opera "was, perhaps, the most astonishing piece of bravura singing which could possibly be heard."

She gave seven concerts in Vienna for charity: one to aid a Swedish composer, another for the Children's Hospital, and the like. She was made court singer by the Emperor Ferdinand.

In 1847, she went to London to fill an engagement at Her Majesty's Theatre. She was to receive forty-eight hundred pounds for the season, — April 14 to Aug. 20, — with a furnished house to live in, horses and carriage, and eight hundred pounds extra for a month in Italy, if she wished to study the language more fully, or for rest. This, of course, was more than she had ever received before.

After her arrival in London, she began to be frightened at the possibility of failure, and begged the manager to cancel the contract. Mr. and Mrs. Grote gave a dinner-party for her, and when she attempted to sing for the pleasure of the company, though Mendelssohn, who was present, accompanied her, she broke down from fright.

The excitement was intense on the night when Jenny Lind was to make her first appearance. The rush for places was so great that men were thrown down, ladies fainted, and dress-suits were torn in pieces. The Queen and Prince Albert were present, with other distinguished people.

Jenny Lind played Alice in "Robert le Diable." The Queen, herself an accomplished musician, was delighted, and threw a wreath at the feet of the artist.

Two evenings later the same opera was given, and the audience rose repeatedly *en masse*, and waved their hats and handkerchiefs. The Queen was again present.

The press was most cordial. The *Illustrated News* said: "Her voice is astonishing. To the fullest, purest, sweetest tone imaginable, it unites a vibrating and penetrating quality that makes its softest whisper audible, no matter where the listener is seated, and that, when exerted to its full extent, is truly glorious; and it may be distinctly heard above the loudest din of the orchestra, and the voices of the other artists."

Clairville Cottage, at Old Brompton, a lovely home among trees and flowers, was provided for the singer. Here, shut out from the eager crowds who wished to meet her, she devoted her time to study. When Mrs. Grote accompanied her, occasionally, to some grand party, she said to her friend, "I would rather have been rambling with you among the Burnham beeches." The queen dowager invited her to visit her, and the Duke of Wellington asked her to his country-seat.

Her part of Amina in "La Sonnambula" gave great satisfaction. In the last act, Amina walks in her sleep over a wooden bridge spanning a mill-stream, the bridge hanging in the air directly over a revolving water-wheel.

When she reaches the middle of the bridge, the planks give way. She starts, lets the lamp fall, and then, without awaking, calmly proceeds on her journey. The perilous feat of crossing the bridge is usually performed by one of the helpers, in place of the prima donna, but Jenny Lind would not deceive the public. She said she was frightened each time, but added, "I should have been ashamed to stand before the audience, pretending that I had crossed the bridge, if I had not really done it."

Queen Victoria records in her diary, of the air, "*Ah! non credea:*" "It was all *piano*, and clear and sweet, and like the sighing of a zephyr, yet all heard. Who could describe those long notes, drawn out till they quite melt away, that shake which becomes softer and softer, those very piano and flute-like notes, and those round fresh tones which are so youthful?"

Jenny Lind appeared for the first time in England in "Norma," by royal command, June 15, 1847. The Queen and Prince Albert came in state. The royal boxes were draped with crimson Genoa velvet trimmed with gold lace, and blue velvet with silver lace. The Queen came at eight, but the crowd began to gather as early as half-past three in the afternoon.

Jenny Lind sang twice at Buckingham Palace, and once at Osborne. She had always refused to take money for Royal concerts, but the Queen gave her a handsome bracelet, saying, "I must again express not only my admiration but my respect for you."

The provinces were eager to hear Jenny Lind, so, in August, she sang at Brighton, Birmingham, Manchester, Liverpool, Norwich, Bristol, Bath, and other towns.

At Bath, she talked with an aged woman, whom she saw walking backward and forward before the almshouse.

"I have lived a long time in the world," said the woman, "and desire nothing before I die but to hear Jenny Lind."

"And would it make you happy?" said the singer.

"Ay, that it would; but such folks as I can't go to the play-house, and so I shall never see her."

"Don't be so sure of that," said the other, as they entered the house. "Sit down and listen."

The old lady heard, and wept at the unusual music. "Now you have heard Jenny Lind," said the stranger, and departed.

At Norwich — a thing most unusual — Jenny Lind was entertained by the Bishop and his wife, the parents of Dean Stanley. Mrs. Stanley wrote to her sister: "Her voice was more wonderful than when I heard it before, — different from all others, in being like the warbling of a bird." Again, she wrote: "I would rather hear Jenny talk than sing, — wonderful as it is."

She returned to Stockholm late in 1847, after an absence of two years. Never after this did she take a penny from Sweden, but gave all the proceeds of her concerts to its charities. During the winter she sang ten times in Donizetti's "Figlia del Reggimento," in which she was a great favorite, four times in "La Sonnambula," four in "Lucia," twice in "Der Freischütz," and in "Norma," "Le Nozze di Figaro," and other operas. The proceeds were given from these plays and several concerts to the educating of gifted but poor children for the stage; to the Theatre Pension Fund; to the machinists of the theatre; to the Artists Guild Pension Fund, and to various composers, singers, and others in need.

The death of Mendelssohn, Nov. 4, 1847, had been a great blow to her. She wrote to a friend in Austria: "For the first two months after it, I could not put a word down on paper, and everything seemed to me to be dead. Never was I so happy, so lifted in spirit, as when I spoke with him! And seldom can there have been in the world two beings who so understood one another, and so sympathized with one another, as we! How glorious and strange are the ways of God! On the one hand, He gives all! On the other, He takes all away! Such is life's outlook!"

For two whole years she could not bear to sing a *Lied* of Mendelssohn's. "As soon as I am obliged to hear or read anything about him," she said, "I get almost incapable of carrying out the great duty which I have taken upon my shoulders."

She wrote to the wife of Mendelssohn: "His 'Elijah' is sublime! In my opinion, he never wrote anything finer; and, assuredly, could not have written anything loftier in the future. . . . You cannot but feel grateful when you consider how much, and in what a lofty manner, you were esteemed and loved by a being, not only exceptionally endowed, but pure and original as he!"

When she left Stockholm in July, 1848, for England, the same love of country was in her heart: "My king, the whole royal family, the country, the ground,—oh! I could have kissed them all, and with tears of profound reverence in my eyes!"

She had become engaged to Herr Julius Günther, the tenor of the Royal Theatre, who had sung for several years with her in Stockholm. He, too, had studied under Garcia, in Paris. The engagement was broken by mutual consent a few months later, largely on account of diverse views about the stage, she having determined to abandon her stage life as soon as it was possible.

May 4, 1848, she appeared again at Her Majesty's

Theatre in London, before a delighted audience. Chopin, who had just come to London, went to hear her. He said, "This Swede is indeed an original from head to foot. She does not show herself in the ordinary light, but in the magic rays of an *aurora borealis*. Her singing is infallibly pure and true; but, above all, I admire her *piano* passages, the charm of which is indescribable."

Her delineation of the madness of Lucy Ashton in "Lucia" was brilliant in the extreme. She gave the play eleven times during the season.

Moved with sympathy for the incurables in the Brompton Hospital for Consumptives, she gave a concert which netted for the inmates about eighteen hundred pounds. Lord Beaconsfield, in 1849, on an anniversary occasion, said: "I know nothing in classic story, or in those feudal epochs when we are taught that the individual was more influential, when character was more forcible — I know nothing to be compared with the career of this admirable woman. It almost reaches the high ideal of human nature when we portray to ourselves a youthful maiden, innocent and benignant, in the possession of an unparalleled and omnipotent charm, alternately entrancing the heart of nations, and then kneeling at the tomb of suffering, of calamity, and of care. To me there is something most beautiful in this life of music and charity — a life passed amid divine sounds and still diviner deeds."

In the fall of 1848 a grand rendering of "Elijah" was given by Jenny Lind at Exeter Hall, to raise money for scholarships in music in memory of Mendelssohn. The soprano parts had been composed expressly for her, therefore there was an especial fitness in her giving this oratorio.

Over one thousand pounds were realized from this concert, which was allowed to accumulate until 1856, when the first Mendelssohn scholar was chosen — Mr. Arthur Seymour Sullivan, now Sir Arthur — for whom Jenny Lind always had high admiration.

After this Jenny Lind gave a concert for the Manchester Royal Infirmary and Dispensary, for the Queen's College Hospital at Birmingham, The Southern Hospital at Liverpool, the sick children of the poor of Norwich, which resulted in "The Jenny Lind Infirmary for sick Children," and other charities, earning and giving away in less than nine weeks about fifty-two thousand dollars. When presents were proposed on account of such generosity she refused to receive them, feeling that the money could be used in a better manner.

At Norwich she hoped the tickets would not be too high. When the bishop proposed one pound for the reserved seats, she said, "Would not ten shillings be better, and then I could sing twice." He did not wish to overtask her.

"Never mind, if the people wish to hear me," she said.

No wonder that Chopin said, "This Swede is indeed an original from head to foot."

April 3, 1849, Jenny Lind gave the "Creation" at Exeter Hall for four prominent charities, and realized about one thousand pounds. The *Times* said: "One of the most general topics of conversation and marked approval was the exceeding clearness with which Mademoiselle pronounced the words of all her songs, duets, and trios," and urged all singers to follow her example.

It began to be noised abroad that Jenny Lind was to leave the stage. The manager of Her Majesty's Theatre was in despair, and the public as well. She consented at last to appear in six operas. In Amina in "La Sonnambula," the *Times* said, "Those high notes, so unrivalled in sweetness, and admitting the finest attenuation without losing a particle of their value, seemed to vibrate through the house with a clearness hitherto unknown."

Her farewell, May 10, 1849, was in Alice in "Robert." At the close three times she came before an enraptured but sorrowing audience, which rose each time she appeared. Tears flowed down her cheeks, while the audience shouted themselves hoarse. For nineteen years, from a child of ten, she had been the idol of the public. She would sing again for a time in concerts, but at twenty-nine she bade adieu to the stage forever.

In eleven years, between her first appearance in opera, in "Der Freischütz," March 7, 1838, and her last in "Robert le Diable," she appeared in thirty operas six hundred and seventy-seven times. Sir Julius Benedict thinks "she held an undisputed sway over her audiences in five operas only." The compass of her voice, says the memoir of the singer, written by Canon Henry Scott Holland and W. S. Rockstro, "extended from B below the stave to G on the fourth line above it — in technical language, from b to G; that is to say, a clear range of two octaves and a sixth. The various registers of this extended compass were so skilfully blended into one, by the effect of art, that it was impossible for the most delicate or attentive ear to detect their points of junction."

The three notes, F, G, and A, of the middle register, were the ones most injured by her hard work and faulty method, before going to Paris to study.

Jenny Lind's voice, says Rockstro, "was not by nature a flexible one. The rich sustained notes of the *soprano drammatico* were far more congenial to it than the rapid execution which usually characterizes the lighter class of *soprano* voices. But this she attained also, by almost superhuman labor. Her perseverance was indefatigable."

Once, when Madame Birch-Pfeiffer left her alone, practising the word *zersplittre*, on a high B flat, in the opening recitative in " Norma," and returned several hours afterwards, she found Jenny Lind practising the same word.

"She takes the greatest care of her voice," Madame Clara Schumann said. " She does not dance, and drinks neither wine, nor tea, nor coffee. . . . Never, perhaps, have I loved and reverenced a woman as I do her."

She disliked the contortions of face made by some singers when delivering impressive passages. She was never satisfied with a song unless the singer " looked pleasant."

She never regretted her decision to leave the stage. She wrote later to Madame Birch-Pfeiffer: " I cannot tell you in words how happy I feel about it. I shall sing in concerts; . . . in this way I shall be able to work at least five years longer; and that is necessary for me, as, for the last twelve months, I have sung only for institutions and charities. Without a beautiful goal one cannot endure life. At least I cannot. I have begun to sing what has long been the wish of my heart — oratorio. There I can sing the music I love; and the words make me feel a better being."

' Years after Jenny Lind had left the stage, an English friend found her sitting by the sea with a Lutheran Bible open in her hands, looking out into a glorious sunset. The friend said, "How was it that you ever came to abandon the stage, at the very height of your success?" " When, every day," was the reply, " it made me think less of *this*," laying a finger on the Bible, " and nothing at all of *that*," pointing to the sunset, " what else could I do?"

The Bible was to her a precious book. She wrote to a friend soon after she left the stage: "My Bible was never more necessary to me than now — never more truly my stay. I drink therein rest, self-knowledge, hope, faith, love, carefulness, and the fear of God; so that I look at life and the world in quite another fashion to what I did before. Would that all men would come to this knowledge, and that we all daily feasted on this Divine Book."

A little time before leaving the stage, Jenny Lind became engaged, in 1848, to a relative of the Grotes, Claudius Harris, a young captain in the Indian army. His admiration for her singing had been so great that he had followed her to Edinburgh, Glasgow, and other places.

She talked with Mrs. Stanley, while at the home of the Bishop in Norwich, about her engagement. "I want a support," she said. "I am quite alone, and just when I want help, the finger of God brings me this heart that can feel with me about all works of charity, just as I do. I never could marry any one who did not think with me about this: I should say to him, 'Good by! good by!'

"We wish to live quiet and uninterrupted somewhere. I want to be near trees, and water, and a cathedral. I am tired, body and soul; but my soul *most!*"

Capt. Harris's mother was opposed to the stage, and all its associations. The son was, also, but the goodness of the singer had blinded his eyes to her profession.

In the marriage settlement, Jenny Lind felt that she must retain the right to sing when she chose, and to have control of her own earnings. This freedom seemed to the young man "unscriptural!" The engagement was broken. The disappointment was painful at first, but she soon felt that good came out of it.

"It has passed over my soul like a beneficent storm," she wrote Madame Birch-Pfeiffer, " which has broken down all the hard shell of my being, and has set free many green plants to find their way to the dear sun! So that now I am always clothed in green, like the fairest hope! And I see quite clearly how infinitely much there is for me to do with my life; and I have only one prayer, that I may yet live long, and that, in the evening of my life, I may be able to show a pure soul to God. . . .

"I am glad and grateful from morning to night! I have a blitheness in my soul, which strains towards heaven! I am like a bird; I do not feel the least changed; quite the contrary; and the '*summa summarum*' is that I have won the greatest profit out of both outer and inner misfortune; and can thank God that I know what trouble is! All makes at last for good! God does not die."

In the early part of 1850, Jenny Lind sang at Göttingen, where the students made her a "Sister-Associate" of one of their famous guilds, and hung her portrait in their Assembly Room. She sang at Hanover twice for charity; at Brunswick, for pensions for the ducal orchestra; at Lübeck, for the poor; for the widow of the orchestral director, Bach, and for the pianist, Schreinzer, and reached Stockholm, May 12, where she gave six concerts for the benefit of the Royal Theatre, which had educated her, and sang at two state concerts in honor of the wedding of the crown prince.

The queen dowager begged her to choose one of several magnificent bracelets placed before her, but she preferred, and accepted instead, a bunch of forget-me-nots, which were in a vase on the table.

A medal in gold, silver, and bronze was struck in her honor, to which the king, and other distinguished persons of Sweden, contributed. At her death, she left these medals to the National Museum at Stockholm.

The fame of Jenny Lind had, of course, spread to the New World. The Emperor of Russia, at this time, offered her $56,000 for five months. P. T. Barnum determined to bring the singer before the American public, if possible. He sent his agent to Europe, who made a contract with Jenny Lind for one hundred and fifty concerts, at one thousand dollars a night, with expenses paid for herself, a companion and secretary, a servant, horses and carriage furnished. This contract was afterwards changed by Mr. Barnum in her interest, she to receive half the profits whenever the receipts were above five thousand five hundred dollars a night, and a right to annul the contract after sixty or one hundred concerts, with fixed penalties in either case. Mr. Barnum had faith in his venture, but the American public had not. He had great difficulty in raising the $187,500, which he had pledged Jenny Lind should be in the hands of London bankers for herself and musicians, as her security. When he asked the president of a bank to aid him, the friend laughed, and said, "It is generally believed in Wall Street that your engagement with Jenny Lind will ruin you. I do not believe you will ever receive so much as three thousand dollars at a single concert." A clergyman loaned him the last five thousand dollars needed.

Jenny Lind gave two concerts in Liverpool before starting for America. On the last night, after singing from Handel's "Messiah," she closed with the national anthem. The *Times* said, "The scene that ensued defies description. The walls of the building reverberated with cheers. Hats, sticks, handkerchiefs were waved in every direction. The platform of the orchestra was covered with bouquets and wreaths, many of which fell upon the head and the shoulders of the songstress."

She visited the new wing of the hospital, whose erection was due to her last year's singing; and then, followed by the shouts of thousands who were assembled on either side of the Mersey, and amid the boom of cannon, she sailed away to America, Aug. 21, 1850.

When she arrived, thousands were on the dock eager to catch a glimpse of her. Triumphal arches, surmounted by the eagle, bore the inscriptions, "Welcome, Jenny Lind! Welcome to America!" That evening she was serenaded at her hotel, the Irving House, by the New York Musical Fund Society, twenty thousand persons being present.

America seemed even more wild with enthusiasm than Europe had been. Tickets for the first concert, Sept. 11, in Castle Garden, were sold by auction, some persons paying as high as six hundred and fifty dollars for a single ticket. The "Jenny Lind Mania," as it was called, swept over the country. Jenny Lind's share, from the first concert, was nearly ten thousand dollars. She immediately sent for the mayor of the city, and divided it, according to his advice, among charitable institutions.

She soon wrote to her parents, "I was met with quite an astonishing reception. I have already given six concerts there [New York], in a hall with room for eleven thousand people; it has been crowded each time."

From Boston, she wrote to her guardian, Judge Munthe, "It is, indeed, a great joy, and a gift from God, to be allowed to earn so much money, and afterwards to help one's fellow-men with it. This is the highest joy I wish for in this life; everything else has disappeared from the many-colored course of my path on earth. Few know, though, what a beautiful and quiet inner life I am living.

Few suspect how unutterably little the world and its splendor have been able to turn my mind giddy. Herrings and potatoes, a clean wooden chair, and a wooden spoon to eat milk-soup with, — that would make me skip, like a child, for joy!"

Mr. George William Curtis, who attended all the Lind concerts in New York except one, heard her first in Berlin, in the part of Amina: he says in his own book of essays, "From the Easy-Chair," written with all his accustomed grace and charm: "The full volume, the touching sweetness of tone, the exquisite warble, the amazing skill and the marvellous execution, with the perfect ease and repose of consummate art, and the essential womanliness of the whole impression, were indisputable and supreme. . . . Other famous singers charmed that happy time. But Jenny Lind, rivalling their art, went beyond them all in touching the heart with her personality. Certainly, no public singer was ever more invested with a halo of domestic purity. When she stood with her hands quietly crossed before her, and tranquilly sang 'I know that my Redeemer liveth,' the lofty fervor of the tone, the rapt exaltation of the woman, with the splendor of the vocalization, made the hearing an event, and left a memory as of a sublime religious function."

In New York, as in Berlin, Jenny Lind was equally a delight to all. When she appeared in Castle Garden, May 24, 1852, "the magnificent voice," says Mr. Curtis, "filled it completely, and in the fascinated silence of the immense throng every exquisite note of the singer was heard. She carried a fresh bouquet, the gift of some friend, each time she appeared. But when at last she came forward to sing the farewell to America, for which Goldschmidt had composed the music, she bore in her hand a bouquet of white rosebuds, with a Maltese cross of deep carnations in the centre. This she held while, for the last time in public, she sang in America; and the young traveller who, five years before, had turned aside at Dresden to hear Jenny Lind in Berlin, alone in all that great audience at Castle Garden knew who had sent those flowers."

One night, in Boston, a girl, plainly dressed, came to the ticket-office, and laying down three dollars, said, "There goes half a month's earnings, but I am determined to hear Jenny Lind."

The remark was repeated to the singer. "Would you know the girl again?" she asked the man. Upon receiving an affirmative reply, she answered, placing a twenty-dollar gold piece in his hand, "Poor girl! Give her that, with my best compliments."

When she was in Havana, she saw one day a crippled Italian, Vivalla, who had come to see Mr. Barnum, passing out of the gate. He had lost the use of his left side by paralysis, and, unable to earn a living, gained a partial support through his dog, which turned a spinning-wheel, and performed other tricks. Jenny Lind was interested in him, and gave him five hundred dollars, while Mr. Barnum made the necessary arrangements for his return to his friends in Italy.

Vivalla called to leave her a basket of fruit, with his thanks. "Mr. Barnum," he said, "I should like so much to have the good lady see my dog turn a wheel; it is very-nice; he can spin very good. Shall I bring the dog and wheel for her?" Mr Barnum replied that she would be too busy to see his dog.

He told the incident to Jenny Lind, who said, "Poor man, let him come; it is all the good creature can do for me. It will make him *so* happy."

Vivalla came, and when she saw him from her window, she hastened down stairs, saying, "This is very kind of you to come with your dog. Follow me. I will carry the wheel up-stairs."

For an hour she devoted herself to the happy cripple. She petted his dog, sang and played for Vivalla, and finally carried his wheel to the door for him. She might be a great singer to all the rest of the world, but to this poor Italian she seemed like an angel, sent directly from Heaven.

From the ninety-three concerts given by Jenny Lind, under Mr. Barnum's management, the proceeds were $712,161. Her portion was $176,675. Sometimes the proceeds from a single concert were over sixteen thousand dollars. In New York City alone she gave away between thirty and forty thousand dollars in charities. When warned against so much liberality, as some unworthy persons were seeking aid, she invariably replied, "Never mind; if I relieve ten, and one is worthy, I am satisfied."

The last sixty nights of the concert series were given under her own management, assisted by Mr. Otto Goldschmidt, of Hamburg, an accomplished musician. At the close of her tour, she was married to Mr. Goldschmidt, at the house of Mr. S. G. Ward, in Boston, by Bishop Wainwright, of New York, Feb. 5, 1852. The Hon. Edward Everett, and a few others, were witnesses. Jenny Lind was, at this time, thirty-one, and her husband twenty-three, he having been born Aug. 21, 1829.

The marriage proved to be a happy one. She had found, she wrote a friend, "all that her heart ever wanted and loved." Her charities in America were unceasing. "While she habitually declined," says Mr. N. P. Willis, "the calls and attentions of fashionable society, she was in constant dread of driving more humble claimants from her door. She submitted, *every day*, to the visits of strangers, as far as strength and her professional duties would any way endure. To use her own expression, she was 'torn in pieces.'"

Mr. Willis thus sums up the charms of Jenny Lind: "That God has not made her a wonderful singer, *and then left her*, is the curious exception she forms to common human allotment. To give away more money in charity than any other mortal, and still be the first of prima donnas! . . . To be humble, simple, genial, and unassuming, and still be the first of prima donnas! To have begun as a beggar-child, and risen to receive more adulation than any queen, and still be the first of prima donnas! . . . It is the *combination* of superiorities and interests that makes the wonder; it is the concentrating of the stuff for half a dozen heroines in one single girl."

Henry F. Chorley, the author, thought her charm due, in part, "to the intense and unworldly, if not supernatural, expression of her countenance, which held fast many an eye that soon tires of regular beauty, or of features the smile or the sorrow of which may be read at a glance."

In 1852, Jenny Lind-Goldschmidt and her husband returned to Europe, and spent some years in Dresden. During the early half of 1854, she sang in Berlin, Leipzig, Vienna, and Budapesth, and, in the following year, at Amsterdam, Rotterdam, the Hague, and many other cities, always receiving the same enthusiastic welcome. In 1856, she sang in England, and later, in Ireland and Germany.

While living in Dresden, she wrote to a friend in Paris of her happy domestic life: "I want to speak to you of my baby. Well, I must tell you that God has given my dear husband and myself an adorable little girl, born on the

21st of March last. She is the perfect image of health and happiness. She laughs, she crows, in a way to delight all sympathetic hearts. We have given her a little Katharine, among other names, but we call her Jenny, — I need not say in honor of whom.

"Our boy, Walter, will be four years old the 9th of August next. He is an intelligent child, very intelligent, very religious, and when he has been naughty it is touching to see the way he prays God to make him good again, poor little chicken. He adores me, obeys me, and I understand the child completely, for he is exactly like myself in nature, — very impressionable, active, gay, high-tempered, affectionate, shy, good-natured, quick to learn, remembering all that he learns, preferring to the finest toys a horrible old doll, because it is one with which he has longest played, caring nothing about dress, but preferring to be loved. Is he musical? No, not the least in the world. That is my great despair. But he is religious, and I think he will be a Christian.

"As to baby, I cannot say as much. The little creature eats, drinks, laughs, and I have nothing to say against her character. My husband is now in England looking for a residence, for we intend, on account of our children, to settle in that country."

After her return to England, Madame Goldschmidt sang on special occasions only. She gave three oratorios for charitable purposes at Exeter Hall during the International Exhibition. In 1865 she appeared in the "Messiah," for the Clergy Fund Corporation; in 1866, at Cannes; in 1867, at the Musical Festival at Hereford; in 1869, in Hamburg and London, in "Ruth," an opera composed by her husband; in Düsseldorf and London, in 1870 and 1871, the latter year, in concert with Madame

Schumann; in 1873, at Northumberland House, before it was taken down; in 1877, in behalf of the Turkish Refugee Fund; in 1880, in behalf of the Albert Institute in a royal concert at Windsor; in 1883, her last public appearance in concert, for the Railway Servants' Benevolent Fund, at the Spa, Malvern Hills.

During her last years she gave much time to training the soprano voices in the Bach choir, founded by her husband in 1875, and helping the Royal College of Music, of whose faculty she was a member.

These last years were very happy, as she saw her children and grandchildren grow up around her. In 1887 she was attacked with paralysis, and was ill for several weeks. As she lay on her death-bed, as her daughter opened the shutters to let in the morning sun, she sang the first bars of the song she loved, "An den Sonnenschein," the last notes she ever sang.

She died Nov. 2, 1887, at Wynds Point, her cottage on Malvern Hills. She was buried Saturday, Nov. 5, in Great Malvern Cemetery. The Queen sent a wreath of white flowers for the woman whom she honored.

In accordance with her oft-expressed desire, the patchwork quilt, which the children of the United States gave her, was buried with her.

The money earned by Jenny Lind in America was entirely set aside for charity, and given away by will at her death. Fifty thousand Swedish crowns were sent to the University of Upsala, and the same to the University of Lund, to be used in scholarships for poor students; that at Upsala to be called "The Geijer Scholarship," and that at Lund, "The Bishop Tegnér." A large portion of the remainder of the fund was given to a hospital for poor children at Stockholm. She provided also for Jenny Lind

Scholarships at the Royal Academy of Music, and the Royal Academy of Fine Arts in Stockholm.

Sir Julius Benedict, who came to America with the singer as musical director, pianist, and accompanist, "regrets," he says, "that Jenny Lind did not turn her powerful influence to better account in America. There, where all the best materials abound, she might have laid the ground-work of a permanent school of music on the largest scale "in that country," which sooner or later will distance old Europe in the fine arts, as it does now in all branches of scientific invention and commercial enterprise."

Jenny Lind's gifts have been estimated at a half million dollars, and this is, perhaps, an under estimate.

Though very modest, she knew and appreciated her genius, and spoke to her friends "of the heavenly career" which she had been permitted to have. "If you knew," she wrote in 1847, "what a sensation of the nearness of a higher power one instinctively feels when one is permitted to contribute to the good of mankind, as I have done, and still do! Believe me, it is a great gift of God's mercy!"

Jenny Lind's voice was so exceptional, and her character so noble, that she will always hold an individual place in the world of art. "I have heard greater artists than the Lind," said a famous physician of the court of Berlin, "but I have never heard but one Lind, or any artist who knew better how to fascinate. She is certainly a marvellous apparition, with an attraction that is irresistible."

As Emerson said, "There must be a *man* behind the work"; so the world loved her, because there was a true woman behind the gifted artist.

"She is simply an angel," said the wife of the Earl of Westmoreland. So thought the rest of the world.

DOROTHEA LYNDE DIX.

DOROTHEA LYNDE DIX.

IN the town of Hampden, Me., April 4, 1802, was born Dorothea Lynde Dix. Neither child nor mother appears to have had any permanent home, as the father, Joseph Dix, was an unsuccessful man, and a wanderer.

Almost the first knowledge which the world has of the child is that when, at twelve years of age, she was stitching tracts together at Worcester, Mass., which her zealous father wrote and published to save the world, forgetting, seemingly, that his family, a wife and three children, were in the meantime destitute, and that there is high authority that "a man should provide for his own."

The little girl, high-spirited, and probably rebelling that she was kept at her task without education, ran away from Worcester, and reached Boston, the home of her paternal grandmother. The latter, Dorothy Lynde, was a woman of strong character, unemotional, living always by the stern rule of duty. The home was not one of love and sunshine for the child, but a home, nevertheless, where she would not want for food or clothing.

Her grandfather, Dr. Elijah Dix, born in Watertown, Mass., in 1747, was a man of unusual force and ability. He became a physician and surgeon at Worcester, Mass., and later removed to Boston, where he opened a drugstore on the south side of Faneuil Hall, and chemical works at South Boston, for refining sulphur and purifying camphor. He had great energy, large public spirit, and will, qualities which seem to have passed over the son Joseph, and lodged in the little granddaughter, Dorothea.

He died when the child was seven years old. She remembered him as the one bright feature of her childhood. She could never be brought to mention these days of poverty and humiliation, not even to tell where she was born, other than to say, pitifully, "I never knew childhood."

Knowing early in life that the support of her mother and her two little brothers, ten and twelve years younger than herself, must inevitably fall upon her, she studied as hard as possible, and at fourteen was back in Worcester, teaching a school for little children.

So girlish was she in looks, though mature in heart, with the burden of care laid upon her, she put on long dresses, and lengthened her sleeves, that she might appear older than she was. She was dignified and strict, and seems to have prospered with the work.

After this experiment in teaching, she returned to the home of her grandmother in Boston, then a town of forty thousand people, and studied till she was nineteen, when she opened a day-school in a little house owned by her grandmother in Orange Court. The school increased till the grandmother's house — euphoniously styled the "Dix Mansion" — was opened for a combined boarding and day school. Children of prominent families came from as far away as Portsmouth, N. H. Later, the two little brothers came, and she brought them up, as she had expected to do, providing for her mother as well.

Her generous heart soon began to manifest itself in work outside of her school. She wrote to her dignified grandmother, — perhaps she preferred that manner to a personal interview, — "Had I the saint-like eloquence of our minister, I would employ it in explaining all the motives, and dwelling on all the good, — good to the poor, the miserable, the idle, and the ignorant, which would follow your giving me permission to use the barn chamber for a schoolroom for charitable and religious purposes. You have read Hannah More's life. You approve of her labors for the most degraded of England's paupers; why not, when it can be done without exposure or expense, let *me* rescue some of America's miserable children from vice and guilt?"

The school was started in the barn, and out of it grew the work of the Warren Street Chapel, says the Rev. Francis Tiffany, of Cambridge, Mass., to whose admirable life of Miss Dix, by which he has done a real service to humanity, I am indebted for most of the facts of this sketch.

These months were full of exhausting labor. She studied hard to improve her mind, "almost worshipping talent," she said. She cared for her aged grandmother, for her brothers, superintended the house, and taught both schools, rising before daylight, and not retiring till after midnight. Besides this, she wrote "Conversations on Common Things," which has gone through sixty editions.

As a result of all this labor, she broke down in health, and was glad to accept the offer of Dr. William Ellery Channing, to care for the education of his children for the six months of the summer of 1827, when the family were at their country home in Portsmouth, R. I. Here she found great rest and pleasure in studying shells and seaweed, as, indeed, in every department of natural history.

She bemoaned her illness, but not for herself. She wrote a friend, "It is for him [her little brother] my soul is filled with bitterness when sickness wastes me; is because of him I dread to die."

For three or four years, being unable to teach very much, she compiled several books, mostly of a devotional character. In 1830, she went with the Channing family to the island of St. Croix, in the West Indies, and there, besides teaching the children, she made collections of tropical plants and birds, which she gave to Professor Benjamin Silliman, Audubon, and others.

In 1831, she opened her school again in the Dix Mansion, ambitious to carry out her ideal of education, and determined to earn a competency, that she might not be impecunious like her parents. To the end of her life she would never be long dependent upon others, or be paid for her benevolent work.

Her school seems to have been an excellent one for those times, with, perhaps, the duty-line too prominent for the sunny life of childhood. The children were requested to write letters to their teacher, which she answered, often long after midnight. One child wrote: "I thought I was doing very well until I read your letter; but when you said that you were 'rousing to greater energy,' all my self-satisfaction vanished. For if you are not satisfied in some measure with yourself, and are going to do more than you have done, I don't know what I shall do. You do not go to rest until midnight, and then you rise very early."

"She was, at this time," says a lady who attended her school, "in the prime of her years, tall and of dignified carriage, head finely shaped and set, with an abundance of soft, wavy, brown hair. Next to my mother, I thought her the most beautiful woman I had ever seen. She fascinated me from the first, as she had done many of my class before me."

Her voice was especially rich, low, and musical in its tone; her eyes were brilliant blue-gray, "their pupils so large and dilating as to cause them often to be taken for black," and her manner modest, yet showing command over self, and power over others.

After five years more of teaching, Miss Dix broke down compeiely, and was obliged to go abroad. Dr. Channing gave her letters of introduction to friends, among whom Mr. and Mrs. William Rathbone, of Liverpool, wealthy Unitarians, proved friends indeed. For a year and a half the invalid found this home one of love and rest. They did not realize, probably, that they were prolonging her life for a wonderful work. She seems to have found here, almost for the first time, the affection of which her woman's heart had been deprived.

During this absence from America, ner mother died in 1836, and her grandmother also, who left her enough property, combined with what she had earned, to support her comfortably through life. Her brothers had now come to self-support. One, Charles, graduated from the Boston Latin School in 1832, and died in the ship which he commanded in 1843, on the western coast of Africa. Joseph became a prosperous merchant in Boston.

Miss Dix came home in the autumn of 1837. Such a woman could not be idle. She was now thirty-five, improving in health, and getting ready for work; and her work was preparing for her.

Coming out of church one Sunday morning in the spring of 1841, it is said that she overheard two men talking of the inhuman treatment of the prisoners and lunatics in the jail of East Cambridge, Mass. About this time, at the suggestion of the Rev. Dr. Nichols, of Saco, Me., then a theological student in Cambridge, Miss Dix was asked to teach, in Sunday school, the women, some twenty in number, in the East Cambridge House of Correction.

With most excellent common-sense, for which she was always remarkable, she reasoned that it was idle to teach Christianity to people who were cold and ill-fed, unless their bodies were cared for as well as their souls. She determined to investigate matters, and found the jail overcrowded, filthy; innocent, guilty, and insane all together; no fires, with the thermometer below zero. She protested, and was told by the jailor that "fire was not needed, and would not be safe."

Duty had too long been the watchword of Dorothea Dix for her to keep silent, and do nothing. She at once applied to that noble philanthropist, Dr. S. G. Howe, who made a careful investigation of the matter, and wrote a letter to the Boston *Advertiser*. Charles Sumner, too, added his voice. Of course, the statements were denied by those in charge of the jail, but the matter was carried to the courts, and the rooms were soon cleaned and warmed.

Miss Dix had begun her life-work at thirty-nine. It was to know little or no cessation for nearly fifty years.

Much had been done both in France and England to ameliorate the cruel condition of the insane. In former times they were chained to their beds, to their walls, and kept worse than dumb beasts. One man in Paris, when Dr. Philippe Pinel undertook his work of mercy, had been in chains for forty years. When his chains were removed, he could not stand at first, but finally tottered to the light, and, looking up to the sky, exclaimed, "Ah, how beautiful!"

The noble Lord Shaftesbury labored in England for seventeen years to do away with the terrible abuses. The insane at that time were lashed into obedience by their keepers, and, for misconduct, chained in wells, the water reaching to their chins. They were kept in dungeons if violent, and fed on bread and water. Lord Shaftesbury found that from seventy-five to eighty per cent might be cured, if treated in the first twelve months; only five per cent, when the treatment was deferred.

Miss Dix, alone and unaided, determined to see if the other prisons and almshouses in Massachusetts were like the one in East Cambridge. She was a delicate and sensitive woman, but heroic when there was a duty to be performed. She went over the State carefully, notebook in hand. Another woman, without the authority of town or State, would not have dared, perhaps, to ask jailors to open doors. She dared, and entered, and observed closely.

When her examinations had been made, she wrote her Memorial to the State Legislature of Massachusetts, stating concisely and clearly *what she had seen*. " I proceed, gentlemen," she said, " to call your attention to the *present* state of insane persons confined within this Commonwealth in *cages, closets, cellars, stalls, pens; chained, naked, beaten with rods*, and *lashed* into obedience."

She told of a young woman at Danvers, nearly nude, confined in a cage, where the air was so offensive that no one could go near her. She told of another, at Sandisfield, who had been chained and beaten, who " was put up at auction (the town's poor), and bid off at the lowest price which was declared for her. One year, not long past, an old man came forward in the number of applicants for the poor wretch; he was taunted and ridiculed. What would he and his old wife do with such a mere beast?

" ' My wife says yes,' replied he; ' and I shall take her.'

" She was given to his charge; he conveyed her home; she was washed, neatly dressed, and placed in a decent bed-room, furnished for comfort, and opening into the kitchen. How altered her condition! As yet, the *chains* were not off. The first week, she was somewhat restless, at times, violent, but the quiet ways of the old people wrought a change. . . . After a week, the chain was lengthened, and she was received as a companion into the kitchen. Soon she engaged in trivial employments.

" ' After a fortnight,' said the old man, ' I knocked off the chains, and made her a free woman.' She is at times excited, but not violently; they are careful of her diet; they keep her very clean; she calls them father and mother."

At Groton, Miss Dix found a young man with an iron collar around his neck, and chained in a small wooden building apart from the almshouse, sitting month after month in darkness and alone. He was declared incurably insane. The keeper of the poorhouse, who had provided the iron collar and chain, spoke of it as his favorite remedy. "I had a cousin," he said, "up in Vermont, crazy as a wildcat, and I got a collar made for him, and he liked it."

"Liked it!" said Miss Dix, in her calm manner, though horrified at the hard-heartedness of the man, "how did he manifest his pleasure?"

"Why, he left off trying to run away."

The man at Groton had become insane while at work, and was taken to the poorhouse. A band of iron, an inch wide, was put about his neck, to which a chain, six feet long, was attached. Manacles were on his wrists. He was finally removed to the McLean Asylum, at Somerville, where his shackles were immediately knocked off, and his swollen limbs gently chafed. The delighted maniac exclaimed to his keeper, " My good man, I must kiss you."

The young man remained for four months, was never

violent, and gave hope of complete recovery when the overseers of the poor, feeling unable to pay three dollars a week, carried him back to the chains of Groton, where, no wonder, he soon became incurable!

At Shelburne, Miss Dix found a man nearly dead, half frozen, his food put into his filthy pen through bars. The keeper poked him about with a stick.

When the memorial of Miss Dix was published, the State was shocked at the revelation. The almshouse keepers pronounced the incidents "sensational and slanderous lies!" The keepers had visions of near-at-hand struggles to obtain new positions, as many would inevitably lose their places.

Some persons delared that this public work of searching out misdeeds was unbecoming in a woman! Alas, this has been the old argument used since the time of Eve! But gentle, yet firm, Dorothea Dix, went quietly on her way, trusting in God, and in the righteousness of her cause.

It was soon found that the State had provision for only five hundred insane, while there were in the Commonwealth nearly one thousand pauper insane and idiotic persons, besides eight hundred cared for privately. Additional buildings were soon erected for the insane, and many evils remedied.

But Miss Dix was satisfied that if such things were found in the progressive State of Massachusetts, other States needed her keen eyes and fearless heart. Perhaps she shrank from the labor and the unpleasantness. All the same, she went forward.

Rhode Island was her next field for operations. She visited, unobtrusively, the institutions, and made notes through several months.

At Little Compton, she found Abram Simmons. He was in a stone structure, like a tomb, unlighted and unventilated. "The place," she says, "was about seven feet by seven, and six and a half high. All, even the roof, was of stone. An iron frame, interlaced with rope, was the sole furniture. The place was filthy, damp, and noisome; and the inmate, the helpless and dependent creature, cast by the will of Providence on the care and sympathies of his fellowman, — there he stood, near the door, motionless and silent; his tangled hair fell about his shoulders; his bare feet pressed the filthy, wet stone floor; he was emaciated to a shadow, and more resembled a disinterred corpse than any living creature. Never have I looked upon an object so pitiable, so woe-struck, so imaging despair.

"I took his hands and endeavored to warm them by gentle friction. I spoke to him of release, of liberty, of care and kindness. Notwithstanding the assertions of the mistress, that he would kill me, I persevered. A tear stole over the hollow cheek, but no words answered to my importunities. . . . In moving a little forward, I struck against something which returned a sharp metallic sound; it was a length of ox-chain, connected to an iron ring which encircled a leg of the insane man. At one extremity it was joined to what is termed 'a solid chain,' — namely, bars of iron eighteen inches or two feet long, linked together, and at one end connected by a staple to the rock overhead. 'My husband,' said the mistress, 'in winter takes out sometimes, of a morning, half a bushel of frost, and yet *he never freezes,*' — referring to the oppressed and life-stricken maniac before us. 'Sometimes he screams dreadfully,' she added; 'and that is the reason we had the double wall, and two doors in place of one; his cries disturbed us in the house.'"

"How long has he been here?" asked Miss Dix.

"'Oh, above three years; but, then, he was kept a long while in a cage first; but once he broke his chains and the bars, and escaped; so we had this built where he can't get off.' Get off! No, indeed; as well might the buried dead break through the sealed gates of the tomb!"

The frost on the inside of this stone cell, where poor, insane Abram Simmons lived, was often half an inch thick, and the outside blanket of his bed was frozen with the drippings from the wall. With wet straw to lie upon, and wet clothing to cover him, the dreary winters passed, one after another. And all this in a Christian State!

All over Rhode Island Miss Dix found mismanagement, lack of accommodation, and inhumanity unknown to the public. When one of the leading men of the State presented the memorial which she had prepared, the people were shocked, as they had been in Massachusetts.

What was to be done? The small asylum in the city of Providence needed enlarging. She determined to visit a well-known millionnaire, and ask his aid. People smiled at her hopeless errand, for Mr. Butler had not been a giver of his wealth. She laid the matter before him, with her almost unsurpassed earnestness and eloquence. He listened, spell bound, and then said abruptly, "What do you want me to do?"

"Sir, I want you to give $50,000 toward the enlargement of the insane hospital in this city."

"Madame, I'll do it!" was his answer; and "Butler Hospital" was the result.

New Jersey was the next State visited, and Hon. Joseph S. Dodd presented her memorial. And then, as usual, followed some of her hardest work. As soon as the memorial was published, she began to write editorials for the press, and letters to prominent persons, urging them to use their pens and their voices for whatever measure was proposed. She was generally given an alcove in the library, or other public building, and hither friends brought member after member of the Legislature that she might convince them with her sincerity and her power. Sometimes, at the parlor of her boarding-house, she would invite fifteen or twenty members for a conference on the memorial, or the bill following it. She had great tact, and was a consummate judge of human nature. She was careful not to give offence, while she was a master in executive ability and leadership.

While thus laboring at Trenton, she wrote to a friend in Philadelphia, says her biographer: "You cannot imagine the labor of conversing and convincing. Some evenings I had at once twenty gentlemen for three hours' steady conversation. The last evening, a rough country member, who had announced in the House that the 'wants of the insane in New Jersey were all humbug,' and who came to overwhelm me with his arguments, after listening an hour and a half, with wonderful patience, to my details, and the principles of treatment, suddenly moved into the middle of the parlor, and thus delivered himself: 'Ma'am, I bid you good night! I do not want, for my part, to hear anything more; the others can stay, if they want to. *I am convinced;* you 've conquered me out and out; I shall vote for the hospital. If you 'll come to the House, and talk there as you have here, no man that is n't a brute can stand you; and so, when a man's convinced, that's enough. The Lord bless you!' — and thereupon he departed."

Miss Dix met with all sorts of obstacles. People did not like to be taxed, either for the sane or the insane.

Some called her a "Heaven-sent Angel of Mercy," and immediately voted against her bill. Some wished she had never come into their State; but always when the hard work had been done, and the bill passed, and a noble institution built, then the Legislature and the people always passed a vote of thanks, and believed, as she herself believed, "that she was called by Providence to the vocation to which life, talents, and fortune have been surrendered these many years."

While working in New Jersey she had also been laboring in Pennsylvania, and in 1845 bills for State insane asylums were carried in each State. Besides work in these two States, she visited the State prisons of Louisiana at Baton Rouge, of Mississippi at Jackson, of Arkansas at Little Rock, of Missouri at Jefferson City, and of Illinois at Alton. During the three years, ending with 1845, Miss Dix travelled, in her arduous labors of love, over ten thousand miles. And yet she was frail in body, and naturally timid! Much of this journeying was over bad roads, the water and mud sometimes coming up to the body of her carriage; "but she always took with her for emergencies," says Mr. Tiffany, "an outfit of hammer, wrench, nails, screws, a coil of rope, and straps of stout leather, which, under many a mishap, sufficed to put things to rights, and enable her to pursue her journey."

"She travelled all over the country," says a friend, "with a moderate valise in her hand, and wearing a plain gray travelling-dress, with snow-white collar and cuffs. Her trunk was sent a week ahead, with the necessary changes of linen, etc., and one plain black-silk dress for special occasions. Neatness in everything indicated her well-directed mind."

She was now but little past forty, and her work seemed

but just beginning. She went to North Carolina where her bill for the Raleigh Insane Asylum had been once defeated. The Hon. James C. Dobbin, afterwards Secretary of the Navy, was her helpful friend. His wife, during an illness, had received great kindness from Miss Dix, and not unmindful of such kindness, Mrs. Dobbin, on her dying bed, besought her husband to see that Miss Dix's bill was passed. When the time came for him to speak upon the bill, his eloquence, the memory of his lovely wife, his own overwhelming sorrow, all added to his brilliant gifts. The bill passed by one hundred and one ayes to ten nays.

Miss Dix went on her way to Alabama rejoicing. Here the work was delayed — though only for a year or two — by the burning of the State Capitol, and other matters; but Miss Dix wrote a friend, "I have recollected amidst these perplexities that God requires no more to be accomplished than He gives time for performing, and I turn now more quietly to my work up the Hill Difficulty. The summit is cloud-capped, but I have passed amidst dark and rough ways before, and shall not now give out."

In Mississippi, where the Legislature determined "not to give a dime," the members voted to give land, and three million brick, and fifty thousand dollars, and wished to name the hospital after her. This she always declined, only in a single instance permitting one in Pennsylvania to be called "Dixmont Hospital," in honor of her grandfather, who founded the town of Dixmont, in Maine.

In many other States — Tennessee, Indiana, Kentucky, Maryland — she accomplished much. She knew no such word as failure. When told, "Nothing can be done here!" she replied, "I know no such word in the vocabulary I adopt." She used to say, "The tonic I need is the tonic of opposition. That always sets me on my feet."

And she had that peculiar tonic administered in large quantity through life.

She was consulted about proper sites for asylums, methods of building, the right persons to be placed in charge, and a thousand matters that taxed heart and brain. When a special piece of ground was desired at Washington, D. C., for the Hospital for the Insane of the Army and Navy, she went to the owner, Mr. Thomas Blagden, and begged him to sell it. He could not bear to part with it, as it was dear to himself and his family. But after a visit from Miss Dix, he sold it for fifteen thousand dollars less than his price, though it cost him much anguish of heart, and wear of body. Neither he nor his wife could stand between Miss Dix and her cherished plans; "regarding you as we do," he wrote her, "as the instrument in the hands of God to secure this very spot for the unfortunates, whose best earthly friend you are, and believing sincerely that the Almighty's blessing will not rest on, nor abide with, those who may place obstacles in your way."

She was always collecting from the many homes where she found a warm welcome, such things as music-boxes, minerals, puzzles, bird's-nests, flowers, toys, with which to amuse the poor insane creatures, whom she had seen shut up alone and in darkness.

What wonder that the people looked upon her as an angel of mercy! Dr. Francis Lieber wrote from Columbia, S. C., to George S. Hillard, of Boston: "What a heroine she is! May God protect her! Over the whole breadth and length of the land are her footsteps, and where she steps flowers of the richest odor of humanity are sprouting and blooming as on an angel's path. I have the highest veneration for her heart, and will, and head."

She wrote Mrs. Hare, of Philadelphia, from Texas: "My eyes fill with tears at the homely heart-welcome, the confidence, the cordial good-will, and the succession of incidents, proving that I do, in very truth, dwell in the hearts of my countrymen. I am so astonished that my wishes in regard to institutions, my opinions touching organization, are considered definitive."

Once she was taking dinner at a small public-house on a prairie. When she offered to pay, the owner said, "No, no, by George! I don't take money from you; why, I never thought I should see you, and now you are in my house! You have done good to everybody for years and years. Make sure, now, there's a home for you in every house in Texas."

Once, when travelling in Michigan, in an uninhabited portion of the country, she observed that her driver, a youth, had a pair of pistols with him. She said, "Give me the pistols; I will take care of them"; to which the lad reluctantly consented.

Going through a dismal forest, a man caught the horse by the bridle, and demanded Miss Dix's purse. With her sweet voice, she said, "Are you not ashamed to rob a woman? I have but little money, and that I want to defray my expenses in visiting prisons and poorhouses, and, occasionally, in giving to objects of charity. If you have been unfortunate, are in distress, and in want of money, I will give you some."

The man turned deadly pale, exclaiming, "My God! that voice!" He told her that he had heard her speak to the convicts in the Philadelphia prison, and expressed sorrow for having disturbed her. She offered him money till he should find some honest employment. He declined at first, but she insisted, telling him that he would be tempted to rob somebody else, if he had no money. But for her presence of mind in taking the pistols, doubtless some one would have been murdered.

She did not confine her work to asylums and prisons. She said, "My conviction of the necessity of search into the wants of the friendless and afflicted has deepened. If I am cold, they are cold; if I am weary, they are distressed; if I am alone, they are abandoned."

While engaged in asylum-work at St. Johns, Newfoundland, there was a dreadful storm, with many shipwrecks. Knowing that at Sable Island, some thirty miles off the southeast coast of Nova Scotia, there had been many wrecks, she determined to visit the place, and see if there could not be some remedy for the frequent loss of lives. While there, a new vessel was wrecked in a dense fog, though all lives were saved. The captain, the last person on board, had become a raving maniac, and refused to leave the wreck. Miss Dix begged the sailors to go back for him in the life-boat, and save his life, if they had to bind him for safety. They did as she requested, and brought him bound hand and foot. Miss Dix loosened his cords, took him by the arm, and led him away, calming him by her persuasive manner and gentle words.

She hurried back to Boston to confer with Capt. R. B. Forbes, of the Humane Society, as to the building of modern life-boats, and other life-saving equipments. She raised funds in Boston, New York, and Philadelphia, for four first-class life-boats, a life-car, mortar, coils of rope, etc., all of which were sent at once to Sable Island, and were the means of saving many lives. She sent also a library of several hundred volumes, contributed by Boston friends and booksellers, to constitute a Mariners' Library for Sable Island. To the end of her life she helped to establish libraries in the life-saving stations all along the coasts of the United States. How barren seems a life given to selfishness or idleness, when compared with that of Dorothea Dix!

As early as 1848 she had endeavored to obtain from Congress a grant of five million acres of land, the proceeds of the sale to be a perpetual fund for the care of the indigent insane, to be divided among the States according to population. Congress had given millions of acres for education and internal improvements, and now she asked five millions for those, she said, " who, through the providence of God, are *wards* of *the nation*, claimants on the sympathy and care of the public, through the miseries and disqualifications brought upon them by the sorest afflictions with which humanity can be visited."

In her memorial to Congress she said, " I have myself seen *more than nine thousand idiots, epileptics, and insane in these United States, destitute of appropriate care and protection.*"

By the courtesy of Congress, an alcove in the Capitol Library was set apart for Miss Dix, where she could converse with the members. The bill was deferred that session, from press of other matters.

In 1850 she appealed again to Congress, this time for 12,225,000 acres, ten millions of which should be used for the benefit of the insane, and the rest for the blind, and deaf, and dumb.

She went to the Capitol Library and worked daily as before. She rose at four or five in the morning, spent an hour in private devotions, to strengthen her for her work, wrote letters on her varied work all over the country, and at ten o'clock was ready to meet and talk with the members about her beloved project. The bill was again deferred, after passing in the House, and 1851 saw her a third time at her post of duty, working and waiting.

This year it passed in the Senate, but was deferred before the House. Two years later, in 1854, she saw her 12,225,000 acre bill carried triumphantly through the House and the Senate, both Democratic. She was, of course, enthusiastic and thankful.

The Democratic President, Franklin Pierce, had assured her personally of his deep interest in the measure. Hereafter the work would be easy, for every State could now care properly for its helpless ones.

To the astonishment of Miss Dix, as well as of all her co-workers all over the country, the President *vetoed the bill!* declaring that he did so from Constitutional reasons, as also from expediency. For the first time in her life, Miss Dix was prostrated by the unexpected disappointment, after six years of labor, since 1848. It seemed necessary for her to go abroad if her life was to be prolonged.

She sailed in September, 1854, in the "Arctic," which, on the return trip, went down with all on board. Mr. E. K. Collins, the chief owner of the line, declined any passage money from Miss Dix, saying, with emotion, when she thanked him, "The nation, madam, owes you a debt of gratitude which it can never repay, and of which I, as an individual, am only too happy to be thus privileged to mark my sense."

She rested for some weeks with her friends, the Rathbones, in Liverpool, and then started for Scotland, to look into the asylums and hospitals of that country.

She found what Lord Shaftesbury had found, no provision for *pauper* lunatics. When this matter was brought before the country, petitions poured in against taxing the land for the insane poor. If rich, they were cared for in private hospitals; if poor! they languished in almshouses, prisons, or police stations.

Miss Dix, ill though she was, went about the work in earnest. She visited the workhouses and private dwellings where the idiots and lunatics were stowed away, and, finding many abuses to be corrected, she determined to ask the Home Secretary, Sir George Grey, in London, for a Committee of Investigation.

The Lord Provost of Edinburgh, learning of her determination and opposing it, also hastened to London, hoping to meet the Home Secretary before she did. "The Lord Provost stopped to have his trunk packed," says Mr. Tiffany, "and to journey comfortably by day. Miss Dix grasped a hand-bag and boarded the night train."

She was twelve hours ahead of the Lord Provost, met the Home Secretary by the aid of the noble Shaftesbury, the commission was appointed, and the report was made to Parliament in 1857.

Of course the country was shocked. The member for Aberdeen characterized the report of the commissioners as "one of the most horrifying documents he had ever seen. It was a state of things which they could not before have believed to prevail in any civilized country, much less in this country, which made peculiar claims to civilization, and boasted of its religious and humane principles. . . . Distressing as were the cases which he had mentioned, there were others ten times worse, remaining behind — so horrible, indeed, that he durst not venture to shock the feelings of the House by relating them."

Sir George Grey deplored, in the House of Commons, that the bringing about of this needed reform should have been left to a "foreigner, and that foreigner a woman, and that woman a dissenter."

Lunacy Laws were passed in 1857, and Sir James A. Clark, Physician to the Queen, wrote Miss Dix, four years afterwards, concerning "the improvement which has been effected in Scotland through your exertions. The treatment of the pauper insane in Scotland is now more carefully attended to than in any other part of Great Britain."

After some noble work in the Channel Islands, Miss Dix went with the Rathbones to Switzerland, the remembrance of which was always a delight. When worn with her great cares in our Civil War, she wrote, "I never find the glorious views of the Alps fade from my mind's eye. A thousand incidents recall and repeat the memory of those grand snow peaks piercing the skies."

On the return of the Rathbones to England, Miss Dix went to France and other countries in her earnest work. At Rouen she visited hospitals for aged men and women; at Paris she had a special permit to visit all the prisons and hospitals, without exception; in Genoa, Turin, Naples, Florence, and Rome, she gave no time to art, but all her time to the suffering. Pope Pius IX. granted her audience, and at her request, drove unannounced to the insane asylum, and made a personal inspection. Cardinal Antonelli entered heartily into her plans.

From the Island of Corfu she wrote to a friend: "You will not be more surprised than I am that I find travelling *alone* perfectly easy. I get into all the hospitals and all the prisons I have time to see or strength to explore. I take no refusals, and yet I speak neither Italian, German, Greek, or Sclavonic."

In Greece and Turkey it was always the same kind reception, the same God-speed to a noble woman who was living to benefit the world.

Dr. Cyrus Hamlin, then President of Robert College,

Constantinople, wrote Mr. Tiffany, that " Miss Dix made the impression at Constantinople of a person of culture, judgment, self-possession, absolute fearlessness in the path of duty, and yet a woman of refinement and true Christian philanthropy. I remember her with the profoundest respect and admiration."

From Constantinople she went to Russia, Sweden, Norway, Denmark, Holland, Belgium, and Germany, always on the one errand of mercy. She returned to America in September, 1856, after an absence of two years, and resumed the work of caring for her various institutions, as though she had been away from school for a brief vacation. She raised money for her work, asking in the various States for more than a third of a million dollars! She was glad of the work to do, otherwise, she said, in 1861, "the state of our beloved country would crush my heart and life."

When Abraham Lincoln was elected, Miss Dix, having been much at the South, felt that war would be the inevitable result. She sought an interview with Mr. Samuel M. Felton, the president of the Philadelphia and Baltimore Railroad, and so impressed upon him the certainty that Mr. Lincoln would be assassinated on his way to the inauguration at Washington (unless the Confederates could, in the meantime, capture Washington, and make it the capital of the Confederacy, thus preventing the inauguration), that President Felton arranged for Lincoln to be conducted thither, privately, by night.

Mr. Tiffany justly thinks it remarkable that " the keen insight and military decision of mind of a woman should have lighted on the precise point where the greatest peril to the nation lay," and thus have preserved Lincoln, and, perhaps, Washington itself, to the country.

The Civil War came with that first gun fired by the Confederates, at Fort Sumter, at daybreak, April 12, 1861. Three days later, President Lincoln called for seventy-five thousand volunteers, for three months' service. Among the first to respond was the Sixth Massachusetts Regiment, some of them lads under twenty,— the first full regiment to enter the war.

Mrs. Mary A. Livermore, in her thrilling book, "My Story of the War," thus describes the departure of the troops from the Boston and Albany Station : " With the arrival of the uniformed troops, the excitement burst out into a frenzy of shouts, cheers, and ringing acclamations. Tears ran down not only the cheeks of the women, but those of the men ; but there was no faltering. A clergyman mounted an extemporized platform, to offer prayer, where he could be seen and heard by all, and a solemn hush fell on the excited multitude as if we were inside a church. His voice rang out to the remotest auditor. The long train backed down where the soldiers were scattered among mothers, wives, sweethearts, and friends, uttering last words of farewell.

" 'Fall into line!' was the unfamiliar order that rang out, clear and distinct, with a tone of authority. The blue-coated soldiers released themselves tenderly from the clinging arms of affection, kissed again and again and again the faces upturned to theirs, white with the agony of parting, formed in long lines, company by company, and were marched into the cars."

A woman had fainted in the crowd, and after she was restored to consciousness Mrs. Livermore turned to speak to her. The poor mother apologized for her weakness ; and a bystander said that Andrew, who had just enlisted, was her only remaining son, as Clement, the other one, had been drowned, the week before, in the Bay of San Francisco.

Mrs. Livermore tried to comfort her by saying, that "he had only gone for three months." "If the country needs my boy for three months, or three years, I am not the woman to hinder him," was the reply of the noble mother. "He's all I've got, now that Clement is drowned; but when he told me he'd enlisted, I gave him my blessing, and told him to go; for, if we lose our country, what is there to live for?"

The Sixth Regiment, in passing through Baltimore, on its way to Washington, was stoned and insulted by a vast mob, and several were killed. These were the first precious lives given for the preservation of the Union, April 19, on the anniversary of the battles of Lexington and Concord.

Only three hours after this bloodshed in Baltimore, Miss Dix reached that city, and, with difficulty, took the last train which was permitted to leave for Washington. Again the work was ready for her, and she was ready for the work. At once she reported herself, with some nurses, at the War Department for free service in the hospitals. She was immediately appointed by Simon Cameron, Secretary of War, "Superintendent of Women Nurses, to select and assign women nurses to general or permanent military hospitals, they *not* to be employed in such hospitals without her sanction and approval, except in cases of urgent need."

She had entered upon a work, Herculean in its proportions. She had thousands of women to superintend, the generous gifts of a great nation to help distribute, the sick and dying to befriend, and many factions to conciliate. What wonder that the frail woman of sixty did not always agree with the surgeons! What wonder if she sometimes seemed arbitrary and severe!

"Her whole soul was in her work," says Mrs. Livermore. "She rented two large houses as depots for the sanitary supplies sent to her care, and houses of rest and refreshment for nurses and convalescent soldiers. She employed two secretaries, owned ambulances, and kept them busily employed, printed and distributed circulars, went hither and thither from one remote point to another in her visitations of hospitals, adjusted disputes, settled difficulties where her nurses were concerned, undertook long journeys by land and by water, and paid all expenses incurred from her private purse. Her fortune, time, and strength were laid on the altar of her country in its hour of trial."

Benson J. Lossing, in his "Pictorial Field Book of the Civil War," gives Miss Dix the same well-deserved praise: "She went from battle-field to battle-field, when the carnage was over; from camp to camp, and from hospital to hospital, superintending the operations of the nurses, and administering, with her own hands, physical comforts to the suffering, and soothing the troubled spirits of the invalid or dying soldiers with a low voice, musical and attractive, and always burdened with words of heartfelt sympathy and religious consolation.

"The amount of happiness that resulted from the services of this woman of delicate frame, which seemed to be incapable of enduring the physical labor required of it, can never be estimated. The true record is only in the great Book of Remembrance."

During the long four years of the war she never took a day's vacation. She had to be reminded often to take her meals, so completely was her mind absorbed by her work. What a pity that she did not keep a record of some of the heroic and pathetic incidents of which these days were full, as she ministered to the soldiers, — incidents that are the only bright gleams amid all the dark shadows of war!

Mrs. Mary V. E. Thomas, one of the nurses in the war, gives this illustration of the supervision of Miss Dix, and its practical results, in "Belford's Magazine" for January, 1892: "One evening, as I was leaving the hospital, a note was handed me from Miss Dix; it read, 'I must see you as soon as possible.' I went direct to the office. As usual, she came at once to the point.

"'I want you to visit the hospital across the river, in Virginia.'

"'What for?'

"'Don't mention my name. Can you go to-morrow?'

"'Yes; but I should like to know for what purpose I am going.'

"'I want to know how the hospital is coming on.'"

The lady went, at the request of Miss Dix, and found at the entrance of the hospital "a highly dressed and highly rouged young woman, with a paper-covered novel in her hand, — French, I saw at once. To my question, 'Can I see the hospital?' she replied, in a saucy tone, 'Go in there,' pointing to the door; 'you'll find somebody.' She proceeded on her way to join the officer of the day, who was awaiting her; this my backward glance revealed to me."

Mrs. Thomas passed about the hospital, observing that the nurses exchanged glances and acted as if they would like to make some communications to her, but scarcely dared. Finally she entered the room of a delicate-looking girl, who told her the real condition of things. The surgeon in charge had brought some disreputable persons from New York, who sat at the officers' table, and ate and drank what was provided for the wounded soldiers, giving the nurses dry bread and weak coffee.

For months they had tried to get a message to Miss Dix, and finally, when a new milkman came, who was not yet in the confidence of the officials, he was given a dollar for getting a note to Miss Dix. Hence the unlooked-for visit by Mrs. Thomas.

When she returned, Miss Dix asked anxiously, " ' What have you to report?'

" ' I went through the hospital; patients seem to be doing pretty well.'

" ' Nothing more?' she questioned, as her countenance fell.

" ' Yes; a painted woman, reading a French novel.'

" ' Ah! What else?'

"Then I opened my budget and told her all. Her face flushed, she clasped her hands nervously, as she said, 'That must be stopped.'

"And it was stopped. Within ten days that hospital was broken up, the patients were removed to Washington, and a certain surgeon was dismissed from the army."

On another occasion, Mrs. Thomas received a slip of paper which read, "Come immediately to my office. D. D."

"The ambulance soon brought me to Miss Dix's office. The windows were filled with plants, many of them in bloom, giving the room a cheerful aspect, while the floors and the corners of the room were piled up with all sorts of hospital stores, bandages, wearing apparel for the invalid soldiers, bedding, etc. Several nurses were receiving directions. I sat down on a box to await my turn. In a few moments we were alone. Miss Dix addressed me excitedly. 'You must go at once to Armory Square Hospital; the wounded are being taken there by the hundreds. You will find enough to do.'

"With nervous haste she filled a basket with such articles as would be needed. She looked tired and worn, and was evidently kept up by excitement which could only find relief in action. All the previous night she and the other ladies had been at the steamboat wharf, ministering to the wounded as they arrived.

"The hospital grounds were crowded with the wounded and the dying, on stretchers. Stepping over several I made my way to a tent already filled to its utmost capacity. Before I could lay aside my bonnet and gloves a pleading voice said, 'Do, please, ma'am, look at this leg.'

"There lay a man of powerful frame and fine, open countenance. I removed the soiled bandage, taking care to notice the way it was put on, as it must be replaced."

"I am afraid I won't be able to put it on like this," said Mrs. Thomas; "of course, the doctor dressed it?"

"Oh, no, ma'am; it was one of them ladies at the front; she was better than any doctor."

Thus did Miss Dix and her noble helpers work for the soldiers.

Mrs. Annie Wittenmyer, whose work was most valuable during the war, and who, since the war, has been a leader in the National Woman's Relief Corps, writes me, concerning Miss Dix: "She was tall and stately in person and manners. She was reserved and imperious in conversation, — on the verge of haughtiness. She was fine-looking, and had certainly in early life been handsome. At sixty there were no wrinkles in her face, or gray threads in her hair. She was neat and always suitably dressed, but very plainly.

"She was a woman of fine mind, which was enriched by culture and much travel. When one could get her to talk she was very entertaining, otherwise she seemed cold and unsocial. . . .

"The people had confidence in her integrity, and she received heavy lots of supplies from this country and England. She worked hard and loyally, and was true and honest."

When the war was over, the Hon. Edwin M. Stanton, who had then become Secretary of War, asked her how the nation could best show her its appreciation of her invaluable services,— either by a great public meeting or a vote of money by Congress. She declined both absolutely, but said, "I would like the flags of my country."

A beautiful pair of flags were made for her by the direction of the Government, and sent to her, "In token and acknowledgment of the inestimable services rendered by Miss Dorothea L. Dix for the Care, Succor and Relief of the Sick and Wounded Soldiers of the United States on the Battle-field, in Camps and Hospitals, during the recent war, and of her benevolent and diligent labors and devoted efforts to whatever might contribute to their comfort and welfare."

These national colors were bequeathed by Miss Dix to Harvard College, and are now suspended over the main portal of Memorial Hall, dedicated to the Sons of Harvard who gave their lives for their country. These flags represent to Harvard College the work of a noble woman, whose memory the students of that institution should never forget to honor.

At the close of the war, for eighteen months Miss Dix carried on a very large correspondence with the families of the soldiers who had died or become invalids under her charge, and obtained pensions for them, or assisted in various ways. She became responsible for the erection of the monument at the National Cemetery at Hampton, Va., near Fortress Monroe, where twelve thousand Union soldiers are buried.

"I had especial direction over most of these, martyred to a sacred cause," Miss Dix wrote a friend; "and never forget the countless last messages of hundreds of dying men to fathers, mothers, wives, and children; never forget the calm, manly fortitude which sustained them through the anguish of mortal wounds and the agonies of dissolution. Nothing, in a review of the past four years' war, so astonishes me as the uniformly calm and firm bearing of these soldiers of a good cause, dying without a murmur as they had suffered without a complaint."

She raised eight thousand dollars among her friends, visited the quarries of Maine and selected the granite, and wrote General Grant for "one thousand muskets and bayonets, fifteen rifled guns, and a quantity of twenty-four-pound shot," for a fence, which he at once granted.

The monument is seventy-five feet high, on a base twenty-seven feet square, inclosed by a circular fence, with the muskets and cannon set in blocks of stone. On it are the words, "In Memory of Union Soldiers who Died to maintain the Laws."

At sixty-five she took up again her work for the insane. For fifteen years, gently but efficiently she did her manifold work for humanity.

At eighty, a home having been urgently tendered her at the asylum in Trenton, N. J., the first one which she had caused to be built in America, she accepted the offer, and there ended her days. She had reared homes for others, but had none for herself. Her marriage in early life was prevented, it is said, by the breaking of an engagement with her cousin.

For six years she lived at the asylum, an honored guest, a great sufferer, but she said that "it was all right it should be so, it was God's will; only it was hard to bear."

Dr. John W. Ward, at the head of the State Lunatic Asylum, of Trenton, writes me: "I saw her daily during her stay with us, and can assure you that her marvellous mind and memory remained intact until almost the hour of dissolution. Her descriptive powers were something phenomenal. I have never met her equal in man or woman. . . . Miss Dix was an indefatigable worker. She allowed scarcely any obstacle to thwart her in her work. Her indomitable will seemed capable of overcoming everything; yet she told me, a short time before her death, that she never planned anything by herself. She always felt fully assured that God directed her from day to day what she should do, and it was this feeling on her part, probably, that during her long life prevented her from working *with* others. She worked *through* others, but never with them. She was always a deeply devout woman; a Unitarian in religious belief, but with a sacred reverence for Bethlehem, Gethsemane, and Calvary."

Precious letters came to Miss Dix in the asylum from all over the country. Whittier wrote from Oak Knoll, Danvers: "Thou hast done so much for others, that it is right for thee now, in age and illness, to be kindly ministered to. He who has led thee in thy great work of benevolence will never leave thee nor forsake thee."

Gen. S. C. Armstrong wrote her: "You are one of my heroes. My ideal is not one who gives the flush and strength of youth to good work, — for who can help doing so when a chance opens? . . . But you kept in the field long past your best days. Your grit and resolve have been wonderful."

She died on the evening of July 17, 1887, at the age of eighty-five, and was buried in Mount Auburn Cemetery, near Boston, a place dear to all Americans, on account of the graves of Lowell, Longfellow, Margaret Fuller, and others who have been an honor and a blessing to their country.

ANN H. JUDSON.

ANN, SARAH, AND EMILY JUDSON.

ON the south side of Washington Square, New York City, is a beautiful Memorial Baptist Church, that should be visited by every one who is interested in helping humanity.

It is a church whose building and methods people will copy in the years to come. Besides the Sunday services, it is used every day in the week for noble purposes. "If a business firm should erect an expensive building, and use it only during six or seven hours a week, could it expect to succeed?" says the Rev. Dr. Edward Judson, the pastor of this church.

"And yet all over Manhattan Island we have vast enclosed spaces, which are actually in use for only a few hours each week. The rest of the time they serve only to circumscribe the cheerful habitations of men, and are occupied by mice, and silence, and gloom."

The Main Auditory, for worship, seats twelve hundred persons; the Memorial Hall, for Sunday-school use, lectures, and other entertainments, seven hundred persons; the School-house, with three light, cheerful rooms, is used for kindergarten, sewing-schools and primary work, both secular and religious; the Young Men's Headquarters, with social room, library, and reading-room, and gymnasium, is open every night; the "Deats Memorial Home for Children," at the base of the tower, with beds for fifty children, provides shelter, food, clothes, school, and church. The expense of all this is borne in part by an adjoining apartment and boarding-house with seven floors, called "The Judson," which already yields a net revenue of $10,000 a year. The current expenses of the church proper are met by voluntary offerings, all the seats being *free*, and the "whole church open all day for any one to come in and rest a while," says its devoted and eloquent pastor. On Sunday evenings the sermon is followed by a Song Service, the congregational singing being led by a choir of fifty voices, accompanied by organ, piano, violins, and flutes.

Besides all the spiritual activities of the church, there is an industrial school for girls, a dress-making establishment for learners, a flower mission, a free ice-water fountain, fresh-air work during the summer, a penny provident fund, and other departments.

Dr. Judson has raised by personal effort over $200,000 of the money needed for these buildings in the heart of the great city. He is the son of the second Mrs. Judson, — Sarah Boardman, — and is an honor to the name of his beautiful and consecrated mother. Preaching in a cultured and wealthy church, he gave up his position to do a greater and more needed work in the lower part of New York. A man of unusual scholarship, most successful in revivals, he is using his great energy and zeal in an imperishable work. Some of the largest churches in the denomination have called him to their pulpits, but he prefers to give his life to his Memorial Church.

Of whom is this grand church a memorial? Of Dr. Adoniram Judson, who wrought such a work in foreign lands as to make his name immortal. He will live in history, forever associated with the three women who shared his sorrows and his successes, whom he loved with a devoted and unchanging affection, and who will always be an inspiration to the womanhood of America.

Ann Hasseltine Judson was born at Bradford, Mass., Dec. 22, 1789. She was an enthusiastic, ardent girl, fond of society, but equally fond of books, of great decision and strength of mind, with indomitable perseverance. So restless was she as a child that her mother once said to her, "I hope, my daughter, you will one day be satisfied with rambling."

She studied at the Academy at Bradford, and at the age of eighteen, with characteristic New England energy, began to teach school, that her time might be spent in a useful manner.

In June, 1810, the Massachusetts Association of Congregational Ministers met at Bradford. It was to inaugurate a most important work. Several young men from the quiet town of Andover, where they had been attending the Theological Seminary, were at the meeting. Samuel J. Mills, James Richards, Luther Rice, and Gordon Hall, who, while in Williams College, had prayed together at night beside a haystack, and had consecrated themselves to the work of saving souls among the heathen, had come to the Bradford gathering.

Another young man was present, slight in physique, with brown hair and eyes, whose history already was interesting, — young Adoniram Judson. He was born in Malden, Mass., Aug. 9, 1788, the son of a Congregational minister; a precocious boy, so excellent in Greek and Latin that he was called by his schoolmates "old Virgil dug up"; equally fond of theology and of the novels of Richardson and Fielding; valedictorian of his class at Brown University when he was nineteen; ambitious, self-dependent, publishing two text-books about the time he graduated, one on grammar, the other on arithmetic; and as restless by nature as was Ann Hasseltine.

He had determined to see the world for himself. He went from the old town of Plymouth, Mass., whither his father had moved some years previously, to Albany, N. Y., that he might see the newly-invented steamer of Robert Fulton. He sailed in her to New York, and then started westward.

At a country inn where he stopped, the landlord apologized for placing him next to the room of a young man who was dying. During the night Judson was much disturbed by the groaning, and wondered whether the young man was ready to meet death. He chided himself for such pious thoughts, for he and his college mate, E——, witty and charming, but a confirmed deist, had often laughed about such fears for the future.

In the morning he inquired about the young man. "He is gone, poor fellow!" said the landlord. "He was a very fine fellow; his name was E——, from Brown University."

Young Judson was stunned. He gave up his journey to see the world, ceased his unbelief, entered Andover Theological Seminary when he was twenty, and became thereafter one of the most devoted men America has ever known.

The following year, 1809, Dr. Claudius Buchanan's "Star in the East," a work showing the spread of the gospel in India, especially under the German missionary, Schwartz, fell into Judson's hands. He began to think seriously of foreign missions, and the next year, when Mills and the others came to Andover, he was ready for the final decision to preach to the heathen.

It was a hard matter for others rather than for himself. He had been offered the position of a tutor at Brown University, and had declined it. Rev. Dr. Griffin had suggested him for his colleague "in the largest church in Boston." His glad mother had said, "You will be so near home"; and he had replied, "I shall never live in Boston. I have much farther than that to go."

His ambitious father had seen his plans for Adoniram thwarted. "The son, also," as says the Rev. Edward Judson in his delightful life of his father, "had nailed his own ambitions to the cross."

As there was no foreign missionary society in America, the young students from Andover proposed to each other to go under the auspices of the London Missionary Society. But first, they would attend the meeting at Bradford, and lay the matter before the Congregational ministers of the State.

During the sessions, the clergymen dined with Deacon Hasseltine, whose youngest daughter, Ann, waited on the table. She listened to the earnest conversation, particularly that of the fearless and dignified Judson. He seemingly paid no attention to the beautiful brunette, though she afterwards learned that he was composing some verses to her in his mind at that very time.

The Bradford meeting came to an end, but not until that grand organization, the American Board of Commissioners for Foreign Missions, had been effected, at the request of these same young men. Judson wrote the petition to the ministers and was the first to sign it.

Fearing that money could not then be raised to support the Andover students, young Judson was sent to England to confer with the London Missionary Society, as to a union of the two nations in missionary effort. He was captured on the journey by a French privateer, taken to Bayonne, and thrown into a damp and moldy prison.

Fortunately, an American from Philadelphia had heard him speak as the prisoners passed along the street, stole into the prison, wrapped his cloak around the slight, boyish Judson, and together they passed out in the darkness.

"Now run!" said the stranger; and Judson heeded the injunction with a will. Later, in France, he was introduced to some of the officers of Napoleon's suite, and travelled through the country in one of the emperor's carriages.

He returned to America in September, 1811, and as the London Society did not deem it best to unite with the American, Judson, Samuel Nott, Samuel Newell, and Gordon Hall were appointed to labor in Asia, under the direction of the American Board.

Judson had already told Ann Hasseltine of his love for her, and had written to her father, asking, "Whether you can consent to part with your daughter early next spring, to see her no more in this world; whether you can consent to her departure for a heathen land, and her subjection to the hardships and sufferings of a missionary life; whether you can consent to her exposure to the dangers of the ocean; to the fatal influence of the southern climate of India; to every kind of want and distress; to degradation, insult, persecution, and perhaps a violent death.

"Can you consent to all this for the sake of Him who left his heavenly home, and died for her and for you; for the sake of perishing, immortal souls; for the sake of Zion, and the glory of God?"

No woman had ever left America to go among the heathen. Many of Ann's friends opposed her going, but she had prayerfully decided the matter in the affirmative, and she and Mr. Judson were married at Bradford, Feb. 5, 1812.

Judson and Samuel Newell were ordained at the Tabernacle Church, in Salem, the following day, and sailed from that town on the 19th, with their wives, for Calcutta.

That it cost Ann Hasseltine a bitter struggle, her journal shows: "My heart bleeds," she writes. "O America, my native land! must I leave thee? Must I leave my parents, my sisters and brother, my friends beloved, and all the scenes of my early youth? Must I leave thee, Bradford, my dear native town, where I spent the pleasant years of childhood; where I learnt to lisp the name of my mother; . . . where I learnt the endearments of friendship, and tasted of all the happiness this world can afford?"

During the long voyage of four months — they reached Calcutta June 18 — the young missionaries read works bearing on their future labors — Paley, and others — and Mr. Judson read several authors on baptism. Since he was going where there were some English Baptists, he must needs be able to show to the natives why a Congregational form was to be preferred.

The result was that he came to believe that the Bible taught immersion, when one becomes a Christian, rather than in infancy, and there seemed to him no alternative but to unite with the Baptist Church. This cost him much pain. He could not look to the American Board for support; there was no Baptist Missionary Society to which he could turn, and it necessarily made him and his companions labor in separate fields. He was greatly blamed by some, but in the end good resulted, as the Baptist churches were stirred to more earnest efforts, and a Baptist Missionary Union was formed, which has done a wonderful work in heathen lands.

Judson and his wife were at once invited by Dr. Carey to the mission-house at Serampore. Here all was strange and interesting to the young couple. Ann wrote home, describing the English Church, where "a number of punkies, something like a fan, several yards in length, hung around, with ropes fastened to the outside, which were pulled by some of the natives, to keep the church cool."

A wedding-procession passed. "The bridegroom was carried in a palanquin, with flowers in his hands, and on his head. He appeared to be about ten years of age. The procession were dressed in uniform, with large branches of flowers, and instruments of music."

The third day after their arrival, the worship of Juggernaut was celebrated. "The idol was set on the top of a stone building. He is only a lump of wood, his face painted, with large black eyes, and a large red mouth. He was taken from his temple, and water poured on him to bathe him. . . . After they had bathed their god they proceeded to bathe themselves."

The Indian Government, which at that time meant the East India Company, being opposed to missionaries, especially those from America, as England and America were not then friendly, ordered the Judsons and others to return to their own land. They begged to go to the Isle of France (Mauritius), which request was granted.

After a voyage of six weeks they reached this island, in the Indian Ocean, four hundred and eighty miles east of Madagascar. They found that the lovely Harriet Newell, the wife of Samuel, who had come thither two months before, had already given her young life, with that of her infant daughter, to the cause of missions. When told that death was near, she lifted her hands, exclaiming, "Oh, glorious intelligence!"

After four months, the Judsons determined again to try India, and went to Madras. They intended to establish a mission on Prince of Wales Island, in the Straits of Malacca, but as the only vessel about to sail was bound for Rangoon, Burma, they took passage, and arrived in July, 1813.

The area of Burma at that time was two hundred and eighty thousand square miles, — four times as large as New England, — with a population of from six to eight millions. The people worshipped Buddha, or Gautama, born about 500 B. C., the son of an Indian prince. He left his home and his wealth, at twenty-nine, and until his death, about eighty, he travelled through India, preaching his gospel. His life was spent in self-denial and charity.

On the arrival of the Judsons at Rangoon, Mrs. Judson, who was ill, was carried in an arm-chair on the shoulders of the natives. When put down to rest the women gathered around her and peered under her bonnet. When she smiled at this they laughed aloud.

The Judsons at once began the study of the language, a matter of great difficulty, as there was neither grammar nor dictionary, nor any English-speaking teacher. These would have been lonely days except for the love they bore each other, and their work

Mrs. Judson wrote to Mr Newell: "We have no society, no dear Christian friends, and with the exception of two or three sea-captains, who now and then call on us, we never see a European face. But, then, we are still happy in each other; still find that our own home is our best, our dearest friend.

"When we feel a disposition to sigh for the enjoyments

of our native country we turn our eyes on the miserable objects around. We behold some of them laboring hard for a scanty subsistence, oppressed by an avaricious government, which is ever ready to seize what industry has hardly earned. We behold others sick and diseased, daily begging their few grains of rice, which, when obtained, are scarcely sufficient to protract their wretched existence, and with no other habitation to cover them from the burning sun or chilly rains than that which a small piece of cloth raised on four bamboos, under the shade of a tree, can afford."

At the end of three years, Judson had completed a grammar of the Burmese language, concerning which the Calcutta *Review* said, "We have seen no work in any tongue which we should compare with it for brevity and completeness." He published also his first Burmese tract, "A View of the Christian Religion in Three Parts, Historic, Didactic, and Preceptive."

One thousand of these tracts were printed at first, and three thousand copies of a catechism prepared by Mrs. Judson. So difficult was the acquisition of the language, that Mr. Judson said he would rather submit to an examination in French after two months of study than in Burman after two years. He thought it the most difficult language on earth, except the Chinese.

Though he had no converts to baptize till he had been in Burma seven years, he was not discouraged. When asked whether he thought the prospects bright for the speedy conversion of the heathen, he would say, "As bright as the promises of God."

He wrote to a friend that, though Rangoon was "a most filthy, wretched place, if a ship was lying in the river, ready to convey me to any part of the world I should choose, and that, too, with the entire approbation of all my Christian friends, I would prefer dying to embarking."

A child had come to brighten the Judson home, a boy, Roger Williams, born Sept. 11, 1815. Mrs. Judson wrote her mother that she "now felt almost in a new state of existence," and added, "We hope his life may be preserved, and his heart sanctified, that he may become a missionary among the Burmans."

But the hope was not to be realized, for the following May she wrote home: "Death, regardless of our lonely situation, has entered our dwelling, and made one of the happiest families wretched. Our little Roger Williams, our only little darling boy, was three days ago laid in the silent grave. Eight months we enjoyed the precious little gift, in which time he had so completely entwined himself around his parents' hearts that his existence seemed necessary to their own. . . . We buried him in the afternoon, in a little enclosure, the other side of the garden. . . . We felt he was our earthly all, our only source of recreation in this heathen land."

Mr. Judson's heart, too, was equally torn by this bereavement. He wrote to a missionary friend at Serampore: "The light of his mild blue eye is quenched, his sweet face has become cold to our lips, and his little mind, which, to a parent's discernment at least, discovered peculiar sensibility and peculiar sweetness of disposition, has deserted its infantile tenement and fled — oh, where? Into what strange scenes is it introduced? Who supports and guides its trembling steps across the dark valley? There a parent's aid could not be extended. But we hope it had a more affectionate and abler guide."

The strong man tried to be comforted, and yet he cried

out in agony of spirit, "We had only *one*. Might not this have been spared?"

Still the childless parents labored on. In May, 1817, Mr. Judson finished his translation of the gospel of Matthew, and he began to compile a Burmese dictionary. But his health became impaired by continuous study, and he was obliged to take a sea voyage

He was constantly urging America to send out more laborers. The work was too great, and the hands of the workers too feeble. "Send us," he wrote, "humble, quiet, persevering men; men of sound, sterling talents, of decent accomplishments, of some natural aptitude to acquire a language; men of an amiable, yielding temper, willing to take the lowest place, to be the least of all, and the servant of all; men who enjoy much closet religion — who live near to God, and are willing to suffer all things for Christ's sake, without being proud of it; — these are the men we need."

In 1819, a *zayat*, or little chapel, costing about two hundred dollars, was built by Mr. Judson, along the roadside leading to one of the pagodas where Gautama was worshipped. In these pagodas, which were supposed to contain a relic of Buddha, expensive offerings were made. One offering, costing $1,200, provided by a member of government, was a bamboo and paper pagoda, ornamented with gold leaf and paintings. It was one hundred feet high, with a man half way up the pagoda, dancing. This was borne by sixty men, preceded by a band of music.

When these people came to worship Gautama, they would see "the teacher," in his little open chapel, ready to teach or to preach in the Burmese language. So eloquent and earnest was Mr. Judson, that those who could not understand a word of the language were held spellbound by his manner. In later years, he found it difficult to preach in his mother tongue, so thoroughly had the Burmese language become his own.

The Burmans learn to read and write on a board a yard long, made black with charcoal and the juice of a leaf, while the letters are made by a white stone.

Meantime, Mrs. Judson had been studying Siamese for a year and a half, and had translated into Siamese the Burmese catechism, tract, and Matthew, besides turning one of their celebrated books into English; an account of the incarnation of one of their deities, when he existed in the form of a great elephant.

As the number of the converts increased, the viceroy of Rangoon began to be alarmed, and persecution was imminent. Mr. Judson resolved to go to the capital of Burma, Ava, and ask the emperor's permission to preach the Christian religion. The journey was made, and the emperor received him with great state, but would make no concessions, dashing Mr. Judson's tract to the ground.

When the missionary returned and told the converts that he must remove the mission, as they were liable to suffer death if they accepted longer the Christian faith, they would not consent, but begged him to remain, and they would suffer death even, if need be.

After eight years in Rangoon, Mrs. Judson's health was such that a change of climate seemed imperative to save her life. She visited England, where she was cordially entertained by the family of Mr. Butterworth, a member of Parliament, meeting Wilberforce and other distinguished persons, and then sailed for America, reaching New York Sept. 25, 1822.

She was met in Philadelphia and Bradford by eager hearts that did not expect to see her again this side the grave. For four nights she was so much overcome by the union with friends that she could not close her eyes in sleep.

Her health still declining, she was obliged to spend the winter in Baltimore, away from the cold of New England. Everywhere she won the love of all who met her.

Dr. Francis Wayland, president of Brown University, says of her in his life of Dr. Judson: "I do not remember ever to have met a more remarkable woman. To great clearness of intellect, large powers of comprehension, and intuitive female sagacity, ripened by the constant necessity of independent action, she added that heroic disinterestedness which naturally loses all consciousness of self in the prosecution of a great object. These elements, however, were all held in reserve, and were hidden from public view by a veil of unusual feminine delicacy. . . .

"As she found herself among friends who were interested in the Burman mission, her reserve melted away, her eye kindled, every feature was lighted up with enthusiasm, and she was everywhere acknowledged to be one of the most fascinating of women."

While in America, her "History of the Burman Mission" was published. Though her health was only partially restored, she was restless for her home in Burma, and in June, 1823, she said, as she was convinced, her final farewell to friends, and arrived in Rangoon late in the fall.

Mr. Judson had received permission to live at Ava, and had been assured of the royal protection. At once, therefore, upon the return of his wife, they hastened thither. It was well that they could not foresee the dreadful things which awaited them.

War soon broke out between Burma and the English Government in India. Refugees from the iron rule of Burma had sought shelter in places under British rule. The Burmese monarch demanded their surrender, and, this not being acceded to, war was begun.

All white foreigners in Ava were suspected of being friends of England, and were thrust into prison. Mr. Judson, with a few others, was confined in the death prison at Ava for eleven months, where their sufferings seemed past belief.

The prison was a long, low building, five or six feet high, with no ventilation except through the cracks between the boards. The atmosphere was a constant poison from its filth. Men and women were fastened in stocks, — heavy logs of timber, bored with holes to admit the feet. Most wore heavy chains besides, and all were nearly naked. The feet of the victims were fastened to a huge pole, which was drawn up by pulleys, so that the head and shoulders rested on the ground, and the blood flowed from the up-lifted feet into the head.

Mr. Judson's five pairs of iron fetters weighed fourteen pounds, so that walking was impossible except by "shuffling a few inches at a time." Each one daily expected death. At three o'clock each afternoon some one was led out to be executed, and no one knew whose turn would come next.

Mrs. Judson's noble heroism now showed itself. She went to the governor and begged to see her husband. Receiving a permit, she hastened to the door, and he crawled to meet her. Then she sought to gain admittance to the queen, but was not allowed. She gave money and presents to the officials, and they clamored for more.

"For the seven following months," writes Mrs. Judson to her husband's brother, Dr. Elnathan Judson, when the terrible ordeal was over, "hardly a day passed that I did not visit some one of the members of government, or branches of the royal family, in order to gain their influence in our behalf; but the only benefit was their encouraging promises preserved us from despair. . . . Sometimes, for days and days together, I could not go into the prison till after dark, when I had two miles to walk, in returning to the house."

She was finally permitted to make for her husband a small bamboo room in the prison, where he could be much by himself. Occasionally she was allowed to spend two or three hours with him.

After Mr. Judson had been six months in prison their little daughter, Maria Elizabeth Butterworth Judson, was born, Jan. 26, 1825. As soon as Mrs. Judson could leave her room she hurried over to the prison. The bamboo room had been torn down, her husband's mat and pillow had been taken by the jailers, and more irons put upon him than before.

One of the jailers opened the pillow and threw away a seemingly hard roll of cotton. Some hours afterward a Burman took the roll home as a relic of the banished prisoners, and months later the manuscript which now makes a part of the Burmese Bible was found within, unharmed.

Mrs. Judson says in the letter to her brother-in-law: "I went immediately to the governor's house. He was not at home, but had ordered his wife to tell me, when I came, not to ask to have the additional fetters taken off or the prisoners released, for *it could not be done.*

"I went to the prison gate, but was forbidden to enter. All was as still as death. I was determined to see the governor and know the cause of this additional oppression, and for this purpose returned into town the same evening at an hour I knew he would be at home. He was in his audience-room, and as I entered looked up without speaking, but exhibited a mixture of shame and affected anger in his countenance.

"I began by saying, 'Your lordship has hitherto treated us with the kindness of a father. . . . You have promised me particularly that you would stand by me to the last. . . . What crime has Mr. Judson committed to deserve such additional punishment?'

"The old man's hard heart was melted, for he wept like a child. 'I pity you, Tsa-yah-ga-dau,'—a name by which he always called me; 'I knew you would make me feel; I therefore forbade your application. But you must believe me when I say I do not wish to increase the sufferings of the prisoners. When I am ordered to execute them, the least that I can do is to put them out of sight. I will now tell you what I have never told you before,— that three times I have received intimations from the queen's brother to assassinate all the white prisoners privately; but I would not do it. And I now repeat it,— though I execute all the others, I will never execute your husband. But I cannot release him from his present confinement, and you must not ask it.'"

Soon after this, without Mrs. Judson's knowledge, the white prisoners were all removed ten miles to a prison in the country, Oung-pen-la. They were chained two-and-two, the official going on horseback, while his slaves drove the prisoners, under a burning sun. Their bare feet were soon blistered, and the soles became destitute of skin. A Greek, in perfect health when they started, fell dead on the way from the heat of the sun, the men beating and dragging him till they were weary. Mr. Judson became so exhausted that he was nearly carried by the man to whom he was chained.

As soon as Mrs. Judson could find out where her husband had been taken she followed him with her baby in her arms, and two little Burmese girls. She obtained a room to live in, which was half full of grain. One of the Burmese girls had small-pox, and the baby and Mrs. Judson soon were prostrated with it. After this Mrs. Judson had spotted fever, and was very near to death. She became so emaciated that she seemed no more her former self. The Burmese neighbors who came in to see her die said: "She is dead; and if the King of Angels should come in, He could not recover her."

All this time the baby, Maria, was half starving for lack of food. Mrs. Judson was unable to nurse her; there was no milk to be had in the village, and the heart-rending cries of the little one nearly distracted the helpless mother.

By making presents to the jailers, Mr. Judson, scarcely able to stand, from the effects of a recent fever, was allowed to come out of prison and take the emaciated little creature to different mothers in the village, that she might share in the sustenance of their own babies. One can scarcely picture a more pathetic scene; the mother daily expecting death, the father daily expecting the executioner (indeed, they learned afterwards that they were taken to Oung-pen-la for that purpose, and were saved only because the "pakan-woon" was himself executed); the brilliant scholar and devoted preacher, with a few inches of heavy chain between his shackled feet, carrying a half-starved child, "a beggar at the breasts of pitying mothers!"

Mrs. Judson partially recovered. At the end of six months in Oung-pen-la and two months at Maloun, where he was obliged to act as an interpreter, Moung Schwaloo, the north governor of the palace, obtained Mr. Judson's release, offering himself as security. Mr. Judson helped the Burmese to negotiate a peace with their British conquerors, under Sir Archibald Campbell, and he and his wife and child were taken to the English camp, where they received every courtesy.

A British officer, Major Calder Campbell, wounded and robbed by his faithless Burmese boatmen, thus speaks of Mrs. Judson: "We were taken on board. My eyes first rested on the thin, attenuated form of a lady — a white lady! the first white woman I had seen for more than a year. . . . She was seated in a large sort of swinging chair, of American construction, in which her slight, emaciated, but graceful form appeared almost ethereal. Yet, with much of heaven, there were still the breathings of earthly feeling about her, for at her feet rested a babe, a little, wan baby, on which her eyes often turned with all a mother's love; and, gazing frequently upon her delicate features with a fond yet fearful glance, her husband.

"Her face was pale, very pale, with that expression of deep and serious thought which speaks of the strong and vigorous mind within the frail and perishing body; her brown hair was braided over a placid and holy brow; but her hands — those small, lily hands — were quite beautiful; beautiful they were, and very wan; for, ah, they told of disease, — of death — death in all its transparent grace, — when the sickly blood shines through the clear skin, even as the bright poison lights up the Venetian glass which it is about to shatter.

"Mrs. Judson's powers of conversation were of the first order, . . . and gained a heightened interest from the beautiful, energetic simplicity of her language, as well as from the certainty I felt that so fragile a flower as she in very truth was, had but a brief season to linger on earth."

On March 6, 1826, Mr. Judson and his wife and child sailed down the Irrawaddy in a British gun-boat, and reached Rangoon March 21. Years afterward, when several persons were discussing what they regarded as the highest type of enjoyment, and giving their experiences, Mr. Judson remarked: "I know of a much higher pleasure than that. What do you think of floating down the Irrawaddy on a cool, moonlight evening, with your wife by your side, and your baby in your arms, free — all free? But *you* cannot understand it, either; it needs a twenty-one months' qualification; and I can never regret my twenty-one months of misery, when I recall that one delicious thrill. I think I have had a better appreciation of what heaven may be ever since."

They found the little church at Rangoon much scattered. The English army held Rangoon only temporarily, and it seemed essential that they should live where they might have the protection of the British flag. A new city had been started, called, in honor of the governor-general of India, "Amherst," where it was expected that the seat of government would be located.

Here Mr. and Mrs. Judson decided to begin anew their work. The English Government, desiring to make a commercial treaty with the Burmese king, Mr. Judson was prevailed upon to go to Ava, as he so well understood the language, with the assurance that the English would do all in their power to secure a clause in the treaty throwing the whole of Burma open to the spread of the gospel.

After his departure Mrs. Judson built a little bamboo dwelling-house, and two school-houses, in which she both taught and held public worship on Sundays.

In the midst of this work, the fatal fever came again. From the first she felt that she should not survive. The terrible prison-life of her husband at Ava had done its work. During the eighteen days of her illness she sometimes said: "The 'teacher' is long in coming, and the new missionaries are long in coming; I must die alone, and leave my little one; but as it is the will of God, I acquiesce in His will. I am not afraid of death, but I am afraid I shall not be able to bear these pains. Tell the 'teacher' that the disease was most violent, and I could not write; tell him how I suffered and died, and take care of the house and things until he returns."

The last two days she was comparatively free from pain. Her last words at evening were: "I feel quite well, only very weak"; and then, with one exclamation of distress in the Burmese language, she ceased to breathe, Oct. 24, 1826, at the age of thirty-seven.

So short the life, and yet the results so blessed! A great work begun in Burma; an example of unsurpassed devotion to a husband; an illustration of heroism, of dignity, and of nobility of mind and character worthy of imitation.

The Burmese converts gathered about their "white mamma," and buried her at Amherst under the hope-tree (*hopia*). Mr. Judson returned to his desolate home three months later, and in the following April made another grave beside that of his young wife, and laid little Maria therein, at the age of two years and three months; "her hands, the exact pattern of her mother's, folded on her cold breast," wrote Mr. Judson to Mrs. Hasseltine at Bradford.

He was but thirty-nine, and had buried his wife and his three children, — his first infant in the Bay of Bengal;

his second, Roger Williams, in the jungle graveyard at Rangoon; and Maria, under the hopia-tree. The blow was a terrible one. "He looks as if worn out with his suffering and sorrows," said one of his missionary friends.

He turned at once to the translating of the Psalms into Burmese, and to the preparation of two works for the schools, — the one, astronomical, and the other, geographical. But the days were desolate for a man of such an affectionate heart. Two years later, on the anniversary of Mrs. Judson's death, he wrote her sisters: "It is the second anniversary of the triumph of death over all my hopes of earthly bliss. . . . It proves a stormy evening, and the desolation around me accords with the desolate state of my own mind."

A year later, he wrote to his mother: "Do not think that I can ever forget you. When I used to carry about my poor little Maria, I thought how much my mother loved her little Adoniram, and carried him about, and took care of him. And though he has now grown almost out of her knowledge, and been parted many years, and will probably see her no more on earth, he can never forget how much he owes to his own dear mother."

Instead of Amherst being made the center of government and the headquarters of the English army, as had been expected, Maulmain was chosen, about twenty-five miles farther north, and it seemed advisable to move thither, Sir Archibald Campbell having given a lot for the mission. The lot, however, was a lonely place, with a thick jungle close at hand, where the howls of wild beasts were often heard at midnight.

Others had come to join the workers in far-off Burma. Young Colman, from Boston, full of promise and devotion, had died after four years of earnest labor. A young man in Waterville College, Me., slight in physique, but strong in heart and purpose, said, "I will go in his place"; and George Dana Boardman made himself ready for his work.

Another was moved by the death of Colman, and wrote: —

> "'T is the voice of deep sorrow from India's shore,
>   The flower of our churches is withered and dead;
> The gem that shone brightly will sparkle no more,
>   And the tears of the Christian profusely are shed.
>
> . . . .
>
> "Mourn, daughters of Arracan, mourn!
>   The rays of that star, clear and bright,
> That so sweetly on Chittagong shone,
>   Are shrouded in black clouds of night,
>   For Colman is gone!"

The author of these lines was Sarah Hall, born in Alstead, N. H., Nov. 4, 1803, and taken, while a child, to Salem, Mass. The eldest of thirteen children, her young life was full of the care incident to such a family circle. Exceedingly fond of poetry, she early showed decided ability as a poet, and a love for knowledge which indicated the rare mind she possessed. Her heart turned toward missions. At thirteen, she wrote a tender poem on the death of little Roger Williams Judson. At seventeen we find her teaching school, that she may gain the means for a better education. She has finished Butler's "Analogy," Paley's "Evidences," Campbell's "Philosophy of Rhetoric," and later she is teaching her little brothers at home, that she may have time for Latin, logic, and geometry.

She has read the "Life of Samuel J. Mills," and is ready to exclaim: "Oh, that I, too, could suffer privations, hardships, and discouragements, and even find a watery grave, for the sake of bearing the news of salvation to the poor heathen! Then I have checked myself in the wild, unreasonable wish. Sinners perishing all around me, and I, an ignorant, weak, faithless creature, almost panting to tell the far *heathen* of Christ!"

When young Boardman met Sarah Hall, "their spirits, their hopes, their aspirations were one." When asked to become the wife of a missionary, Sarah's mother said, in the agony of her heart, "Oh, I cannot part with you!" but a month later, as she embraced her tenderly, she said, "I *hope* I am willing."

And even after the marriage, July 4, 1825, when not yet twenty-two, Sarah was leaving the paternal roof, she bent her fair head out from the carriage window, and said, "Father, are you willing? Say, father, that you are willing I should go." And the grieving father said, "Yes, my child, I am willing." "Now I can go joyfully," she said, and was soon on her way to India.

"She was, at this time," says one who knew her, "a gentle, confiding, persuasive being, who would sweeten the cup of life to those who drank it with her. Further acquaintance would develop strength as well as loveliness of character. It would be seen that she could do and endure as well as love and please. Sweetness and strength, gentleness and firmness, were in her character most happily blended."

After their arrival in India, Mr. and Mrs. Boardman spent some time in Calcutta studying the language. Mrs. Boardman was said to possess "faultless features, molded on the Grecian model, beautiful transparent skin, warm, meek blue eyes, and soft hair, brown in the shadow, and gold in the sun."

The Boardmans reached Amherst just before little Maria Judson was buried, and rendered all the assistance possible. "After leaving the grave," writes the consecrated Boardman, "we had a delightful conversation on the kindness and tender mercies of our heavenly Father. Brother Judson seemed carried above his grief."

Mrs. Boardman became very ill at Amherst. As soon as she was able, they went to Maulmain, Dr. Judson coming a little later; he had been given the title of D. D. some years before by his own college, Brown University, though he preferred not to use it, but the world has thus designated him.

The work went on encouragingly at Maulmain, but after seven months the Boardmans decided to go to Tavoy, the only important point within one hundred and fifty miles, thus to broaden the field of labor. Here Mrs. Boardman, after "unwearied toil, repeated repulses and discouragements," established a school for girls.

The next year, 1829, Mr. Boardman made his first tour among the Karens, *wild* men, as their name indicates, scattered throughout Burma, Siam, and parts of China. They number from two hundred thousand to four hundred thousand.

"Of all the people in the world," wrote Mr. Boardman, "the Karens, I believe, are the most timid and irresolute. And the fable that when some superior being was dispensing written languages and books to the various nations of the earth a surly dog came along and drove away the Karens and carried away their books agrees better with their indolent and timid character than half the other fables in vogue among the wise and learned Burmans do with truth or common-sense. . . . They are in general as careless about the future as the present, except those who have heard the gospel, and those who have been encouraged by the Burmans to build kyoungs and pagodas, in the hope of avoiding in the next world the state of hogs and dogs, and snakes and worms. They are too idle to be quarrelsome or ambitious, and too poor to gamble, or eat or drink to very great excess."

When Mr. Boardman went among them he learned that they kept a mysterious book, carefully preserved, which, although they did not know its contents, they had worshipped for twelve years. He found that it was the "Book of Common Prayer with the Psalms," published at Oxford, England.

Mr. Boardman endured great privations in his jungle trips among the Karens. "The paths which lead to their settlements," he said, "are so obscurely marked, so little trodden, and so devious in their course, that a guide is needed to conduct one from village to village, even over the best part of the way. Not unfrequently the path leads over precipices, over cliffs and dangerous declivities, along deep ravines, frequently meandering with a small streamlet for miles. . . . There are no bridges, and we often have to ford or swim over considerable streams, particularly in the rainy season, — when, however, the difficulties of travelling are so great as to render it next to impossible. Sometimes we have to sleep in the open air in the woods, where, besides insects and reptiles, the tiger, the rhinoceros, and the wild elephant render our situation not a little uncomfortable and dangerous."

Mr. Boardman's health was becoming undermined. Death had entered the household and taken the firstborn, "the bright, beautiful, darling Sarah Ann," two years and eight months old. "I knew all the time that she was very ill," wrote Mrs. Boardman; "but it did not occur to me that she might die, till she was seized with the apoplexy, about three hours before she closed her eyes upon us forever. Oh, the agony of that moment! . . .

"A few hours before she died she called us to her, kissed us, and passed her dear hand, still full and dimpled as in health, softly over our faces. The pupils of her eyes were so dilated that she could not see us distinctly, and once, for a moment or two, her mind seemed to be wandering; then, looking anxiously into my face, she said, 'I frightened, mamma! I frightened!'" But the child had to go alone over the same journey which so many have taken before her.

She was a most affectionate and attractive child, with her blue eyes and rosy cheeks, and could speak Burmese like a native. A little over a year later, Mr. and Mrs. Boardman buried their youngest child, a boy of eight months.

Mr. Boardman was admonished that his own work was near its close. His eyes were brighter and his cheeks more hollow. He longed to go once more among his beloved Karens to baptize several that had become Christians. He was carried, therefore, on a litter several days' journey into the wilderness, and by the waterside, though so weak that he could not breathe without being fanned, he saw thirty-four make the covenant with their Lord.

A storm coming up, his mattress and pillows were drenched with rain, though his friends tried to shield him with their umbrellas. "How kind and good our Father in heaven is to me," said the dying man to his wife; "how many are racked with pain, while I, though near the grave, am almost free from distress of body. I suffer nothing, *nothing* to what you, my dear Sarah, had to endure last year, when I thought I must lose you. And then I have you to move me so tenderly! I should have sunk into the grave ere this but for your assiduous attention. . . . I have long ago, and many times, committed you and our little one into the hands of our covenant God. . . . He will be your stay and support when I am gone. The separation will be but short. Oh, how happy I shall be to welcome you to heaven!"

Mr. Boardman died in the jungles, and was borne back to his home on the litter, to be buried beside his little Sarah.

Mrs. Boardman was urged to return to America, with her only remaining child, George, two years and a half old, now minister of the First Baptist Church in Philadelphia, but she had come to spend her life for the heathen, and she could not leave her work.

The gentle Mrs. Boardman went on in her self-denying labors. She made tours among the Karens, as her husband had done. "Perhaps you had better send the chair," she wrote a friend; "as it is convenient to be carried over the streams when they are deep. You will laugh when I tell you that I have forded all the smaller ones."

She often spoke to two or three hundred Karens. Her village schools were so successful that when an appropriation was made by government for schools throughout the provinces it was stipulated that they "be conducted on the plan of Mrs. Boardman's schools at Tavoy."

She wrote: "Every moment of my time is occupied, from sunrise till ten o'clock in the evening. . . . The superintendence of the food and clothing of both the boarding-schools, together with the care of five day-schools, under native teachers, devolves wholly on me. My day-schools are proving every week more and more interesting."

A little more than three years after the death of Mr. Boardman, Mrs. Boardman became the second wife of Dr. Judson. Ann Hasseltine had been dead for nearly eight years, and the lonely missionary needed an educated and devoted helper like Sarah Boardman. They were married April 10, 1834.

When Mr. Boardman died, Dr. Judson had written her concerning her child: "If you should be prematurely taken away, and should condescend, on your dying bed, to commit him to me, by the briefest line or verbal message, I hereby pledge my fidelity to receive and treat him as my own son, to send him home in the best time and way, to provide for his education, and to watch over him as long as I live. More than this I cannot do, and less would be unworthy of the merits of his parents." And now Dr. Judson was to receive and treat George "as his own son," a promise which he lovingly kept.

The work had grown wonderfully since those seven years when Dr. Judson waited for his first convert. In 1832 there were one hundred and forty-three baptisms,— over five hundred since his arrival in Burma.

Mrs. Judson was devoting much of her time to the study of the Peguan,— a large portion of the population of Maulmain and Amherst were Peguans,— and translated the New Testament and several tracts from the Burmese into the Peguan.

Dr. Judson was just completing his first rough draft of the Burmese Bible, on which he had spent nearly seventeen years. He preferred to preach, and did so every Sunday, and every evening of the week, but he knew that for all who labored after him this arduous translation was a necessity. Seven long and laborious years he gave to its revision. The work was accurate and thorough. "Long and toilsome research among the biblical critics and commentators, especially the German, was frequently requisite to satisfy my mind," he says, "that my first position was the right one. . . . I never read a chapter without pencil in hand and Griesbach and Parkhurst at my elbow; and it will be an object to me through life to bring the translation to such a state that it may be a standard work."

"The best judges," says Dr. Francis Wayland, "pronounce it to be all that he aimed at making it; and, also, what with him never was an object, an imperishable monument of the man's genius. . . . We honor Wycliffe and Luther for their labors in their respective mother-tongues, but what meed of praise is due to Judson for a translation of the Bible, *perfect as a literary work*, in a language so foreign as the Burmese?"

In October, 1835, the Judsons welcomed the birth of a daughter, Abby Ann, named after Dr. Judson's only sister and his first wife. She came to a lonely house, for Mrs. Judson the previous December had sent her only child, George, a boy of six, to America to be educated.

She writes to her sister: "After deliberation, accompanied with tears and agony and prayers, I came to the conviction that it was my duty to send away my only child, my darling George, and yesterday he bade me a long farewell. . . . My eyes are rolling down with tears, and I can scarcely hold my pen. . . . I shall never forget his looks as he stood by the door and gazed at me for the last time. His eyes were filling with tears, and his little face red with suppressed emotion. But he subdued his feelings, and it was not till he had turned away, and was going down the steps, that he burst into a flood of tears."

To another, she writes: "Let George call the persons with whom he finds a home 'uncle' and 'aunt,' if they desire it, but I do not like to have him call others 'papa' and 'mamma' while we live. Let him often be reminded of us, and let the love which he now feels for us be carefully cherished. I could not bear to be forgotten by the little one who was so long my only earthly comfort."

Mrs. Judson's friends in America said they almost feared to take charge of little George, "for so perfect had been his mother's work in training him thus far that they should fear they would only mar what had been done."

A son, Adoniram, was born to Mrs. Judson in Maulmain, April 7, 1837, called by the natives, "Pwen," meaning a flower, and the following year, July 15, 1838, another son, Elnathan.

In 1839, when Dr. Judson was a little past fifty, his health failed from an affection of his lungs, entailing a loss of voice, but he partially recovered after a sea voyage. These were anxious days for Mrs. Judson, who wrote him: "I have often wondered that I should have been so singularly blessed as to possess that heart, which is far more precious than all the world beside. . . . At times, the sweet hope that you will soon return, restored to perfect health, buoys up my spirit; but perhaps you will find it necessary to go farther, a necessity from which I cannot but shrink with doubt and dread; or you may come back only to die with me. This last agonizing thought crushes me down in overwhelming sorrow."

At the close of 1839, a third son was born, Henry, who died under two years of age, at Serampore, where Mrs. Judson had gone for the health of herself and children.

Three years later another son was born, named Henry Hall, after the child buried in the mission burial-ground at Serampore. Luther had died at birth in 1841.

Dr. Judson, after his twenty-four years spent on the Burmese Bible, had carried forward, at the urgent request of the Board at home, his Burmese dictionary, and Mrs. Judson, of whom her husband said, "It is no more than truth to say that there is scarcely an individual foreigner now alive who speaks and writes the Burmese tongue so acceptably as she does," was translating "Pilgrim's Progress" into Burmese, and editing the Burmese newspaper, during the absence of Mr. Stevens.

In 1843, her seventh child, Charles, was born, who died nearly two years later, at Maulmain, and Dec. 27, 1844, Edward, who has been so blessed in his labors in New York City.

Still in early middle life, but with her constitution broken by such frequent illness and consequent care, it became evident that only a trip across the ocean could prolong the years of the gifted woman.

On April 26, 1845, Dr. and Mrs. Judson, with Abby, Adoniram, and Elnathan, embarked on the ship "Paragon" for London. Henry, Charles, and Edward were left in the care of the missionaries at Maulmain. The vessel sprang aleak, and put in for repairs at Port Louis, Isle of France. Mrs. Judson had so improved that it was deemed best for Dr. Judson to return to his work, though he longed once more to see his native land. Thinking that she must part from her husband, Mrs. Judson wrote him this touching poem: —

> "We part on this green islet, love, —
> Thou for the Eastern main,
> I for the setting sun, love;
> Oh, when to meet again!

. . . .

"My tears fall fast for thee, love;
  How can I say farewell!
But go; thy God be with thee, love,
  My heart's deep grief to quell.

"Yet my spirit clings to thine, love;
  Thy soul remains with me,
And oft we'll hold communion sweet
  O'er the dark and distant sea.

"And who can paint our mutual joy,
  When, all our wanderings o'er,
We both shall clasp our infants three,
  At home, on Burma's shore!

"But higher shall our raptures glow,
  On yon celestial plain,
When the loved and parted here below
  Meet, ne'er to part again."

. . . .

Mrs. Judson soon experienced a relapse, and Dr. Judson decided to continue with her to America. They took passage on the "Sophia Walker," bound for the United States, leaving Port Louis July 25.

Mrs. Judson rallied once, but again failed rapidly. The ship reached St. Helena Aug. 26, and remained there for a few days. Mrs. Judson longed to see her parents, from whom she had been separated twenty years, and especially her son George, then seventeen years old; but she was equally ready for the unseen world, saying to her husband: "I am longing to depart. . . . What can I want beside?"; but was constrained to say, "I am in a strait betwixt two; let the will of God be done."

She was so resigned about the children remaining in Burma, that Dr. Judson said: "You seem to have forgotten the little ones we have left behind." "Can a mother forget?" she replied, and was unable to proceed. Charlie had then been dead three weeks, but the parents did not know it.

On Sept. 1, at two o'clock in the morning, her husband said to her: " Do you still love the Saviour?" "Oh, yes!" she replied, "I ever love the Lord Jesus Christ." "Do you still love me?" he asked. She answered in the affirmative. "Then give me one more kiss," he said. An hour later she had passed away.

During the day a coffin was procured from the shore, and in the afternoon the body was taken to the land, and buried at six o'clock, near the grave of Mrs. Chater, a missionary from Ceylon, who also had died on the passage home. The ship sailed away that evening. "In the solitude of my cabin, with my poor children crying around me," writes Dr. Judson, "I could not help abandoning myself to heart-breaking sorrow. . . . I exceedingly regret that there is no portrait of the second as of the first Mrs. Judson. Her soft blue eye, her mild aspect, her lovely face and elegant form have never been delineated on canvas. They must soon pass away from the memory even of her children, but they will remain forever enshrined in her husband's heart." Dead at forty-two, but Sarah Boardman Judson's work had been most helpful and lasting. "Her translation of Mr. Boardman's 'Dying Father's Advice,'" writes Dr. Judson, "has become one of our standard tracts; and her hymns, in Burmese,— about twenty in number — are probably the best in our 'Chapel Hymn Book,' a work which she was appointed by the mission to edit. Besides these works, she published four volumes of Scripture questions, which are in constant use in our Sabbath Schools. The last work of her life — and one which she accomplished in the midst of overwhelming family cares, and under the pressure of declining health — was a series of Sunday cards, each accompanied with a short hymn adapted to the leading subject of the card. . . .

"Her acquaintance with, and attachment to, the Burmese Bible were rather extraordinary. She professed to take more pleasure and derive more profit from the perusal of that translation than from the English, and to enjoy preaching in the native chapel more than in any other."

As teacher, scholar, mother, and wife, Mrs. Judson has left a fragrant and enduring memory; a woman rising above obstacles, using her time to remarkable advantage; gentle yet fearless in her work. "The most finished and faultless specimen of an American woman," said her English friends in Calcutta, "that they had ever known"

Dr. Judson reached Boston Oct. 15, 1845, in feeble health, with his three motherless children. He found homes, and churches, and colleges, all eager to see and hear him. Everywhere, and at all times, he showed the same devotion to missions. When, at a convention held in New York City, it was proposed to abandon the Arracan Mission, he rose to his feet, and, though unable to speak above a whisper, said: "Though forbidden to speak by my medical adviser, I must say a few words. I must protest against the abandonment of the Arracan Mission. . . . If the convention think my services can be dispensed with in finishing my dictionary, I will go immediately to Arracan; or, if God should spare my life to finish my dictionary, I will go there afterward and labor there, and die, and be buried there." These words were repeated to the audience by Dr. Cone. The mission was not abandoned.

Years before, when he had received nearly four thousand dollars for his work for the government, in the treaty at Ava, and as a diplomat, he gave all the money to the mission. His private property he gave also to the mission. Though he said that he and others received "less than any English missionaries of any denomination, in any part of the East," he lessened his yearly allowance from the Board by one quarter.

His son Edward, in his father's Life, tells this amusing incident: "The railroad system had sprung into existence during his absence. He entered the cars at Worcester one day, and had just taken his seat, when a boy came along with the daily newspapers. He said to Mr. Judson, 'Do you want a paper, sir?' 'Yes, thank you,' the missionary replied; and, taking the paper, began to read. The newsboy stood waiting for his pay, until a lady passenger, occupying the same seat with Mr. Judson, said to him, 'The boy expects to be paid for his paper.' 'Why!' replied the missionary, with the utmost surprise. 'I have been distributing papers gratuitously in Burma so long that I had no idea the boy was expecting any pay.'"

In January, 1846, Dr. Judson met in Philadelphia Miss Emily Chubbock, then known in the literary world as "Fanny Forester." He wished some competent Christian person to write a life of Sarah Boardman Judson, as the Rev. James D. Knowles, of Boston, had written one of Ann Hasseltine Judson. Miss Chubbock was well fitted for the work, undertook it, and it was published two years later, soon having a sale of twenty-eight thousand copies.

Emily Chubbock's history had been an interesting one. She was born, Aug. 22, 1817, in Eaton, in the central part of New York State, whither her parents had removed from New Hampshire, the same State in which Sarah Boardman was born. They had been in comfortable circumstances,

EMILY C. JUDSON.

but having lost their money, the father never seemed able again to win support for his family. Emily's mother was a woman of fine intellect, with the will-power and sagacity which the father seemed to lack.

Emily was a delicate child, the fifth in a large family. At the early age of eleven she was working in a woollen factory, earning one dollar and twenty-five cents a week. "My principal recollections during this summer," she wrote afterwards, "are of noise and filth, bleeding hands and aching feet, and a very sad heart."

She worked twelve hours a day, — too long for either child or adult, — "and," she wrote, "came home completely worn out with fatigue." One May day, when she was twelve years old, the carding-machine broke, and she, having the afternoon to herself, used all her money in hiring a horse and wagon to take her sick sister, Lavinia, out driving. "We spread a buffalo-robe on a pretty, dry knoll, and father carried her to it in his arms. I shall never forget how happy she was, nor how Kate and I almost buried her in violets and other wild spring flowers. It was the last time that she ever went out."

When Emily was thirteen she saw in the "Baptist Register" the words, "Little Maria lies by the side of her fond mother." She knew at once that Mrs. Ann H. Judson was dead, and she pitied Dr. Judson in his loneliness. She even made up her mind to be a missionary herself, though it seemed like a far-off possibility.

She says: "We suffered a great deal from cold this winter, though we had plenty of plain food. Indeed, we *never* were reduced to hunger. But the house was large and unfinished, and the snow sometimes drifted into it in heaps. We were unable to repair it, and the owner was unwilling. Father was absent nearly all the time distributing newspapers," — one can but respect a man who is willing to work to the uttermost, at any occupation however menial, to help care for the children whom he has brought into the world, — "and the severity of the winter so affected his health that he could do but little when he was at home. Mother, Harriet, and I were frequently compelled to go out into the fields and dig broken wood out of the snow to keep ourselves from freezing. Catharine and I went to the district school as much as we could."

They now moved to a farm, partly on account of the poor health of Emily. Mr. Chubbock's experiment at farming proved a complete failure, and they moved back to the village into a poor shelter, with two rooms below and a loft above, reached by means of a ladder. Emily got employment of a Scotch weaver at twisting thread, and the others took in sewing, or tried to earn a living in various ways.

Finally, the slight girl of fifteen, who seems to have had a large part of the energy of the family, obtained a position as school-teacher at seventy-five cents a week, with the not altogether enjoyable feature of "boarding round." The young, enthusiastic teacher was much liked. She taught in the neighboring towns till she was twenty.

There were, of course, home troubles: "failure in stage-coach business. The family removed to Hamilton, but returned in the spring; home lost; horses, coaches, etc., seized and sold at auction." Her father seems to have made the mistake of thousands of men who prefer to do business for themselves on small capital rather than work for others on a limited salary, the latter often being a hundred times more conducive to the happiness and comfort of wife and children. Mrs. Chubbock, crushed with this constant failure, and care, had brain-fever and inflammation of the lungs.

Emily Chubbock, besides teaching a hundred pupils, was studying Greek with a student in the theological seminary, and mathematics with a minister, writing poetry and prose for the village newspapers, and showing an ability that surprised and delighted all who knew her. She said to a friend at this time; "I have felt ever since I read the memoir of Mrs. Ann H. Judson, when I was a mere child, that I must become a missionary. I fear it is but a childish fancy, and am making every effort to banish it from my mind; yet the more I seek to divert my thoughts from it, the more unhappy I am." One recalls how the life of Samuel J. Mills influenced Sarah Hall in her missionary desires; who shall estimate the power of a book?

Finally, friendship did for Emily Chubbock what it can often do, if we only think for others instead of selfishly living for ourselves. What are we in the world for if not to use our thoughts, our eyes, our hands, and our money to help others?

Miss Allen, of Morrisville, where Emily had taught, had become her friend. When the former went to the then well-known Utica Seminary, she told the principal, Miss Sheldon, of the girl who was struggling for an education. Miss Sheldon at once proposed to Emily to spend two or three years at her seminary, and pay for it by subsequent teaching. This proposition was gladly accepted.

"She was at this time," says a friend, "a frail, slender creature, shrinking with nervous timidity from observation; yet her quiet demeanor, noiseless step, low voice, earnest and observant glance of the eye, awakened at once interest and attention. . . . Miss Chubbock had a heart full of sympathy; and no grief was too causeless, no source of annoyance too slight, for her not to endeavor to remove them. She therefore soon became a favorite with the younger, as with the older and more appreciative scholars. Her advice was asked, her opinions sought, and her taste consulted."

Through the kindness of Mr. Hawley, of a bookselling firm in Utica, a publisher in New York City agreed to bring out a little volume for Emily of one hundred and twelve pages, "Charles Linn; or, How to Observe the Golden Rule": a book for children. She was to receive ten per cent of the net price of the books, and to be paid twice a year.

For the first edition, of fifteen hundred, sold in eleven weeks, she received fifty-one dollars. All authors know how rejoiced the young teacher's heart must have been.

She was working far beyond her strength. Prof. A. C. Kendrick, in his "Life of Emily Chubbock," says: "With throbbing head and tingling nerves and an aching heart she sat down to her papers, and it was only by sending her thoughts away to the humble roof which sheltered those who were dearer to her than life, and reflecting on the sweetness of ministering to their wants, that she could spur her flagging energies to their work. . . .

"As Miss Sheldon was at one time passing, near midnight, through the halls, a light streaming from Emily's apartment attracted her attention, and softly opening the door, she stole in upon her vigils. Emily sat in her nightdress, her papers lying outspread before her, grasping with both hands her throbbing temples, and pale as a marble statue. Miss Sheldon went to her, whispered words of sympathy, and gently chided her for robbing her system of its needed repose. Emily's heart was already full, and now the fountain of feeling overflowed in uncontrollable weeping. 'O Miss Sheldon!' she exclaimed; 'I *must* write, I *must* write; I must do what I can to aid my poor parents.'"

She wrote her sister Kate: "Miss Sheldon has given me some slips of geranium, but I am afraid they will die, because I cannot get any jars to put them in. If they live, I will bring them to you. I could get pretty flower-pots for eighteen cents apiece. O Poverty, how vexatious thou art!"

"The Great Secret; or, How to be Happy," soon followed; then "Effie Maurice," "Allen Lucas; or, The Self-made Man," and some other Sunday-school books.

The income was comparatively little, but Emily at once bought for her parents, in Hamilton, a small house and garden for four hundred dollars, and hoped that her brain and health would last till it was paid for. She wrote to a friend, "There is nothing like coining one's brain into gold — no, bread — to make the heart grow sick."

While on a visit to New York, when she was twenty-seven, she wrote a bright letter to the *Evening Mirror*, then edited by George P. Morris and N. P. Willis, signing the letter "Fanny Forester." The letter pleased Mr. Willis, and he gladly accepted her sketches.

At once people began to ask about the new and sprightly author. Magazine editors wrote, seeking her productions at the highest prices then paid. They had returned them to her, or let them lie for months unnoticed and unanswered, before Mr. Willis "discovered" her. It is gratifying that every now and then there is an editor like Mr. Willis, who "discovers" genius. Though she never met Mr. Willis but once, she always felt the deepest gratitude for his kindness and appreciation. "I shall go on glorifying you in our new daily paper," he wrote her, "until the magazine people give you fifty dollars an article," — and so he did.

When fame came, health failed. Emily Chubbock had struggled long for recognition, and now the frail body was too weak for its added work. She was invited to the house of a minister, Dr. Gillette, of Philadelphia, a friend of Miss Sheldon's, though a stranger to her, to see if the mild climate and rest would not restore the waning life.

She partially regained her health, and brought out several of her magazine sketches on her return to Utica, in a book entitled, "Trippings in Author Land." The book was heartily welcomed. Her taste, her powers of reasoning, her sense of humor, her refinement, her graphic descriptions, were everywhere talked about. When she spent the following winter with the family of Dr. Gillette, all doors were opened to her, and a new life seemed, indeed, begun.

But other paths were opening to her. Dr. Judson was on his way to Philadelphia to attend some missionary meetings, and was to be escorted thither from Boston by Dr. Gillette. On their way, a slight accident detaining them for two or three hours, Dr. Gillette, seeing that a friend had the newly published "Trippings in Author Land," borrowed it and handed it to Dr. Judson. He took it hesitatingly, as the title seemed to him rather frivolous, but was soon charmed by the grace of the style, and vivacity of the writer.

Handing back the book, he said that it was written with great beauty and power. He asked if the author was a Christian, and said, "I should be glad to know her. A lady who writes so well ought to write better. It is a pity that such fine talents should be employed upon such subjects."

Upon being told that he would soon meet her, as she was a guest at the Gillette home, he asked, "Is she a Baptist?" and was answered in the affirmative.

The next morning the devoted and scholarly missionary of fifty-seven met the refined and charming author of twenty-eight. He was pleased with her intellect and sympathetic nature; she admired his mind and his devotion to his work. As the acquaintance grew, both loved each other with an ardor that not even death could quench. Neither did he forget the two noble women who had blessed his life already.

The letters which passed between Dr. Judson and Emily after they were betrothed to each other, while they show great depth of affection on the part of each, show no forgetting of the departed. He writes from Boston: "I have just been having a good cry here alone, in Mr. Colby's chamber, about my poor dear children. I left the two boys yesterday crying as they set off in the cars for Worcester. Abby Ann I took on to Bradford, and this morning I left her crying at the Hasseltines'. And thoughts of the children bear my mind to their departed mother, and I review the scenes on board the 'Sophia Walker' and at St. Helena. And then I stretch away to my two little forsaken orphans in Burma; and then I turn to you, whom I love not less, though but a recent acquaintance."

And Miss Chubbock writes back: "I am longing to see the little darlings. And, dearest, my own dearest, best friend, God helping me, they shall never feel the loss of the sainted one. Do not call them 'orphans' any more. I will love them and watch over them, and when I fail in anything you will point out the faults and teach me better." And when she had become Emily Judson, she kept nobly her promise.

Death had come so often to Dr. Judson that he almost feared it again: "And must this face ever become settled," he writes her, "cold, lifeless, like those other faces that I once feasted on? And must I again press down the stiffening eyelids on the extinguished orbs of love?"

The world did not favor the marriage. Many friends even could not believe that a writer of fiction was suited to be a missionary's wife, and they felt sure that to place a brilliant author in desolate India was a sacrifice too great to be thought of.

But "Fanny Forester" wrote to her friends: "I am a great admirer of greatness — real, genuine greatness; and goodness has an influence which I have not the power to resist. . . . I would go with him the world over. There is a noble structure within, singularly combining delicacy and strength, which will afford me protection and shelter in this world, — a place where my own weak nature may rest itself securely, — a thing that never will grow old, and that I shall love in eternity. So you see that in going to Burma I make no sacrifices; for the things that I resign, though more showy, are not half as dear to me as those which I gain."

Dr. Judson was not moved by all the adverse comment, and when Emily wrote, "I dread the coming of something that may separate us, or make us less happy in each other," he replied, "I wonder whether you think that anything I hear or can hear will ever make me regret the blessed Providence that carried me to Delaware 12th, or feel ungrateful for your kind love, which has allowed my spirit to mingle with yours in a union which neither time nor death can ever dissolve. . . .

"I have been so cried down at different periods of my life — especially when I became a Baptist, and lost all, all but Ann — that I suppose I am a little hardened. But I feel for you, for it is your first field. Whatever of strength or shield is mine, or I can draw down from Heaven, is yours."

The copyright of "Trippings" was purchased from the publisher, and Ticknor, Read & Fields, of Boston, brought out the work in two handsome volumes, under the title of "Alderbrook."

Dr. Judson and Emily Chubbock were married June 2, 1846, and July 11 they sailed from Boston, many friends coming to say good-by, among them the slender boy of eighteen, George Dana Boardman, whom his mother had so longed to see once more before she died, at St. Helena.

They were four months on the journey to Maulmain. In passing the island of St. Helena, Dr. Judson thought of Sarah Boardman, and said, "Farewell, rock of the ocean! I thank thee that thou hast given me a 'place where I might bury my dead.'" And when the promontory of Amherst loomed in sight he discerned with a small telescope on the green bank "the small enclosure which contains the sleeping-place of my dear Ann and her daughter, Maria."

And when later he was absent from home for a time he wrote to his wife, "Here we lie, with Amherst in sight from my cabin window, — Amherst, whither I brought Ann, and returned to find her grave; Amherst, whither I brought Sarah, on returning from my matrimonial tour to Tavoy, and whence I took her away in the 'Paragon' to return no more; Amherst, the terminus of my long voyage in the 'Faneuil Hall' with Emily. The place seems like the centre of many radii of my past existence. . . .

"I seem to have lived in several worlds; but you are

the earthly sun that illuminates my present. My thoughts and affections revolve around you, and cling to your form and face and lips. Other luminaries have been extinguished by death. I think of them with mournful delight, and anticipate the time when we shall all shine together as the brightness of the firmament and as the stars for ever and ever."

What wonder that a man who could love earnestly, yet not forget, was a kind and thoughtful husband! Mrs. Judson wrote long after: "He was always planning pleasant little surprises for his family and neighbors, and kept up through married life those little lover-like attentions which I believe husbands are apt to forget. . . . If he went out before I was awake in the morning, very likely some pretty message would be pinned to my mosquito curtain. If he was obliged to stay at a business meeting, or any such place, longer than he thought I expected, some little pencilled line that he could trace without attracting attention would be despatched to me. . . . He was always earnest, enthusiastic, sympathizing, even in the smallest trifles; tender, delicate, and considerate — *never moody*."

Dr. Judson and his wife were met by warm hearts at Maulmain. The natives scrambled up the sides of the vessel, and could scarcely wait to clasp the hand of the missionary.

Mrs. Judson took the two motherless children, Henry and Edward, to her heart. "I do love the dear children that a saint in heaven has left me," she wrote home to America. "I love them for their own sakes; for sweeter, more lovely little creatures never breathed; brighter, more beautiful blossoms never expanded in the cold atmosphere of this world. . . . Edward is the loveliest child that I ever saw; there is something which seems to me angelic in his patience and calmness."

Dr. Judson wrote to his sister that "Emily makes one of the best wives and kindest mothers to the children that ever man was blessed with"; and to his boys in America, that his wife had just put their little brothers in bed, and that "Henry is singing and talking aloud to himself; and what do you think he is saying? 'My own mamma went away, away in a boat. And then she got wings and went up. And Charlie, too, went up, and they are flying above the moon and the stars.'"

Dr. Judson determined to try again if Burmese intolerance could not be overcome, and moved his family from Maulmain to Rangoon. They hired the upper part of a brick house, which Mrs. Judson called "Bat Castle." Maulmain had not been altogether a perfect abode, when, as Mrs. Judson wrote, "Frogs hop from my sleeves when I put them on, and lizards drop from the ceiling to the table when we are eating"; and the floors were black with ants; but Rangoon was far less desirable.

She wrote to her sister Kitty: "The floor overhead is quite low, and the beams, which are frequent, afford shelter to thousands and thousands of bats, that disturb us in the daytime only by a little cricket-like music, but in the night, — oh, if you could only hear them carouse! . . . We have had men at work nearly a week trying to thin them out, and have killed a great many hundreds. . . . Besides the bats, we are blessed with our full share of cockroaches, beetles, spiders, lizards, rats, ants, mosquitoes, and bedbugs. With the last, the wood-work is all alive, and the ants troop over the house in great droves, though there are scattering ones besides. Perhaps twenty have crossed my paper since I have been writing. Only one cockroach has paid me a visit, but the neglect of these gentlemen has been fully made up by a company of black bugs, about the size of the end of your little finger, — nameless adventurers."

Despite all this, the missionaries worked on unceasingly, Dr. Judson preaching and preparing his great Burmese dictionary, two volumes, containing over one thousand pages, and Mrs. Judson learning the language, conducting prayer-meetings, caring for her children, "and so, *so* happy in each other; ten times happier than if in America in a palace" — "a deliciously happy family," Dr. Judson wrote to his daughter Abby. After seven months, the appropriations for Indian missions having been curtailed, they returned to Maulmain, where their house, in which all their best clothing and most valuable goods were kept, had been burned, with all its contents; but Dr. Judson said, "The Lord gave and the Lord hath taken away; *blessed be the name of the Lord!*"

On Dec. 24, 1847, Emily Frances was born to Mrs. Judson, whose welcome the mother has so beautifully sung in "My Bird": —

"Ere last year's moon had left the sky,
  A birdling sought my Indian nest,
And folded, Oh, so lovingly!
  Her tiny wings upon my breast.

"From morn till evening's purple tinge
  In winsome helplessness she lies;
Two rose leaves, with a silken fringe,
  Shut softly on her starry eyes.

"There's not in Ind a lovelier bird;
  Broad earth owns not a happier nest;
O God! Thou hast a fountain stirred,
  Whose waters never more shall rest.

> "This beautiful, mysterious thing,
>   This seeming visitant from heaven,
> This bird with the immortal wing,
>   To me, to me, Thy hand has given.
>
> "The pulse first caught its tiny stroke,
>   The blood its crimson hue, from mine, —
> This life which I have dared invoke,
>   Henceforth is parallel with Thine.
>
> "A silent awe is in my room;
>   I tremble with delicious fear;
> The future with its light and gloom, —
>   Time and Eternity are here.
>
> "Doubts, hopes, in eager tumult rise;
>   Hear, O my God! one earnest prayer:
> Room for my bird in paradise,
>   And give her angel-plumage there."

Dr. Judson wrote to Abby, "Emily Frances is the sweetest little fairy you ever saw." Somewhat later Mrs. Judson became very ill, and fears were entertained of her death. The children, too, became ill. In helping to care for them, Dr. Judson took a severe cold, and broke down so rapidly that a sea voyage seemed the only possible restorative. His wife accompanied him to Amherst, where they spent a month, but he did not improve.

He longed to live to complete his dictionary. "People will call it a strange providence," he said, "if I do not live to finish my dictionary. But to me it will be a strange providence if I do. Men almost always leave some work, that they or their friends consider vastly important, unfinished. It is a way God has of showing us what really worthless creatures we are, and how altogether unnecessary, as active agents, in the working out of his plans." He did not live to finish his dictionary, and other hands completed the great work.

It was decided that he should take a longer sea voyage, and so he embarked, April 3, 1850, on the "Aristide Marie," bound for the Isle of France. He could not bear to leave his family, and often said, "Oh, if it were only the will of God to take me now, — to let me die here! I cannot, cannot go. This is almost more than I can bear"; and yet his face would brighten as he repeated, "Oh, the love of Christ! the love of Christ! We cannot understand it now, — but what a beautiful study for eternity!"

Again, he said, when told by his wife that it was the opinion of the mission that he would not recover, "I know it is, and I suppose they think me an old man, and imagine it is nothing for one like me to resign a life so full of trials. But I am not old, at least in that sense; you know I am not. Oh, no man ever left this world with more inviting prospects, with brighter hopes or warmer feelings — warmer feelings"; and he burst into tears.

"It is not because I shrink from death that I wish to live, neither is it because the ties that bind me here, though some of them are very sweet, bear any comparison with the drawings I at times feel towards heaven; but a few years would not be missed from my eternity of bliss, and I can well afford to spare them, both for your sake and for the sake of the poor Burmans. I am not tired of my work, neither am I tired of the world; yet, when Christ calls me home, I shall go with the gladness of a boy bounding away from his school. . . . I am ready to go *to-day*, if it should be the will of God, — this very hour; but I am not *anxious* to die."

The "Aristide Marie" did not sail till Monday, April 8, five days after Dr. Judson had embarked. His wife was unable to accompany him. On Wednesday evening, a friend said, "I hope you feel that Christ is now near, sustaining you." "Oh, yes!" he replied; "*it is all right there.*"

On Friday afternoon, April 12, he said, in Burmese, to a servant, "It is done; I am going. . . . Take care of poor mistress." He died at a quarter past four.

A strong plank coffin was soon constructed, sand was poured in to make it sink, and at eight o'clock the crew assembled, and, in perfect silence, the body was committed to the sea, in latitude thirteen degrees north, and longitude ninety-three degrees east, three days out of sight of the mountains of Burma.

A man of devoted piety, rare scholarship, sunny nature, and indomitable will, Dr. Judson wrought a wonderful work in his lifetime; a work that has gone on in an ever-increasing ratio since his death. When he died there were sixty-three churches among the Burmans and the Karens, under the charge of one hundred and sixty-three missionaries, native pastors and assistants, with seven thousand native Christians. The Rev. J. E. Clough, D. D., of the Telugu Mission in southeastern India, a people numbering eighteen millions, says in the *Independent* for May 19, 1892, of the twenty-one Baptist mission stations among the Burmese, Karens, and Shans, "There are about thirty thousand communicants, with five hundred churches and chapels, of which one stands on the site of the prison of Oung-pen-la, where Dr. Judson was imprisoned, and where his devoted wife heroically struggled for long months to preserve his life."

Since Dr. Judson's death, the American Board, the Baptist Union, and kindred organizations in the Episcopal, Methodist, and Presbyterian churches, have grandly carried on the labors in which he was the pioneer. The American Baptist Missionary Union statistics for 1891 show four hundred and seventeen missionaries, two thousand and thirty native preachers, fourteen hundred and fifty-nine churches, and more than one hundred and sixty-three thousand members, over eighteen thousand persons having been baptized in 1891.

Mrs. Judson did not learn of her husband's death till four months had passed. Ten days after his death, April 22, his son Charles was born, dying the same day, of whom his mother wrote in "Angel Charlie":—

> "He came — a beauteous vision —
>   Then vanished from my sight,
> His wing one moment cleaving
>   The blackness of my night;
> My glad ear caught the rustle,
>   Then, sweeping by, he stole
> The dew-drop that his coming
>   Had cherished in my soul.
>
> . . . .
>
> "Oh, I would not recall thee,
>   My glorious angel boy!
> Thou needest not my bosom,
>   Rare bird of light and joy;
> Here dash I down the tear-drops,
>   Still gathering in my eyes;
> Blest — oh! how blest! — in adding
>   A seraph to the skies!"

To Mrs. Judson, as to the world, the loss of a man like Dr. Judson was very great. She longed to stay in Burma, "for," she said, " my heart is *here*. I love the missionaries, love the work, and love the precious Christians that have been accustomed to gather round me for prayer and instruction. They sobbed like so many children when I announced my purpose of returning."

When failing health made a change of climate a necessity, she bade adieu to Maulmain, Jan. 22, 1851, after five short years of her married life, and, spending a little time in England, reached Boston in October of the same year, with her three fatherless children, Henry, Edward, and Emily Frances.

She assisted Dr. Wayland in preparing a life of her husband, published a little volume of poems, a collection of essays, entitled "The Kathayan Slave," its title taken from the first narrative in the volume; a memorial of Lavinia and Harriet Chubbock, entitled "My Two Sisters"; and was hoping to prepare an abridged memoir of her husband, for Sabbath schools and for the young.

But a constitution never robust was breaking from its early struggles with poverty. Indeed, even now, many were dependent upon her, and her life was not an easy one.

Toward the middle of the year 1854, consumption had so wasted her vital forces that she longed for rest. "It is not," she said, "the pearly gates and golden streets of heaven that attract me; it is its perfect rest in the presence of my Saviour. It will be *so* sweet, after a life of care and toil like mine, though a very pleasant one it has been, and I am only weary of the care and toil because I have not strength to endure them. This lack of strength is dreadful. . . . It is so sweet to die at home. I could not bear the thought of being buried elsewhere than here, where you all will probably rest by and by at my side."

"It is bright either way," she said to a friend, who had expressed the hope that God would restore her to health.

She died June 1, 1854, in the month of roses, as she had wished, at the early age of thirty-seven. Though she said, "There is *one* who will be inconsolable," referring to her little Emily, she made no provision for her in her will other than for the rest of the children, to whom she had been a loving mother.

On a simple headstone, in the cemetery at Hamilton, N. Y., one may read the words, "Dear Emily." She had been dear to the lamented Judson, dear to the Burmese, whose language she spoke admirably, writing many hymns in their native tongue, and dear to the tens of thousands who appreciated her gifted mind, and the strength and beauty of her character.

AMELIA B. EDWARDS.

AMELIA BLANDFORD EDWARDS.

DURING the winter of 1889-90, at the request of twenty-five college presidents, and such men as Lowell, Whittier, Holmes, and Howells, Miss Edwards came to America to deliver a course of lectures on Egypt, which she had given with great success in England and Scotland. All who heard the gifted Englishwoman will always remember her cheerful manner and her warm heart, coupled with rare scholarship and such an enthusiasm for her subject as made everybody long to visit and explore the ancient country.

In every city where she spoke she was the recipient of social courtesies from the most distinguished. Columbia College had already, in 1887, given her the degree of Doctor of Letters (L. H. D.), and Smith College made her a Doctor of Laws, the first time such a distinction was accorded in America to a woman.

In England she had won an honored place. The Crown had recognized her services to knowledge by awarding her a pension from the Civil List. When the Orientalists held their Congress in Vienna in 1886, at the invitation of the Emperor, Miss Edwards's important paper was so much appreciated that it was at once published in French, German, and English.

When King Oscar invited the Congress to Stockholm, in

1889, Miss Edwards's paper treating of the Cypriote, Phœnician, and other signs upon the potsherds recently discovered in Egypt was of so much interest that the renowned Dr. Brugsch and others caused it to be read again in the African section of the Congress.

In 1883, in conjunction with Sir Erasmus Wilson and Prof. Reginald Stuart Poole, LL. D., she helped to found the Egypt Exploration Fund, which has done, and is still doing, an invaluable work. The collecting of money fell largely upon her; also the correspondence with the explorers who were carrying forward the researches in the Egyptian tombs and elsewhere; and the editing of the works of these men, besides presenting the results of their labors to the public through the London *Times*, the *Athenæum*, the *Academy*, and other journals. She watched every new discovery with delight. In *Harper's Magazine* for July, 1882, she wrote of the finding of the royal mummies now in the Bûlak Museum in Cairo. Prof. Maspero, in July, 1881, caused the arrest of some Arabs whom he suspected of concealing valuable treasures. These Arabs pointed out, at last, a buried tomb in Dayr-el-Bahari, where were found some thirty-six mummies of kings, queens, and high-priests. These are now in the Bûlak Museum.

In *Harper's* for October, 1886, she wrote on Tanis, the Joan of the Bible; in *The Century* for January, 1890, on the Temple of Bubastis.

Her last illness was brought on by a visit to the London docks, in November, 1891, to examine antiquities from Ahnas, which were to be distributed in England and America. In January and later, she rallied from pneumonia, but a relapse came, and she died, not at her home, "The Larches," near Bristol, but at Weston-Super-mare, on April 15, 1892, at five A. M. on Good Friday. She was a little more than sixty-one years of age.

The end came suddenly and unexpectedly, bringing sorrow to thousands of hearts in both hemispheres.

Miss Edwards was born June 7, 1831, in London. She was the daughter of an army officer prominent in the Peninsular Campaign under Wellington, and of an able mother, descended from the Walpole family. Her maternal grandfather was an Irish barrister, Robert Walpole.

Her early education was begun by her mother, and carried on by a tutor who fitted boys for college. At four years of age she wrote a story, printing it in capital letters; at seven, "The Knights of Old," a poem, printed in a weekly journal; at twelve, a long historical novel, of the time of Edward III,, published in a penny paper, the London *Pioneer*.

When she was fourteen she sent a story to "The Omnibus," a periodical edited by the late George Cruikshank. On the back of the manuscript she drew sketches of her chief characters. The great caricaturist was so pleased with the art work that he visited the author and was surprised to find her still a child. He offered to train her in his special work, but as she had decided to devote herself to music she declined his offer. For seven years she studied music becoming a composer as well as a performer. At the age of twenty-one she had become so successful with her short stories in *Chambers's Journal* and elsewhere, that, having lost her property, she decided upon literature as a profession, rather than singing in concerts and operas.

From this time onward her life was one of continuous labor, happy labor, and yet none the less exhausting and constant. She wrote regularly for the press; reviews of books, musical, dramatic, and art criticisms, stories and sketches for *Household Words*, *Chambers's Journal*, and *Good Words*, and was on the staff, at different times, of several journals; the *Saturday Review*, the *Graphic*, the *Illustrated London News*, and the *Morning Post*. Miss Edwards says in the *Arena* for August, 1891: " Time is precious to me, and leisure is a thing unknown. . . . When I am asked what are my working hours, I reply, ' All the time when I am not either sitting at meals, taking exercise, or sleeping'; and this is literally true. I live with the pen in my hand, not only from morning till night but sometimes from night till morning. . . . For at least the last twenty-five years, I have rarely put out my lamp before two or three in the morning. Occasionally when work presses and a manuscript has to be despatched by the earliest morning mail, I remain at my desk the whole night through, and I can with certainty say that the last chapter of every book I have ever written has been finished at early morning."

Her first novel, at least the first which attracted any attention, was " My Brother's Wife," published in 1855, when Miss Edwards was twenty-four. Two years later, in 1857, " The Ladder of Life " appeared, followed by " Hand and Glove " in 1858, and " Barbara's History " in 1864, the latter becoming a general favorite, being translated into German, French, and Italian.

Meantime, in 1856, Miss Edwards had written " A Summary of English History"; in 1858, " A Summary of French History," and a translation of " A Lady's Captivity among Chinese Pirates "; in 1862, " Sights and Stories," a holiday tour through North Belgium; in 1863, " The Story of Cervantes," and the same year, " Rachel Noble's Experience." The next novel after " Barbara's

History" was "Half a Million of Money," published in 1865, and the same year a volume of poems called "Ballads," and one of short stories, called "Miss Carew."

"Debenham's Vow," a story of the blockade at Charlestown, appeared in 1870; "The Sylvesters," in 1871; "In the Days of My Youth," in 1873; and a volume of short stories, "Monsieur Maurice," also in 1873.

She was now forty-two, and had published nearly twenty volumes, besides her large amount of journalistic work. This meant a busy life indeed, varied by occasional visits to Germany, Greece, and Italy.

In 1873, "Untrodden Peaks and Unfrequented Valleys" was published. It is a breezy and interesting record of a journey in the South Eastern Tyrol, among the limestone mountains called the "Dolomites." The book shows Miss Edwards as ever the educated and energetic woman; skilled in botany, knowing how to measure mountains, to paint pictures, as well as to study character, to get much of cheer out of the discomforts of an almost unknown land.

The wedding scene in Cortina, where the bride and groom exchange rings and receive the blessing of the priest with their lighted candles in their hands, the husband then going away to play at bowls, and the young wife to exchange her finery for her shabby, every-day clothes, is a graphic picture. No tourist will ever go over the route taken by Miss Edwards without looking for the buried villages at the bottom of the lake of Alleghe, whose church-spires and house-tops can still be seen. The four villages were buried in this lake in 1771, through a landslide. It is said that a charcoal-burner, who had been at work in the woods all day, ran through the villages telling that the mountain was moving, but nobody heeded this

Eastern Paul Revere, and in the night the mountain swept down upon the sleepers and none escaped. Two villages were buried and two were drowned.

Especially interesting is her description of Cadore, forever immortalized as being the home of the great painter, Titian. She saw the white-washed cottage where he was born, with this inscription in Italian on the side wall: "In 1477, within these humble walls Titian Vecellio entered a celebrated life, whence he departed, at the end of nearly a hundred years, in Venice, on the 27th day of August, 1576." Adjoining is the old house where he is believed to have painted, when eleven years of age, the Madonna and the child standing on her knee, while a boy (an angel), supposed to have the face of Titian, kneels at the feet of the Virgin.

In the old Duomo Miss Edwards saw some pictures believed to be genuine Titians, and found that the pastor of the church thought "Cadore the axis on which the world goes round." When one sees how thousands attach themselves to any who have achieved fame, one marvels why so many are unwilling to do the hard work which is necessary to bring fame or success.

A second edition of "Untrodden Peaks" was published in 1890, seventeen years after the first edition, dedicated to "My American Friends in all Parts of the World."

In 1877 a book was published which was eagerly read, and at once acknowledged to be the work of a scholar, and an authority upon Egyptology, "A Thousand Miles up the Nile." Heretofore Miss Edwards had been a musician, a painter, a novelist, a charming woman socially: now she was indeed a woman of whom her sex could be proud, the accepted equal of prominent scholars, an indefatigable worker, and one of comprehensive grasp.

No one can read the book without becoming forever afterwards deeply interested in Egyptian history, having a desire to see for one's self the wonders of architecture in that strange land, and the proofs of that remarkable civilization, from which we may learn so much. She said she had found that hieroglyphics could be read, "for the simple reason that I find myself able to read an Egyptian sentence."

Miss Edwards and her friends sailed up the Nile in a dahabeeyah, a flat-bottomed boat with two masts, with a crew and other helpers, numbering twenty in all. The Nile sailors she describes as a docile, good-tempered set, who are paid a little more than two pounds a month. Bread is their chief article of food, which they bake at large public ovens along the river, cut in slices and dry in the sun, and then soak in hot water, flavor with oil, pepper, and salt, and stir it into boiled lentils till the whole becomes like pea-soup. A little coffee twice a day and a handful of dates, with this soup, constitute their food for the journey.

Of course Miss Edwards saw the great pyramid at Ghizeh, seven hundred and thirty-two feet long and four hundred and eighty feet high, begun by King Khufu, or Cheops, and supposed to have been over four thousand two hundred years old at the time of the birth of Christ.

At Sakkârah, after seeing more pyramids, she visited the Serapeum, — the long-lost sepulchral temple of the sacred bulls. These animals lived in the great temple of Apis, at Memphis, when they were alive, and at death, after being prepared like mummies, were buried in catacombs in the desert.

In 1850, Mariette Bey, exploring in the interests of the French Government, discovered this temple, and the avenue six hundred feet long, leading to it, bordered with sphinxes. At the end of the main avenue was found a semi-circular platform, around which stood statues of famous Greek philosophers and poets. Besides the great temple of the Serapeum there were found three smaller temples, and three groups of Apis catacombs, vaults and passages hewn out of the solid rock on which the temples were built.

In these tombs Miss Edwards saw immense stone coffins, fourteen feet in length, by eleven in height, each coffin a single block of highly finished black granite. Three of the sarcophagi bear the oval of Cambyses, the second king of Persia, 529 B. C., who, being enraged at one of the sacred bulls, drew his dagger and stabbed him in the thigh. The bull died of his wound, according to Herodotus. Mariette found in one of these sepulchral chambers the footprints of the workmen, made four thousand years before, in the thin layer of sand on the pavement.

Memphis, the once great city, with sacred groves, obelisks, temples, and palaces, is now little more than dust heaps. Apis, the sacred bull, once lived here in state, taking his exercise in a courtyard where every column was a statue.

Going up the river, the travellers were honored with a visit from "Holy Sheykh Cotton," a well-fed man of thirty, whose blessing makes the sailors sure of a successful voyage. "He has two wives," says Miss Edwards; "he never does a stroke of work, and he looks the picture of sleek prosperity. Yet he is a saint of the first water, and when he dies miracles will be performed at his tomb, and his eldest son will succeed him in the business."

Another saint is Sheykh Selim, "holiest of the holy, dirtiest of the dirty, white-pated, white-bearded, withered, bent, and knotted up, — he who, naked and unwashed, has sat on that same spot every day, through summer heat and winter cold, for the last fifty years, never providing himself with food or water; never even lifting his hand to his mouth, depending on charity, not only for his food but for his feeding."

Worse, almost, than the ignorance and superstition of the people is their filth. "The children of the very poor," says Miss Edwards, "are simply encrusted with dirt and sores, and swarming with vermin. To wash young children is injurious to health, therefore the mothers suffer them to fall into a state of personal uncleanliness, which is alone enough to engender disease. To brush away the flies that beset their eyes is impious; hence, ophthalmia and various kinds of blindness. I have seen infants in their mothers' arms with six or eight flies in each eye. I have seen the little helpless hands put down reprovingly if they approached the seat of annoyance."

At Denderah, Miss Edwards saw the massive temple begun by Ptolemy XI. upon a site where other temples had been erected since the era of King Cheops. The names of Augustus, Caligula, Tiberius, Nero, and others are found in the royal ovals. The building must have been comparatively new when in A. D. 379 the ancient religion was abolished by the edict of Theodosius, and forty thousand statues of divinity were destroyed. The walls of the enclosure about the temple, with its groves of palm and acacia, were one thousand feet in length, thirty-five in height, and fifteen feet in thickness.

Here is a famous external bass-relief of Cleopatra, the beautiful queen who knew ten languages, and who turned the heads of Julius Cæsar and Mark Anthony. The hair is plaited as the women of Egypt dress their hair to-day, in an almost infinite number of tiny plaits, the ends covered with Nile mud dipped in yellow ochre.

The temple of Denderah contained store chambers, where the vestments of the priests and the holy vessels must have been kept, with cloisters and vast enclosures surrounded by walls, where the solemn rites of the priesthood were probably observed.

The king is represented in his double character of Pharaoh and high-priest in all the hieroglyphics of this vast temple. He is conducted to the gods by goddesses. He is purified and crowned, and then presented in the supreme presence of Hathor, the Goddess of Truth, and of the Beautiful. Later he presents flowers, bread, and wine as offerings to Osiris.

The latter, the Good, was killed in a fight with Typhon the Evil, and his body thrown into the Nile. His wife, Isis, found it, and his soul was believed to enter into the bull Apis.

In a dark chamber of the temple was the Holy of Holies, where the golden sistrum or timbrel of the goddess was kept. The king alone could take this mysterious emblem from its niche, and enclosing it in a costly shrine, put it in one of the sacred boats, to be hoisted on poles and carried in procession on the shoulders of the priests.

At the temple of Luxor, in Thebes, Miss Edwards and her party looked upon the representations of the battles of Rameses II., usually called Rameses the Great. He is said to have met his enemies single handed, and to have charged upon the foe six times, overthrowing twenty-five hundred chariots and one hundred thousand warriors. Those whom he did not kill he forced into the river. Rameses II., called also Sesostris, began to reign at the age of twelve, about 1405 B. C., with his father, Seti I., the son of Rameses I., the founder of dynasty XIX. Rameses II. had three wives, as is told by the hieroglyphics, an extensive harem, and his children numbered one hundred and seventy. He was a wonderful ruler, building more than one hundred temples, digging artesian wells and canals, and effecting the greatest improvements and enterprises in his kingdom, through the forced labor of slaves and captives taken in war. He is believed by scholars to have been the Pharaoh of the captivity of the Israelites, and his son, Menepthah, the Pharaoh of the Exodus.

In 1881, Prof. Maspero found the mummy of this famous chieftain, Rameses II., among the stolen and hidden bodies in Dayr-el-Bahari. On the top of the mummy case is an effigy of the body within. The hands are crossed upon the breast. The right hand holds the royal flail, and the left the royal crook. The eyes are inserted in enamel, while the eyebrows and eyelashes are painted black.

The body itself was wrapped in orange and rose-colored linen, very fine, with white bands to keep the shroud in place. On these bands were written the name and history of the king.

The Rev. Charles S. Robinson, D. D., in his "Pharaohs of the Bondage of the Exodus," thus describes the mummy of Rameses II.: "The initial wrapping was removed, and there was disclosed a band of stuff or strong cloth rolled all around the body; next to this was a second envelop, sewed up and kept in place by narrow bands at some distance each from each; then came two thicknesses of small bandages, and then a new winding-sheet of linen, reaching from the head to the feet. Upon this a figure representing the goddess Nut, more than a yard in length, had been drawn in red and white color, as prescribed by the ritual for the dead. Beneath this amulet there was found one more bandage; when that was removed a piece of linen alone remained, and this was spotted with the bituminous matter used by the embalmers; so at last it was evident that Rameses the Great was close by — under his shroud. . . .

"A single clip of the scissors, and the king was fully disclosed. The head is long, and small in proportion to the body. The top of the skull is quite bare. On the temple there are a few sparse hairs, but at the poll the hair is quite thick, forming smooth, straight locks about two inches in length. White at the time of death, they have been dyed a light yellow by the spices used in embalmment. The forehead is low and narrow . . . the eyes are small and close together; the nose is long, thin, arched like the noses of the Bourbons; the cheek-bones very prominent; the ears round, standing far out from the head, and pierced, like those of a woman, for the wearing of ear-rings; the jawbone is massive and strong; the chin very prominent; the mouth small but thick-lipped."

The mummy is six feet long. At Dayr-el-Bahari were found also the bodies of King Pinotem I., King Pinotem II., Queen Isi-em-Kheb, and many others. With the mummy of the queen were found mummified meats, — trussed geese, calves' heads, dried grapes and dates, all packed in a large rush hamper, and sealed with her husband's seal.

Besides food for her future needs, her toilet was not forgotten: her ointment bottles, several full-dress wigs, curled and frizzed, a set of alabaster cups, and exquisite goblets of variegated glass.

A wooden and ivory cabinet of the great woman Pharaoh of dynasty XVIII., Queen Hatasu, was found, containing a desiccated human liver, possibly her own. She was famous as a builder of ships and promoter of commerce. She was the wife of her brother, Thothmes II.

As the rites of mummification were performed for every man, woman, and child, slave and criminal, it is estimated that there have been in Egypt not less than 731,000,000 mummies.

Formerly a stately avenue two miles long bordered by sphinxes about ten feet in length led from the temple at Luxor to the one at Karnak. Miss Edwards thinks there must have been two hundred and fifty sphinxes on each side of the avenue.

At Karnak the travellers studied the Great Temple with its doorway one hundred feet in height. The twelve central columns of the hypostyle hall built by Seti, the father of Rameses the Great, are sixty-two feet high, and so large that six men with extended arms, finger-tip to finger-tip, can barely span any one of them. The remaining one hundred and twenty-two columns are gigantic also. All are buried between six and seven feet in the alluvial deposits.

Of this hall Miss Edwards says: "The Pyramids are more stupendous. The Colosseum covers more ground. The Parthenon is more beautiful, yet in nobility of conception, in vastness of detail, in majesty of the highest order, the Hall of Pillars exceeds them every one. This doorway, — these columns are the wonder of the world."

Miss Edwards became so absorbed in her water-color paintings at these various places that she sometimes forgot to eat. The faithful Arab servant would touch nothing at such time, saying, "By my prophet, am I a pig or a dog, that I should eat when the Sitt is fasting?"

They explored Nubia, with its temples, tombs, and strange people. They went among the natives, bought girdles soaked in castor-oil, and other souvenirs of the country.

Of the Nubian, Miss Edwards says: "He reckons castor-oil among his greatest luxuries. He eats it as we eat butter. His wives saturate their plaited locks with it. His little girls perfume their fringes with it. His home, his breath, his garments, his food are redolent of it. It pervades the very air in which he lives and has his being. Happy the European traveller who, while his lines are cast in Nubia, can train his degenerate nose to delight in the aroma of castor-oil!"

At Abou Simbel, in Nubia, they visited the temples with the colossal statues of Rameses II. and his queen, Nefertari, each thirty feet high, and their infants, ten feet high. The superb hieroglyphics are cut half a foot deep in the rock: "Rameses, the Strong in Truth, the Beloved of Amen, made this divine abode for his royal wife, Nefertari, whom he loves." In another place in the temple one reads that "his royal wife, who loves him, Nefertari, the Beloved of Maut, constructed for him this Abode in the Mountain of the Pure Waters." The name of Nefertari means perfect, good, or beautiful companion. Evidently love was in the world in those days, as now.

Miss Edwards describes the monster battle scene with 1,100 figures, on the north side of the Great Hall. Rameses drives before him the fugitives, after the battle. The work must be seen at sunrise to be appreciated.

At Abou Simbel Miss Edwards and her party made some interesting discoveries of rock-cut chambers in the buried sand. They were sculptured and painted in the best style of the best period of Egyptian art, bearing the portraits of Rameses the Great and his queen. The coloring was very brilliant. That these chambers had never been discovered before, as have many of the others, either in the times of the Ptolemies or the Cæsars, was shown by the fact that there were no interpolated inscriptions, or "pious caricatures of St. George and the Holy Family," in the time of the early Christians. Miss Edwards thinks it probable that an earthquake which visited that country in the time of Rameses II. made the chambers ever after inaccessible. Dr. S. Birch thinks the newly-discovered place might have been the library of the Great Temple of Abou Simbel, where the Egyptian books, huge rolls of papyrus, were stored.

In this excavating Miss Edwards worked with the greatest enthusiasm. "Unconscious of fatigue," she says, "we toiled upon our hands and knees, as for bare life, under the burning sun. We had all the crew up, working like tigers. Every one helped; even the dragoman and the two maids. More than once, when we paused for a moment's breathing space, we said to each other: ' If those at home could see us, what would they say!'"

On their return down the Nile, they joined the excavators at work in the Necropolis of Thebes, and saw mummies taken out of the rock tombs. Sometimes the mummies were in the mountain side; these tombs had been numbered half a century before by Sir Gardner Wilkinson in "The Manners and Customs of the Ancient Egyptians." "This book," says Miss Edwards, "as a child, had shared my affections with 'The Arabian Nights.' I had read every line of the old six-volume edition over and over again. I knew every one of the six hundred illustrations by heart. Now I suddenly found myself in the midst of old and half-forgotten friends. . . . It seemed to me that I had met all these kindly brown people years and years ago, perhaps in some previous stage of existence; that I had walked with them in their gardens; listened to the music of their lutes and tambourines; pledged them at their feasts "

Bab-el-Molûk, or the Valley of the Tomb of the Kings, was found to be a most interesting study. The longest tomb in the valley, that of Seti I., measures four hundred and seventy feet in length, with a total depth of descent of one hundred and eighty feet. The sarcophagus was taken to England, and is in the Sir J. Sloane Museum. It is carved from a single block of the finest alabaster.

The tomb of Rameses III., one of the greatest of the monarchs of Egypt, measures four hundred and five feet in length, and descends only thirty-one feet. The sarcophagus is in the Fitz-William Museum at Cambridge, England, and its lid is in the Louvre. Many of these tombs were opened and rifled of their jewels and other treasures in Ptolemaic times. The vases, sandals, clothing, food, and other articles in the tombs were placed there for the use of the dead, when they should awake, after the return of the soul to the body. The wealthy often left a portion of their estate to the priests to provide for these sepulchral meals.

The immense colossi of the plain, at Thebes, fifty feet high, without their pedestals, and eighteen feet and three inches across the shoulders, representing Amenhotep III., who reigned about one hundred and fifty years before the time of Rameses the Great, and began the Temple of Luxor, were of intense interest to the travellers. One of these statues formerly gave out a musical sound during the first hour of the day, and was supposed to have a miraculous voice. The Greeks thought it the son of Tithonus and Aurora, and called it Memnon. Hadrian and other famous emperors and writers came to hear Memnon. Some have supposed the music was produced by the priests, as there is a hollow space inside the throne of the statue; others, that it was produced by rarefied air through the crevices of the stone, caused by the sudden change of temperature consequent on the rising of the sun.

Miss Edwards's " A Thousand Miles up the Nile " at once became a classic on Egypt. The " Literary World " well called it " one of the brilliant, fascinating books of travel for all time."

In 1879 she published "A Poetry Book of Elder Poets." She also wrote three hundred biographies for Colnaghi's Photographic Historical Portrait Gallery," and " Home and Foreign Lyrics," besides several translations and compilations.

She published only one novel after this, " Lord Brackenbury," in 1880, which appeared first as a serial in the London *Graphic*. It went through twenty editions, and has been translated into French, German, and Russian.

The story turns upon the mysterious disappearance of Lord Brackenbury, after he has purchased one hundred and fifty thousand dollars' worth of diamonds, ostensibly for Winifred, to whom he is betrothed. He is not in love with her, but expects to marry her through the wish of his father.

He prefers to lead a seafaring life rather than take upon himself the cares of an estate; uses the diamonds for his support for a term of years, marries the one he loves, and returns seventeen years later, to find that his brother

Lancelot has married Winifred. He asks for and receives a portion of the estate, and, without seeing his brother or Winifred, goes back to his quiet, untitled life. The description of an eruption of Vesuvius in 1872 is very graphic.

After the publication of this book Miss Edwards gave herself more fully than ever to her beloved Egyptian study. She translated Maspero's "Egyptian Archæology," and after her lectures in America, brought out, in 1891, her "Pharaohs, Fellahs, and Explorers," the substance of the lectures, with much added. Every page is full of interest. Her friend and co-laborer in Egyptology in this country, the Rev. William C. Winslow, D. D., LL. D., of Boston, the efficient and scholarly vice-president of the Egypt Exploration Fund, well says of her in "Biblia" for May, 1892: "Her profound knowledge of ancient Egypt and her exhaustive study of the remarkable results of the explorations in that historic wonderland, combined with her graphic and picturesque powers of description, made her articles of popular as well as scholastic value.

"It is not too much to say that Miss Edwards will live in biography as one of the most remarkable women of the latter half of this century. . . . We thank heaven for what her busy, varied, suggestive life accomplished, and for the splendid example she has set to her own sex in showing what women can do in scholarly research, and, more important yet, in causing its light to shine out and enlighten the world."

Miss Edwards describes the finding, in 1883, of Pithom, one of the "treasure cities" built by the forced labor of the Hebrews. It was discovered by M. Naville, of Geneva, the first explorer sent out by the Exploration Fund.

Tanis, or Zoan, was discovered in 1884, by Mr. W. M. Flinders Petrie.

The great temple of Tanis — Zoan — was one of the grandest in Egypt, dating probably from the time of the Pyramids. It was rebuilt centuries later by Rameses II. Mr. Petrie found here fragments of the largest colossus ever sculptured by man. It was cut out of the red granite of Assûan, and once stood erect and crowned, one hundred and twenty-five feet high, including the pedestal. The minimum weight of this statue of Rameses II. must have been about twelve hundred tons; probably one massive block. The foot of the statue measured fifty-seven and two eighths inches in length.

In one buried house in Tanis, that of Bakakhin, Mr. Petrie found seven ancient waste-paper baskets full of deeds, letters, and other manuscripts. One proved to be a mathematical treatise, another an almanac.

In other places Mr. Petrie found most interesting papyri. One, in 1889, was a complete copy of the Second Book of the "Iliad," written in uncial Greek by a scribe of the second century after Christ. It was buried under the head of a young woman in the Græco-Egyptian Necropolis of Hawara. The inscription upon her coffin was illegible. "We only know," says Miss Edwards, "that she was young and fair, and that she so loved her Homer that it was buried with her in the grave. Her head and her beautiful black hair are now in the Ethnographical Department of the Natural History Museum at South Kensington, and her precious papyrus is in the Bodleian Library at Oxford."

Miss Edwards regarded as the three most interesting historic documents yet found in Egypt the "Chart of Victory," engraved on a large black granite tablet found in the temple of Karnak, at Thebes, the "Epic of Pentaur," and the treaty between Rameses II. and the allied princes of Syria.

The "Chart of Victory" records the conquests of Thothmes III., the Alexander of ancient Egypt. The "Epic of Pentaur" records the campaign of the great Rameses II. against the allied forces of Syria and Asia Minor. It is sometimes called the Egyptian Iliad. A copy of this poem on papyrus is in the British Museum.

Several papyri have been found containing moral precepts. The maxims of Ptah-hotep are found in the famous Prisse papyrus, the oldest papyrus known. It is in the Bibliothèque Nationale, of Paris, written by a scribe in the XIth dynasty. Some of it is copied from a Vth dynasty document, written nearly four thousand years before our era. An excellent translation is in the Bibliothecra Sacra, 1888, made by Prof. Howard Osgood, D. D., of Rochester, N. Y. The maxims are applicable to us of the nineteenth century: —

"Be not proud because of thy learning," says Ptah-hotep. "Converse with the ignorant as freely as with scholar; *for the gates of knowledge should never be closed.*"

"If thou art exalted after having been low, if thou art rich after having been needy, harden not thy heart because of thy elevation: thou hast but become a steward of the good things belonging to the gods."

"If thou wouldst be of good conduct and dwell apart from evil, beware of bad temper; for it contains the germs of all wickedness."

"Work for thyself. Do not count upon the wealth of others: it will not enter thy dwelling-place."

"He who speaks evil reaps evil."

"Ill-treat not thy wife, whose strength is less than thine: be thou her protector."

Miss Edwards's lecture tour in America was fatiguing. While at the house of Mrs. Francis Collins, at Columbus, Ohio, a friend who had travelled with her in the Eastern Mediterranean twenty years before, she broke her arm, and from this, added to the wear of body, she never fully recovered. She did not lose a single lecture engagement, being scrupulous about her word, and knowing the disappointment her absence would occasion those who had prepared for her coming. She even lectured on the evening of the day on which her arm was broken, and travelled several hundred miles the day afterward.

Mrs. Collins writes me concerning her: "She was, as you know, a most accomplished woman, and very agreeable in manner, with nothing pedantic about her. She was a fine artist, and her sketches were spirited and finished. She told me she had studied music sufficiently to be able to write it for a full band, and on all subjects which came up for discussion during the *dolce far niente* days of our voyage she showed herself very familiar with science, literature, and art.

"Singularly destitute of near relatives, she was extremely devoted to an aged friend who had lived with her for years, and on both occasions when I met her she was hastening home to her; the last time, if I remember correctly, to keep her friend's birthday.

"She was very conscientious in her writing. She said she always wrote as well as she possibly could, never doing slovenly work for the sake of quicker remuneration."

Miss Edwards was a woman of indomitable courage and perseverance, else she could never have done the work which she did. From a child, she was an omnivorous reader. At fourteen she had read Scott, Bulwer, Cooper, Dickens, and others, as her own words in the *Arena* for August, 1891, attest: "The shelves of her library devoted to the British poets carry me back to a time when I read them straight through without a break, from Chaucer to Tennyson. . . . An equally voluminous series of histories of Greece and Rome, and of translations of the Greek and Latin poets, marks the time when I first became deeply interested in classic antiquity. To this phase also belong the beginnings of those archæological works which I have of late years accumulated, almost to the exclusion of all other books, as well as my collection of volumes upon Homer, which nearly fill one division of a bookcase.

"When I left London, some six and twenty years ago, to settle at Westbury-on-Trym, I also added to my library a large number of works on the fine arts, feeling, as every lover of pictures must do, that it is necessary in some way or another to make up for the loss of the National Gallery, the South Kensington Museum, and other delightful places which I was leaving behind. At this time, also, I had a passion for Turner, and eagerly collected his engraved works, of which I believe I possess all. I think I may say the same of Samuel Prout. Of Shakespeare I have almost as many editions as I have translations of Homer; and of European histories, works of reference generally, a writer who lives in the country must, of course, possess a goodly number."

Miss Edwards also had among her books many valuable gifts from authors: the "Ring and the Book," from Browning; "Many Moods," from John Addington Symonds, dedicated to her; a presentation copy of Sir Theodore Martin's translation of the "Odes of Horace," and Lord Lytton's version of the Odes, with a letter addressed to her at the time of its publication.

"My books," says Miss Edwards, "have for many years been my daily companions, teachers, and friends. Merely to lean back in one's chair, now and then — merely to lean back and look at them — is a capital pleasure, a stimulus, and, in some sense, a gain. . . . The tired brain is consciously refreshed by it."

Beside books, pictures, and pottery, treasures from Egypt abound in her home: shrivelled dates, lentils, nuts, and a piece of bread from the tombs of Thebes, three mummied hands, and the heads of two ancient Egyptians "in a wardrobe in her bedroom."

Miss Edwards was a brilliant woman mentally and socially; esteemed not less for her sympathetic heart and her warm feeling for America than for her learning and her ability. The "London Academy," to which she contributed often, and would accept no remuneration, says of her articles: "We know not whether to admire in them most the brilliance of their narrative style or the accuracy with which each detail was verified. She was in truth a model contributor — never declining a request, punctual to her promises, writing in a clear, bold hand, and considerate of the convenience of printer as well as editor."

Her home was "The Larches," a rambling and picturesque house set in the midst of larches and high shrubs, in an acre of ground, at Westbury-on-Trym, four miles from Bristol, in the west of England. Flowers grew everywhere, and birds were welcome visitors. Under the larch-trees Miss Edwards walked two miles daily for exercise: a half mile before breakfast, a half mile after breakfast, and a mile or more late in the afternoon.

"To walk these two miles *per diem*," she said, "is a

Draconian law which I impose upon myself during all seasons of the year. When the snow lies deep in winter it is our old gardener's first duty in the morning to sweep 'Miss Edwards's path,' as well as to clear two or three large spaces on the lawn, in which the wild birds may be fed. The wild birds are our intimate friends and perennial visitors, for whom we keep an open *table d'hôte* throughout the year. By feeding them in summer we lose less fruit than our neighbors; and by feeding them in winter we preserve the lives of our little summer friends, whose songs are the delight of ourselves and our neighbors in the springtime."

Miss Edwards's death, humanly speaking, came all too early, just as she was in the midst of her greatest work. She had planned much more labor, but other hands must do it, if it be done at all. Her winsome presence and generous nature will be gratefully remembered; while her scholarship and her usefulness in the world of thought will ever be an inspiration.

She was a member of many learned societies, such as the Biblical, Archæological, and the Society for Hellenic Studies. She wrote the article upon Egyptology in the Encyclopædia Brittanica, and the supplementary article for the American edition on Recent Discoveries in Egypt. By her will she endowed a chair of Egyptology, and gave her valuable library to Somerville Hall, a college for women at Oxford.

A PARTIAL
Catalogue of Books

PUBLISHED BY

THOMAS Y. CROWELL & CO.

46 East Fourteenth Street, New York.

100 Purchase Street, Boston.

STANDARD AND MISCELLANEOUS.

AD LUCEM. By Mary Lloyd. Selections of Prose and Poetry for suffering ones. Parti-colored cloth, gilt top, 18mo $1.00
Seal leather, flexible. Gilt edge 1.75
Levant, padded. Gilt edge 2.50

AT HOME AND IN WAR. By Col. A. V. Verestchagin. 12mo . 1.50

BRAMPTON SKETCHES. New England Life Seventy Years Ago. By Mrs. Mary B. Claflin. Illustrated 1.00

BROWN'S CONCORDANCE 50

CAMBRIDGE BOOK OF POETRY AND SONG. By Charlotte Fiske Bates. *New and Revised Edition. New Cover Designs.* With 40 fac-simile poems in autograph, and 32 full-page illustrations from original designs by Church, Dielman, Fredericks, Fenn, Gifford, Murphy, Schell, Smillie, and others. Engraved by Geo. T. Andrew. Over 900 pages, royal 8vo, cloth, gilt edges, boxed 5.00
Full Levant, gilt 10.00
Tree calf, gilt 10.00

CAPTAIN COIGNET, Soldier of the Empire, 1776-1850 (The Narrative of). An autobiographical account of one of Napoleon's Body Guard. Fully illustrated, 12mo, half leather, gilt top 2.50
Half calf 5.00

CENTURY OF AMERICAN LITERATURE (A). Selected and arranged by Huntington Smith. Cloth, 12mo 1.75
Half calf 3.50

CONVENIENT HOUSES AND HOW TO BUILD THEM. By Louis H. Gibson, architect, comprising a large variety of plans, photographic designs, and artistic interiors and exteriors of Ideal Homes, varying in cost from $1,000 to $10,000. 8vo, cloth $2.50

CONYBEARE AND HOWSON, Life of St. Paul. 12mo, cloth	1.00
CRIME AND PUNISHMENT. By Feodor M. Dostoyevsky. 12mo.	1.50
DAILY FOOD. New Illustrated Edition. 18mo. Gilt edges. With 12 Photo Engravings, white back, fancy sides	.75
Lavender and gold. Gilt edges	.75
French silk and gold. Gilt edges	1.25
32mo. Plain	.15
32mo. Gilt	.20
32mo. Morocco, flexible, round corners, gilt edges	.60
DEAD SOULS. By Nikolai V. Gogol. 12mo	1.25
DOCTOR LAMAR. A Novel. By Elizabeth P. Train. 12mo	1.25
DICTIONARY OF QUOTATIONS FROM THE POETS (A). Based upon Bohn's Edition. *Revised, Corrected,* and *Enlarged.* By Anna L. Ward. Crown 8vo, cloth, bevelled boards	2.00
Half calf	4.00
DICTIONARY OF PROSE QUOTATIONS (A). By Anna L. Ward. Crown 8vo, cloth, bevelled boards	2.00
Half calf	4.00

Ely's Works:

ELEMENTS OF SOCIALISM. By Prof. Richard T. Ely	1.25
LABOR MOVEMENT IN AMERICA. By Prof. Richard T. Ely	1.50
PROBLEMS OF TO-DAY. A discussion of Tariff, Taxation, and Monopolies. By Prof. Richard T. Ely. 12mo. Revised and enlarged edition	1.50
SOCIAL ASPECTS OF CHRISTIANITY. By Prof. Richard T. Ely	.90
TAXATION IN AMERICAN STATES AND CITIES. 12mo	1.75
EMINENT AUTHORS OF THE NINETEENTH CENTURY. By Dr. Georg Brandes ("The Taine of the North"). 12mo	2.00
Half calf	4.00
EQUITABLE TAXATION. Six essays on the subject, three of which received prizes from "The Public Opinion." By Walter E. Weyl, Robert Luce, Bolton Hall, J. W. Graham, J. W. Cabot, W. H. Cowles. With an Introduction by the Hon. Jonathan A. Lane, biographical sketches of the authors, and portraits. 12mo, cloth	.75
FIFTY YEARS, THREE MONTHS, TWO DAYS. By Julius Wolff.	1.25
FOSTER'S CYCLOPÆDIAS OF ILLUSTRATION. 8vo, cloth	5.00
Sheep	6.00

1st Series Prose.	Cloth.		1st Series Prose.	Sheep.
2d " "	"		2d " "	"
1st " Poetical	"		1st " Poetical	"
2d " "	"		2d " "	"

FOSTER'S INDEX AND CATALOGUE FOR ANY LIBRARY.	2.25
Sheep	3.00
FOSTER'S SCRAP HOLDER	1.25
FOUNDING OF THE GERMAN EMPIRE BY WILLIAM I. By Heinrich von Sybel. Translated by Prof. Perrin of Boston University. 5 vols. 8vo. Cloth	10.00
Half morocco	20.00

FROM HEART AND NATURE. By Sarah K. Bolton and Chas. K. Bolton. 12mo, cloth, gilt top $1.00

GOLD NAILS TO HANG MEMORIES ON. A Rhyming Review, under their Christian Names, of old acquaintances in History, Literature, and Friendship. By Elizabeth A. Allen. 8vo, gilt edge . . 2.50

GOLDEN WORDS FOR DAILY COUNSEL. Selected and arranged by Anna H. Smith. Cloth, 16mo, red edges 1.00
Gilt edge 1.25
Seal leather, flexible, gilt 2.00
Levant morocco, flexible gilt 2.50
Levant morocco, padded 2.50

GOTTHOLD'S EMBLEMS. By Christian Scriver. 12mo . . . 1.25

GREAT MASTERS OF RUSSIAN LITERATURE. By Dupuy. 1.25

HAPPY FIND (A). From the French of Mme. Gagnebin. 12mo . 1.25

HER MAJESTY'S TOWER. By W. H. Dixon. With 47 illustrations. Complete in 1 volume. Royal 12mo, cloth 2.00
Half calf 4.00

HER ONLY BROTHER. From the German of W. Heimburg. 12mo, 1.25

HISTORY OF FRANCE. By Victor Duruy. Translated by Mrs. M. Carey, under the supervision of J. F. Jameson, Professor of History in Brown University. 2.00
Half calf 4.00

HUBBELL'S S. S. TREASURER'S CASH ACCOUNT 75

HUBBELL'S S. S. LIBRARY RECORD 1.25

IMPRESSIONS OF RUSSIA. By Dr. Georg Brandes. 12mo . . 1.25

INITIALS AND PSEUDONYMS. A Dictionary of Literary Disguises. By Wm. Cushing and Albert R. Frey. First Series. Royal 8vo, cloth 5.00
Half morocco 7.50
Half morocco, interleaved 10.00

INITIALS AND PSEUDONYMS. Second Series. Royal 8vo,
Cloth, ... 3.00
Half morocco 6.00
Half morocco, interleaved 8.00

JANE EYRE. By Charlotte Brontë. With 48 illustrations. Engraved by Andrew. 2 vols. 12mo. Cloth, gilt top 5.00
Half calf 9.00
Edition de Luxe, limited to 250 numbered copies, large paper; Japan proofs, mounted; cloth box and slip jackets 10.00

LES MISERABLES. By Victor Hugo. Translated by Isabel F. Hapgood. New edition. Complete in two volumes, with 32 full-page illustrations. 12mo. Cloth, gilt top, boxed 3.00
White back, fancy paper sides, gilt top 3.00

MARQUIS OF PENALTA (Marta y Maria). 12mo. By Valdés . 1.50

MAXIMINA. By Don Armando Palacio Valdés. 12mo. . . . $1.50
MEDITATIONS OF A PARISH PRIEST. Thoughts by Joseph
    Roux. 12mo, gilt top 1.25
MEMOIRS OF NAPOLEON BONAPARTE. By Bourrienne. 34
    portraits engraved on wood. 4 vols. 12mo, cloth, plain . . . 5.00
    Cloth, gilt top, uncut edges, paper label 6.00
    Half calf 10.00
    Half levant morocco 15.00
    Limited edition with over 100 illustrations, gilt top, half leather . . 10.00
METZEROTT, SHOEMAKER. A powerful novel, by Katharine
    Pearson Woods, treating of modern socialism. 12mo . . . 1.50

Miller's Works:
MAKING THE MOST OF LIFE. By Rev. J. R. Miller, D.D. 16mo.
    White back, gilt top, boxed 1.00
    Levant morocco, flexible, gilt edge 2.50
SILENT TIMES. By Rev. J. R. Miller, D.D. 16mo. White back, gilt
    top, boxed 1.00
    Levant morocco, padded, gilt edge 2.50
THE EVERY DAY OF LIFE. By Rev. J. R. Miller, D.D. 16mo.
    White back, gilt top, boxed 1.00
    Levant morocco, flexible gilt edges 2.50

MULLER'S LIFE OF TRUST. 12mo 1.50
PAYING THE PENALTY. By Gibbon, Fenn, and others. 12mo . 1.00
PELOUBET'S NOTES. 8vo 1.25
PLEA FOR THE GOSPEL, A. By the Rev. George D. Herron, author
    of "The Larger Christ," "The Message of Jesus to Men of Wealth."
    12mo 75
POLISHED STONES AND SHARPENED ARROWS. By C. W.
    Bibb. A manual for Christian Workers. Cloth, 12mo . . . 1.25
POLLY BUTTON'S NEW YEAR. By Mrs. C. F. Wilder, author of
    "Sister Rednour's Sacrifice," "Land of the Rising Sun," etc. 18mo,
    unique ornamental binding 75
PORTABLE COMMENTARY. By Jamieson, Fausset, and Brown.
    2 vols. Crown 8vo 3.50
RECOLLECTIONS OF A PRIVATE. A Story of the Army of the
    Potomac. By Warren Lee Goss, author of "Jed; a Boy's Adven-
    tures in the Army of '61-'65," "The Soldier's Story of his Captivity
    at Andersonville and other Prisons." Illustrated with over 80 spirited
    engravings by Chapin and Shelton. 8vo.
    Cloth 3.00
    Seal Russia. Marbled edges 4.00
    Half morocco. Marbled edges 5.00
ROGET'S THESAURUS OF ENGLISH WORDS AND PHRASES.
    New edition, revised and enlarged by the author's son, J. L. Roget.
    Crown 8vo, cloth 2.00
    " " " indexed 2.50
    " " half calf, indexed 4.00

ROBBER COUNT, THE. By Julius Wolff	1.25
SALTMASTER (THE) OF LUNEBURG. By Julius Wolff. 12mo,	1.50
SHILLABER'S (Mrs.) COOK BOOK. 12mo, cloth	1.25
Kitchen edition in oilcloth	1.25
SISTER SAINT SULPICE. By Valdés. With portrait. 12mo.	$1.50
SHIPTON'S (Anna) WORKS. 11 vols. 16mo, cloth	6.60

    Asked of God.
    Lost Blessing.
    Sure Mercies of David.
    "Tell Jesus."
    Waiting Hours.
    Promise and Promiser.
    Secret of the Lord.
    Wayside Service.
    The Watch-Tower.
    Precious Gems.
    The Lord was There.

SIGRID. An Icelandic Love Story	1.25
SOUL'S INQUIRIES ANSWERED. 18mo	.50
Interleaved, red edges	.75
" gilt edges	1.00
" seal leather, flexible	1.50
ST. JOHN'S EVE. By Nikolaï V. Gogol. 12mo	1.25
SUMMER LEGENDS. By Rudolph Baumbach. Translated by Helen B. Dole. 16mo, gilt top, laid paper, parti-color binding	1.00
SURE MERCIES OF DAVID. Presentation edition, cloth, 18mo, boxed	1.00
TARAS BULBA. By Nikolaï V. Gogol. 12mo	1.00
TELL JESUS. Presentation edition. Cloth, 18mo, boxed	1.00
TENNYSON'S POEMS. New edition. Complete in two volumes. Illustrated with two photogravures and numerous wood engravings by the best artists. 2 vols. 12mo. Gilt top	3.00
White back, fancy paper sides, gilt top	3.00
TENNYSON'S POEMS. A new and complete edition. Illustrated by Church, Dielman, Schell, Harry Fenn, and other artists. With portrait, 24 full-page illustrations, and vignette titles, engraved by Andrew. The finest edition of Tennyson ever published in this country. Royal 8vo, full morocco, gilt edge	6.00
TENNYSON'S WORKS. Handy volume edition. 8 vols. Cloth, gilt top, neat cloth case	6.00
Half Russia, gilt edges, leather box uniform with binding	12.00
Half calf, gilt edges, fancy leatherette case	12.00
American seal Russia, gilt edges, round corners, fancy leatherette case,	15.00
Tree calf, gilt edges, in calf box	30.00
THREE TIMES TRIED. By Farjeon, Allen, and others. 12mo	$1.00

TOLSTOI'S WORKS. 9 vols. 12mo, cloth 13.00
  Half calf, extra 25.00
    Anna Karénina 1.25
    Childhood, Boyhood, and Youth } 1.50
    What to do
    Ivan Ilyitch } 1.50
    Family Happiness
    My Confession
    My Religion } 1.50
    Life
    Napoleon's Russian Campaign
    Power and Liberty } 1.50
    The Long Exile
    The Invaders } 1.50
    A Russian Proprietor
    Sevastopol } 1.50
    The Cossacks
    War and Peace, 2 vols. 3.00
    War and Peace, 4 vols. Gilt top 5.00
    Gospel Stories. 12mo 1.25

TOM BROWN'S SCHOOL DAYS. By Thomas Hughes. With 53 illustrations. Engraved by Andrew. 12mo, cloth 2.00
  Full gilt edges 2.50
  Edition de Luxe, limited to 250 numbered copies, large paper, Japan proofs mounted; cloth box and slip jackets 5.00

VAGRANT, THE, AND OTHER TALES. By Vladimir Korolenko. 1.25

WALTON'S COMPLETE ANGLER. New edition. Complete in two volumes. With all the original 86 illustrations of Major's edition, and two additional photogravures. 2 vols. 16mo. Gilt top . . . 2.50

WEB OF GOLD, A. By the author of "Metzerott, Shoemaker." 12mo, 1.25

WORDSWORTH'S POEMS. Selected by Matthew Arnold, and illustrated in photogravure by Edmund H. Garrett. Printed from new plates on fine dekle edge laid paper. 12mo. *Cloth*, ornamental design, gilt top. Cloth box 2.50
  Full leather, gilt top, boxed 3.50

MONICA, THE MESA MAIDEN. By Mrs. Evelyn H. Raymond, author of "Mixed Pickles." Illustrated. 12mo 1.25

STANDARD WORKS IN SETS.
FINE ILLUSTRATED EDITIONS.

LES MISÉRABLES. By Victor Hugo. Illustrated Edition. 100 full-page illustrations. Translated by Isabel F. Hapgood. 12mo, cloth, gilt top, 5 vols. $7.50
Half calf, extra 15.00
Half crushed morocco 17.50
Half crushed levant 20.00

HUGO'S (Victor) Works. Illustrated Edition. Over 600 illustrations. Calendered paper. *Cloth, gilt top, 15 vols.* 12mo 22.50
Half calf, extra 45.00
Half crushed morocco 52.50
Half crushed levant 60.00

Volumes in this set boxed and sold separately in cloth and half calf as follows:—

Les Misérables. 5 vols.	cloth	7.50	Half calf	15.00
Notre-Dame. 2 vols.	"	3.00	" "	6.00
Ninety-three. 2 vols.	"	3.00	" "	6.00
Toilers of the Sea. 2 vols.	"	3.00	" "	6.00
History of a Crime. 2 vols.	"	3.00	" "	6.00
By Order of the King. 2 vols.	"	3.00	" "	6.00

HUGO (Victor) Works. Library Edition. Illustrated. The above fifteen volumes bound in 10 *volumes*, cloth, gilt top. (Sold only in sets), 15.00
Half calf 30.00

POPULAR EDITIONS.

HUGO'S (Victor) Works. Popular Edition. 6 vols. 12mo, cloth . . 7.50
Half calf, 7 vols. 14.00
Half pebble calf, Roger Payne Finish, gilt top, 7 vols 13.00

Volumes in this set sold separately in cloth.
Les Misérables 1.25
Notre-Dame 1.25
Ninety-three 1.25
Toilers of the Sea 1.25
History of a Crime 1.25
By Order of the King 1.25

LES MISÉRABLES. Popular Edition. 5 vols. 12mo.
Half Russia 6.00
Half pebble calf, Roger Payne Finish, gilt top 7.50

IRVING'S (Washington), Complete Works. Popular Edition. 8 vols 8.00
Library Edition, leather titles, gilt top 10.00
Half calf 12.00
Half Russia 10.00
Half pebble calf, Roger Payne Finish, gilt top 11.00

COUNT TOLSTOI'S MASTERPIECES. 6 vols. 12mo. Half Persian levant 12.00
War and Peace. 4 vols.
Anna Karénina. 2 vols.

CHARLES DICKENS'S COMPLETE WORKS.

A NEW EDITION IN 15 AND 30 VOLUMES.

Printed from new electrotype plates made from new, large-faced type, well leaded. All the mechanical details — paper, press-work, illustrations, and binding — are first class in every respect.

15 VOLUME EDITION. Carefully printed on fine machine-finish paper, with 240 full-page illustrations. Large 12mo.

Popular Edition.	15 vols., cloth . . . . . Per set . .	$18.75
" "	15 vols., half calf, marbled edges " . .	37.50
Library Edition.	15 vols., cloth, gilt top . . . " . .	22.50
" "	15 vols., half calf, gilt top . . " . .	45.00

Volumes sold separately in cloth styles as follows:—

Pickwick Papers,	16 illus.,	popular,	cloth,	$1.25	Library,	cloth,	1.50
Nicholas Nickleby,	16 "	"	"	1.25	"	"	1.50
Martin Chuzzlewit,	16 "	"	"	1.25	"	"	1.50
Old Curiosity Shop and Reprinted Pieces,	16 "	"	"	1.25	"	"	1.50
Barnaby Rudge, and Hard Times,	16 "	"	"	1.25	"	"	1.50
Dombey and Son,	16 "	"	"	1.25	"	"	1.50
David Copperfield,	16 "	"	"	1.25	"	"	1.50
Our Mutual Friend,	16 "	"	"	1.25	"	"	1.50
Bleak House,	16 "	"	"	1.25	"	"	1.50
Little Dorrit,	16 "	"	"	1.25	"	"	1.50
Uncommercial Traveller and Christmas Stories,	16 "	"	"	1.25	"	"	1.50
Oliver Twist, Pictures from Italy, and American Notes,	16 "	"	"	1.25	"	"	1.50
Christmas Books and Great Expectations,	16 "	"	"	1.25	"	"	1.50
Tale of Two Cities and Sketches by Boz,	16 "	"	"	1.25	"	"	1.50
Child's History of England and Edwin Drood, etc.	16 "	"	"	1.25	"	"	1.50

DICKENS'S WORKS — Continued.

30 VOLUME EDITION. With all the original illustrations by Phiz, Cruikshank, etc., and many later ones, to which have been added 65 new cuts from etchings by Pailthorpe, contained in no other edition, and a steel portrait, making, in all, 799 full-page illustrations. Printed on fine calendered paper, large 12mo.

30 volumes, gilt top, cloth, gilt back . . . Per set . .	$40.00
" " gilt top, cloth, plain back . . . " . .	40.00
" " half calf, gilt top . . . . . " . .	80.00
" " half crushed levant . . . . . " . .	110.00

Volumes sold separately in the plain back, cloth binding, as follows: —

Title	Vols.	Illustrations	Price
Pickwick Papers	2 vols.,	66 illustrations	3.00
Nicholas Nickleby	2 "	39 "	3.00
Martin Chuzzlewit	2 "	40 "	3.00
Old Curiosity Shop	2 "	79 "	3.00
Barnaby Rudge	2 "	82 "	3.00
Dombey and Son	2 "	40 "	3.00
David Copperfield	2 "	40 "	3.00
Our Mutual Friend	2 "	40 "	3.00
Bleak House	2 "	40 "	3.00
Little Dorrit	2 "	40 "	3.00
Uncommercial Traveller		8 "	1.50
Christmas Stories		14 "	1.50
Oliver Twist		45 "	1.50
Pictures from Italy and American Notes		8 "	1.50
Christmas Books		65 "	1.50
Great Expectations		37 "	1.50
Tale of Two Cities		16 "	1.50
Sketches by Boz		40 "	1.50
Child's History of England		19 "	1.50
Edwin Drood and Miscellaneous		41 "	1.50

STANDARD BOOKS FOR YOUNG PEOPLE.

MRS. BOLTON'S BOOKS.

FAMOUS TYPES OF WOMANHOOD. By Sarah K. Bolton. With portraits of Queen Louise, Madam Recamier, Desirée, Miss Dix, Jenny Lind, Susanna Wesley, Harriet Martineau, etc. 12mo . . $1.50

FAMOUS ENGLISH STATESMEN. By Sarah K. Bolton. With Portraits of Gladstone, John Bright, Robert Peel, etc. 12mo . . $1.50

FAMOUS ENGLISH AUTHORS OF THE NINETEENTH CENTURY. By Sarah K. Bolton. With Portraits of Scott, Burns, Carlyle, Dickens, Tennyson, Robert Browning, etc. 12mo . . 1.50

FAMOUS EUROPEAN ARTISTS. By Sarah K. Bolton. With portraits of Raphael, Titian, Landseer, Reynolds, Rubens, Turner, and others. 12mo 1.50

FAMOUS AMERICAN AUTHORS. By Sarah K. Bolton. With Portraits of Longfellow, Holmes, Emerson, Lowell, Aldrich, and other noted writers. 12mo, ... 1.50

FAMOUS AMERICAN STATESMEN. By Sarah K. Bolton, with portraits of Sumner, Clay, Jackson, Webster, etc. 12mo . . . 1.50

FAMOUS MEN OF SCIENCE. By Sarah K. Bolton. With Portraits of Agassiz, Darwin, Linnæus, etc. 1.50

GIRLS WHO BECAME FAMOUS. By Sarah K. Bolton. With 20 Portraits. Companion book to "Poor Boys Who Became Famous." 12mo 1.50

POOR BOYS WHO BECAME FAMOUS. By Sarah K. Bolton. With 24 portraits. 12mo 1.50

STORIES FROM LIFE. By Sarah K. Bolton. 12mo 1.25

MRS. FARMER'S BOOKS.

BOYS' BOOK OF FAMOUS RULERS. By Lydia Hoyt Farmer. With portraits. Lives of Agamemnon, Julius Cæsar, Charlemagne, Frederick the Great, Napoleon, etc. 12mo 1.50

FRENCH REVOLUTION (THE), A short history of. By Lydia Hoyt Farmer. Fully Illustrated 1.50

GIRLS' BOOK OF FAMOUS QUEENS. By Lydia Hoyt Farmer. With portraits. Lives of Cleopatra, Queen Elizabeth, Catherine de Medicis, Josephine, etc. 12mo 1.50

LA FAYETTE. The Knight of Liberty. By Lydia Hoyt Farmer. Fully illustrated. 12mo 1.50

TOM CLIFTON; or, Western Boys with Grant and Sherman. By Warren Lee Goss, author of "Jed," etc. Fully illustrated. 12mo. 1.50

JED: A BOY'S ADVENTURES IN THE ARMY IN "61." By Warren Lee Goss. Fully illustrated. 12mo 1.50

JO-BOAT BOYS, THE. By Rev. J. F. Cowan, D.D., editor of "Our Young People." Illustrated by H. W. Peirce. 12mo . . . 1.50

MOTHER OF THE KING'S CHILDREN, THE. By Rev. J. F. Cowan, D.D., author of "Jo-Boat Boys." Illustrated by H. W. Peirce. 12mo 1.50

FAMOUS COMPOSERS, A SCORE OF. By Nathan Haskell Dole. With portraits of Beethoven, Wagner, Liszt, Haydn, etc. 12mo . 1.50

AN ENTIRE STRANGER. By Rev. T. L. Baily. Illustrated. 12mo,	$1.25
BOYHOOD OF LIVING AUTHORS. By Wm. H. Rideing. 12mo,	1.00
CAPTAIN'S DOG (The). By Louis Énault. 12mo, 18 Illustrations	1.00
CHRISTMAS COUNTRY. Translated from the Danish and German	1.25
CECIL'S KNIGHT. By E. B Hollis. 12mo.	1.25
CUORE. An Italian Schoolboy's Journal. By Edmondo de Amicis. 12mo	1.25
"FAIRY LEGENDS OF THE FRENCH PROVINCES"	1.25
GENERAL GORDON, The Christian Hero. 12mo	1.25

Homer Greene's Books:

BLIND BROTHER (The). 12mo, illustrated	.90
BURNHAM BREAKER. 12mo, illustrated	1.50
RIVERPARK REBELLION (The). 12mo, illustrated	1.00

HINTS TO OUR BOYS. Square 16mo	.50
HOME IN THE HOLY LAND. 12mo illustrated	1.50
IN PERILS OFT. By W. H. Davenport Adams. 12mo. Illustrated	1.50

J A K Books:

BIRCHWOOD. By J A K. 12mo, illustrated	1.25
FITCH CLUB. By J A K. 12mo, Illustrated	1.25
GIANT DWARF (The). By J A K. 12mo, illustrated	1.25
PROFESSOR JOHNNY. By J A K. 12mo, illustrated	1.25
RIVERSIDE MUSEUM. By J A K. 12mo, illustrated	1.25
ROLF AND HIS FRIENDS. By J A K. 12mo. Illustrated	1.25
SCOTCH CAPS. By J A K. 12mo. Illustrated	1.25
WHO SAVED THE SHIP? By J A K. 12mo. Illustrated.	1.25

LED IN UNKNOWN PATHS. By Anna F. Raffensperger. 12mo	1.25
LITTLE ARTHUR'S ENGLAND. 12mo, Illustrated	1.25
LITTLE ARTHUR'S FRANCE. 12mo, illustrated	1.25
LITTLE ARTHUR'S ROME. By Hezekiah Butterworth. 12mo	1.25
MAKERS OF ENGLISH VERSE. By Mrs. Blanche W. Bellamy. 12mo, illustrated	1.25
MARTIN THE SKIPPER. By James F. Cobb. Illustrated	1.50
MIXED PICKLES. By Mrs. Evelyn Raymond. 12mo, illustrated	1.25
MUSICAL JOURNEY, THE, OF DOROTHY AND DELIA. By the Rev. Bradley Gilman. Profusely illustrated. 12mo, unique binding	.50
MUTINY ON THE LEANDER. By Bernard Heldmann. Illustrated.	1.50
OFF TO THE WILDS. By George Manville Fenn. 12mo. Illustrated,	1.50
PHILIP. A Story of the First Century. By Mrs. Mary C. Cutler. 12mo,	1.00
PRINCES, AUTHORS, AND STATESMEN OF OUR TIME. By Canon Farrar, James T. Fields, and other popular writers. Edited by James Parton. 60 illustrations. 1 vol. 8vo, cloth	2.50

Anna Chapin Ray's Books:

HALF A DOZEN BOYS. 12mo, illustrated	1.25
HALF A DOZEN GIRLS. 12mo, illustrated	1.25
IN BLUE CREEK CANON. 12mo, illustrated	1.25
CADETS OF FLEMMING HALL. 12mo, illustrated	1.25

RED CARL. From the German of J. J. Messmer. 12mo, Illustrated	1.25
SEARCH FOR THE STAR; or, Life in Wild Woods of Maine. By Edward Willett. 9 illustrations, 12mo.	1.25

SHORT STUDIES IN BOTANY FOR CHILDREN. By Harriet C. Cooper. Fully illustrated. 12mo. 1.00
THROWN UPON HER OWN RESOURCES; or, What Girls Can Do. By Jenny June. 12mo, with portrait of the author . . . 1.00
WALKS ABROAD OF TWO YOUNG NATURALISTS. From the French of Charles Beaugrand, by David Sharp, M.B., F.L.S., F.Z.S., President of Entomological Society, London. Fully illustrated. 8vo, $1.50
WATCHERS ON THE LONGSHIPS. By James F. Cobb. Illustrated, 1.50
WHAT FIDE REMEMBERS. By Faye Huntington. Illustrated . 1.25
WHITE CROSS AND DOVE OF PEARLS. By the author of Laura Linwood 1.50
WRECKED ON LABRADOR. By Winfrid A. Stearns. 12mo . . 1.50

CLASSIC JUVENILES, BY JACOB ABBOTT.

"The Prince of Writers for the Young."

ABBOTT'S AMERICAN HISTORIES FOR YOUTH. Illustrated By Darley, Herrick, Chapin, and others. 4 vols. (2 vols. in one) . $6.00
AUGUST STORIES. 4 vols. Illustrated. 16mo 4.50
JUNO STORIES. 4 vols. Illustrated. 16mo 4.50
JONAS BOOKS. 6 vols. bound in 3. Illustrated. 16mo . . . 3.75
LUCY BOOKS. 6 vols. bound in 3. Illustrated. 16mo . . . 3.75
ROLLO BOOKS. 14 vols. in 7. Illustrated. 16mo 8.75
WALTER'S TOUR. 6 vols. 6.00

ADVENTURE LIBRARY. Fully illustrated. New and uniform style of binding. 5 vols. 12mo 7.50
  In Perils Oft. By W. H. Davenport Adams. 12mo.
  Mutiny on the Leander. By Bernard Heldmann. 12mo.
  Martin the Skipper. By James F. Cobb. 12mo.
  Off to the Wilds. By George Manville Fenn. 12mo.
  Watchers on the Longships. By James F. Cobb. 12mo.

BIRCHWOOD SERIES. By J A K. 8 vols. 12mo 10.00
DOVE SERIES. 6 vols. Illustrated. 16mo 5.00
FARMER BOY SERIES. By Rev. Wm. M. Thayer. 16mo. 4 vols. 4.25
  Farmer Boy.   Good Girl and True Woman.
  Poor Boy and Merchant Prince. Country Boy in the City.

GEORGEY'S MENAGERIE. By Madeline Leslie. 6 vols. Illustrated. 16mo 4.50

HANDY VOLUME CLASSICS.

An entirely new line of standard books in prose and poetry. Handy in size, carefully printed on good paper, and bound in faultless styles. Each volume is illustrated with a frontispiece and title-page, in photogravure, and most of the volumes have numerous additional illustrations by the best artists.

PARTI-COLORED CLOTH: white back, gilt side, gilt top, boxed, 23 vols., 18mo. Per vol., $1.00.

1. Browning (Robert) selections, 2 vols.
2. Burns's Poems. "
3. Lady of the Lake.
4. Lalla Rookh.
5. Lucile.
6. Poe's Poems.
7. Tennyson's Idylls of the King.
8. " In Memoriam.
9. " The Princess.
10. " Early Sonnets, etc.
11. " Locksley Hall, etc.
12. Wordsworth (selections).

13. Carlyle's Heroes and Hero Worship.
14. " Sartor Resartus.
15. Emerson's Essays, 2 vols.
16. Paul and Virginia
17. Pilgrim's Progress.
18. Ruskin's Crown of Wild Olive.
19. " Sesame and Lilies.
20. Vicar of Wakefield.
21 Cranford.

(Other volumes in preparation.)

All of the above volumes are bound uniformly in the following additional styles:

Cloth, Vellum Finish, neat gold border, full gilt edges, boxed, 18mo, per vol. $1.00
Silk, stamped in gold, full gilt edges, boxed, 18mo, per vol. 1.50
Half Calf, gilt top, boxed, 18mo, per vol. 2.00
Half Levant, gilt top, boxed, 18mo, per vol. 2.50

This attractive series is sure to be a favorite with those desiring something new and dainty for gifts or for the drawing-room table, and with the general reader or student who prefers his reading in small, companionable volumes.

For sale by all Booksellers, or sent postpaid by the publishers upon receipt of price.

CROWELL'S POETS.

HALF RUSSIA, Marbled Edges. Without Red Lines. In new and attractive style of binding. 108 vols., 12mo $1.00

1. Arnold (Edwin).
2. Arnold (Matthew).
3. Aurora Leigh.
4. Aytoun.
5. Beauties of Shakespeare.
6. British Female Poets.
7. Browning (Mrs.).
8. Browning (Robert).
9. Bryant.
10. Burns.
11. Byron.
12. Calverley.
13. Campbell.
14. Chaucer.
15. Childe Harold.
16. Christian Year.
17. Coleridge.
18. Cook (Eliza).
19. Cowper.
20. Crabbe.
21. Dante.
22. Dryden.
23. Eliot (George).
24. Familiar Quotations.
25. Famous Poems.
26. Favorite Poems.
27. Faust (Goethe's).
28. Frenau's Poems.
29. Gems, 1001.
30. Goethe's Poems.
31. Golden Treasury.
32. Goldsmith.
33. Gray, Thomas.
34. Greene, Marlowe and Jonson.
35. Half Hours with the Poets.
36. Halleck, Fitz-Greene.
37. Heber, Bishop.
38. Heine.
39. Hemans.
40. Herbert.
41. Hood.
42. Hugo (Victor).
43. Iliad.
44. Imitation of Christ.
45. Ingoldsby Legends.
46. Irish Humorous Poems.
47. Jean Ingelow.
48. Keats.
49. Kingsley.
50. Lady of the Lake.
51. Lalla Rookh.
52. Lay of the Last Minstrel.
53. Longfellow (Early Poems).
54. Lowell (James Russell) (Early Poems).

55	Lucile.	82	Schiller.
56	Macaulay.	83	Scott.
57	Marmion.	84	Shakespeare (1 vol.).
58	Meredith (Owen).	85	Shakespeare (2 vols.).
59	Milton.	86	Shelley.
60	Moore.	87	Smith, Alex.
61	Motherwell.	88	Songs, Household.
62	Mulock (Miss).	89	Songs, Sacred and Devotional.
63	Odyssey.	90	Southey.
64	Ossian.	91	Spanish Ballads.
65	Paradise Lost.	92	Spenser.
66	Percy's Reliques.	93	Swinburne.
67	Petrarch.	94	Tasso.
68	Pilgrim's Progress.	95	Taylor's Philip Van Artevelde.
69	Poe.	96	Thackeray.
70	Poetry of Flowers.	97	Tupper.
71	Poetry of Love.	98	Tennyson.
72	Poetry of Passion.	99	Thomson.
73	Poetry of Sentiment.	100	Vers de Société.
74	Poets of America.	101	Virgil.
75	Pope.	102	War Songs.
76	Praed.	103	Wesley.
77	Procter.	104	White, Kirke.
78	Red Letter Poems.	105	Whittier (Early Poems).
79	Religious Poems.	106	Willis.
80	Rogers.	107	Wordsworth.
81	Rossetti.		

THE IMPERIAL EDITION OF STANDARD POETICAL WORKS.

All of the volumes in this new line of poets are printed from *our own plates* on fine paper, illustrated with 8 full-page illustrations by the best artists, and bound in a durable and tasteful style. The volumes are *complete* (with the one exception indicated), and have biographical and critical notes when essential. These volumes will, therefore, fill the need of good editions of standard poets suitable for library or holiday use at popular prices.

CLOTH, Full Gilt Edges. 20 vols. Full 12mo. Per vol. . . $1.50

1 Browning (Mrs.).
2 Browning, Robert (selections).
3 Burns.
4 Byron.
5 Dictionary of Quotations.
6 Favorite Poems.
7 Golden Treasury.
8 Goldsmith.
9 Jean Ingelow.
10 Lady of the Lake.
11 Lalla Rookh.
12 Lucile.
13 Meredith.
14 Milton.
15 Moore.
16 Red Letter Poems.
17 Scott.
18 Shakespeare.
19 Tennyson.
20 Wordsworth.

www.ingramcontent.com/pod-product-compliance
Lightning Source LLC
Chambersburg PA
CBHW021337300426
44114CB00012B/983